Management for Professionals

The Springer series "Management for Professionals" comprises high-level business and management books for executives, MBA students, and practice-oriented business researchers. The topics cover all themes relevant to businesses and the business ecosystem. The authors are experienced business professionals and renowned professors who combine scientific backgrounds, best practices, and entrepreneurial vision to provide powerful insights into achieving business excellence.

The Series is SCOPUS-indexed.

Dominik Schwizer • Michael Burch

Data Excellence in Sports

A Practical Guide for Sports Organizations

Springer

Dominik Schwizer
Chur, Graubünden, Switzerland

Michael Burch
Buch-Gannertshofen, Germany

ISSN 2192-8096 ISSN 2192-810X (electronic)
Management for Professionals
ISBN 978-3-032-10992-7 ISBN 978-3-032-10993-4 (eBook)
https://doi.org/10.1007/978-3-032-10993-4

This Springer imprint is published by the registered company Springer Nature Switzerland AG
The registered company address is: Gewerbestrasse 11, 6330 Cham, Switzerland

Preface

Sports and all its aspects are a huge topic worth investigating from several points of view. On the one hand, sports are interesting as a discipline to bring together people from various backgrounds from all over the world creating some kind of universal language that everybody understands and everyone can speak, hence creating social contacts. The Olympic Games are a good example for this because they can be understood as a nation- and culture-connecting event. Not only is the competition of interest but also the social contacts in the Olympic village. On the other hand, sports can also be part of one's own individual life, in a more isolated fashion, without the need to communicate and interact with other people. However, if sports are used as a means of communicating and building social relationships, it builds some kind of bridge between communities and cultures that are people, which can be an important ingredient in our daily lives. As a concrete example of a real-world sporting event, we can mention the politically explosive football match between Iran and the United States in the 1998 World Cup in France (Burch et al., 2020; Longman, 2022) that ended peacefully.

In reality, the field of sports might be understood from at least two main perspectives: passive vs. active participation. The passive aspect focuses on sports consumers, while the active aspect describes real sportsmen who are athletes. A sportsman can fall into two main categories that can be described as professional vs. amateur sports, for example, based on a hobby or to avoid health issues by practicing sports on a regular basis. Moreover, big and popular sports events are crucial for the future existence of the field of sports, individual sports disciplines, and their variations, in particular, for the inspiration of youth, i.e., future athletes. It might be noted that digitalization is a means to support sports consumers, which can have the positive effect that people—maybe the future, young athletes or hobby sportsmen—become motivated to practice more sports or at least become inspired by it. Novel digital technologies (e.g., the broadcast on TV Meneses et al., 2022 or on the World Wide Web Huang et al., 2018) might accelerate these developments in the field of sports.

Sports is not just an activity, in light of digitalization in the computer era, it generates vast amounts of data, with varying data types, static, dynamic, even being real-time data, making data analyses and visual depictions of it to challenging tasks. The data creates a source of information that is sleeping until powerful data analysis and visualization concepts make them understandable in the sense of finding patterns that can hint at problems worth improving, problems that might neither be detected nor solved without an additional data analysis and visualization process. The number of interested people in such data analyses is getting larger, not only the athletes themselves might be interested in such data analysis results but any related discipline that somehow makes use of sports data, for example, the mass media, betting agencies, sponsors, or even forms of industrial and academic partners that find a certain value in the data. The age of digitalization does not only bring into play the fact that data about sports is measured, collected, stored, processed, analyzed, and visualized, it even tries more to link the data sources between various sport disciplines and actors—athletes and sports consumers—to build synergy effects for all involved people—a methodology that was not possible before the invention of the computer and other related hardware and software, also with the steady progress in hardware technologies and software systems. The hardware technologies, for example, also bring a huge field into play that steadily advances measurement devices like sensors, video cameras, or very sport-specific technologies including intelligent sports wear and wearable technologies (Zadeh et al., 2021).

All these points bring into play powerful ideas, concepts, and academic and industrial research fields worth studying. The digitalization age brings opportunities for faster and more accurately measuring sports data over space and time, with a multitude of integrated hardware components getting cheaper and cheaper over time. Digitalization is a mighty field that is actually responsible for creating vast amounts of data; however, the data itself has to be stored, managed, handled, linked, transformed, and so on, to make it useful for data analysis techniques typically involving efficient and effective algorithms and interactive visualizations to derive patterns, insights, and knowledge from the data. The technological concepts progress in at least two major ways, focusing on the data generation, made possible by digitalization and sensor technology, and on the data analysis, creating value and insights from the recorded data. Both concepts build some kind of synergy effect, i.e., one can only survive with the other in combination, as stand-alone concepts they would not be useful at all.

This book originated from a collaboration between researchers from the field of sports management, sports economics as well as data science and visual analytics. We saw the need to describe the concepts and technologies of this emerging field in light of the progress of digitalization and the impact of it on many involved fields, including data science with all of its algorithms but also visualization with the interactive intervention of the users-in-the-loop. The invention of the computer or other devices such as mobile phones, video cameras, eye trackers, and the like brought a huge step into the field that again led to technologies never imaginable without those devices and technologies. Sports itself has a long history, also in the digital world (English, 2016), but the opportunities to measure, record, store, and analyze the involved data has made it to a field that makes it even more visible to many actors, including research institutions or the industry, for example, producing sports wear, advertisement banners, food, e-tickets and printed tickets with and without bar or QR codes, and the like, all products and services focus on a certain market that might be somehow important for a sports event, either before, during, or after it.

Moreover, not only products and services around sports events get more advanced and flexible, research in academia and industry also focuses on the involved data which is steadily growing and linking several heterogeneous data sources, while such data analyses focus on improving and enhancing certain aspects, not only due to reasons of earning or saving money. Scientific research fields like artificial intelligence (AI), machine learning (ML), deep learning (DL), data mining (DM), statistics, interactive visualization, visual analytics (VA), and many more are standard ingredients when it comes to sports events with a variety of involved data. All of them focus on finding insights and knowledge in the vast amounts of data, with the ultimate goal to improve certain aspects, to even predict future effects based on an existing repertoire of data elements, or to create a statistical overview that summarizes sports events to inform interested people, for example, for a newspaper, on TV, or on the World Wide Web. We might categorize the aforementioned ideas into data producers who can be the sportsmen themselves during the training phase but also during the real competition. But we might also see the spectators in this group as the people who have a sports watching behavior as well as a browsing behavior when reading sports news, for example, on the web or in the mass media. Another major category can be the data consumers who can have different roles such as trainers, the mass media, sports managers, sportsmen themselves, organizations, the medical staff, and so on. The people in those roles are typically responsible on the data analysts to get insights and knowledge from their data. Moreover, sports marketing is interested in an improvement and steady progress of the field of sports and sports events based on data analyses.

The goal of the book is manifold which is already stated as data excellence in sports in its title. However, as a major goal it makes an attempt to provide an overview about the field of sports in the light of digitalization and data science, while it describes when and in which areas digitalization has taken place so far and in which ones it still has to come. Moreover, it tries to summarize the roles of various people participating in sports events, not only the athletes themselves, while it also comes up with lots of statistical numbers, figures, and tables to illustrate the value and impact of digitalization in the history of sports, for different sports types, as well as in different countries and regions. We discuss many varying topics related to sports data. Some of the topics might be more related to sports while others are more linked to general data science and related disciplines like visualization or human-computer interaction (HCI). However, both research areas, sports and data science, are interesting and timely topics that it makes sense that one must be discussed under the light of the other and that one can also learn from the other, building some kind of synergy effect. As a wrap-up, we also look into scalability issues and limitations and even more, we discuss challenges with respect to sports and data science.

Chur, Switzerland | Dominik Schwizer
Buch-Gannertshofen, Germany | Michael Burch
September 2025

References

Burch, M., Wallner, G., Angelescu, S. L., & Lakatos, P. (2020). Visual analysis of FIFA world cup data. In *Proceedings of the 24th International Conference on Information Visualisation, IV* (pp. 114–119). IEEE.

English, P. (2016). Sport history in the digital era. *New Media and Society, 18*(4), 684–686.

Huang, Y., Shen, C., & Li, T. (2018). Event summarization for sports games using Twitter streams. *World Wide Web, 21*(3), 609–627.

Longman, J. (2022). Enmity past, U.S. meets Iran and suffers bitter 2-1 defeat.

Meneses, J., Souto, L., Sil, S., Silva, T., & Au-Yong-Oliveira, M. (2022). Sports streaming: Transition from TV to digital—an analysis of traditional and new media companies in the online environment. In Á Rocha, H. Adeli, G. Dzemyda & F. Moreira (Eds.), *Proceedings of Information Systems and Technologies, WorldCIST*, volume 469 of *Lecture Notes in Networks and Systems* (pp. 220–232). Springer.

Zadeh, A. H., Taylor, D., Bertsos, M., Tillman, T., Nosoudi, N., & Bruce, S. (2021). Predicting sports injuries with wearable technology and data analysis. *Information Systems Frontiers, 23*(4), 1023–1037.

Acknowledgments Sport, business, and technology come together in this book on data management in sports organizations. The increasing interdisciplinarity poses new challenges not only for sports managers but also for researchers. This book is also the result of an extremely constructive and benevolent collaboration with my co-author Michael Burch. His experience, patience, and perseverance contributed significantly to the publication of the book in its current form. Without this interdisciplinary collaboration, the work would not have been possible. In addition, a book project like this also requires a lot of energy and time. Special thanks therefore go to Layla, who always stood by my side with encouragement even in difficult phases and showed a lot of patience and understanding for the project. My greatest thanks go to my parents, Ida and Kilian, for their tremendous support on my journey through life. I dedicate this book to them.

Data science is an important research field that is suitable for almost any kind of discipline related to data. Sports is such a discipline with big, heterogeneous, dynamic, and partially unstructured data that can only be analyzed when the right algorithms, visualizations, and interactions are applied to find answers to the tasks of the users. For a data scientist and visualization expert, it is extremely valuable to be able to count on the experience of a domain expert, in my case a sports expert who can guide the data-related thoughts into the right direction and make data science a powerful application to sports. Dominik Schwizer is a great choice in this respect to get the right input at the right time, and only based on these synergy effects was it possible to create this book. However, without the support of my loving family, my partner Tina Gaiser, and my three children Colin, Annalina, and Milena, such a book project would never be imaginable. I dedicate this book to them.

Competing Interests The authors have no competing interests to declare that are relevant to the content of this manuscript.

Contents

Acronyms

3D	Three dimensional
AFL	Australian Football League
AI	Artificial intelligence
ANOVA	Analysis of variance
API	Application programming interface
AR	Augmented reality
BASPO	Federal Office of Sport
BC	Before Christ
BMI	Body mass index
C++	High-level programming language
CDO	Chief data officer
CO_2	Carbon dioxide
CPU	Central processing unit
CRM	Customer relationship management
CSR	Corporate social responsibility
CSV	Comma separated values
DEKRA	German Technical Inspection Association
DL	Deep learning
DM	Data mining
DOSB	German Olympic Sports Confederation
EEG	Electroencephalography
ESG	Environmental, social, governance
EURO	UEFA European Championship
FC	Football club
FIFA	International Federation of Association Football
FPL	Fantasy Premier League
GLT	Goal line technology
GmbH	Gesellschaft mit beschränkter Haftung
GPS	Global positioning system
GPU	Graphics processing unit
GSR	Galvanic skin response
HCI	Human-computer interaction
HR	Human resources
IBM	The International Business Machines Corporation

IMU	Inertial measurement unit
IOC	International Olympic Committee
IoT	Internet of things
IT	Information technology
KMS	Knowledge management system
KNVB	Royal Dutch Football Association
KPI	Key performance indicator
LHRD	Large high-resolution display
LPS	Local positioning system
LZR	Stands for Laser in the Speedo LZR Racer swimsuit
MCV	Multiple and coordinated views
ML	Machine learning
MLB	Major League Baseball
MR	Mixed reality
NFL	National Football League
NHL	National Hockey League
NHV	Royal Dutch Hockey Association
NP	Nondeterministic polynomial time
OOI	Object of interest
PCA	Principal component analysis
PhD	Doctor of Philosophy
POI	Person of interest
POS	Point of sale
PR	Public relations
Q&A	Questions and answers
QR	Quick response code
RPE	Rate of perceived exertion
SIPS	Sports injury prevention screen
t-SNE	t-Distributed stochastic neighbor embedding
TLX	Task load index
TV	Television
UCI	International Cycling Union
UEFA	Union of European Football Associations
UK	United Kingdom
USA	United States of America
UX	User experience
VA	Visual analytics
VAR	Video assistant referee
VARS	Video assistant referee system
VR	Virtual reality
WADA	World Anti-Doping Agency
WWW	World Wide Web
XAI	Explainable artificial intelligence
XML	Extensible markup language
XR	Extended reality

Introduction 1

Sports activities have already been reported in ancient times, not only for entertainment reasons but also for rituals and cultural circumstances. Physical and also mental activities played a crucial role in these times and are still important today. The biggest difference to sports, as we know it today, is the fact that nowadays we are able to measure, record, store, manage, analyze, and visualize any kind of data related to sports in a much more efficient and effective way as it could have been done centuries ago. This effect is due to the growing impact of digitalization (Marcenko & Nikiforova, 2021; Xiao et al., 2017) and not only caused by the growing interest in sports fields but also mainly by the progress in hardware and software technologies, typically in the computer and data science domains, that have to keep pace with the growing amount of sports data. Hardware, in particular, is becoming cheaper, allowing one to record and store larger and larger datasets, which was still a problem a few decades ago (Batistic & van der Laken, 2019). However, just storing data does not lead to success, researchers and data consumers have to dig in the data with modern advanced analysis methods to identify patterns and anomalies that hint at certain issues worth improving.

Not only do athletes themselves participate in typical sports events, but even more people, activities, and processes are crucial ingredients to make each sports event a success, no matter what level and in which region it takes place. Sports involve a variety of connected people building some kind of network structure, and most of them focus on having any kind of joy, entertainment, or profit from the event. However, not only sports activities conducted by sportsmen of any kind of sports field themselves build the core of all sports events, but also managers, clubs, cities and event locations, spectators, the mass media, sponsors, sports organizations, as well as additional services and institutions involved, play an important role in the entire event—before, during, or after the event, in various roles and environments. This whole army of people involved in each sport event—individual, group, or team sports—makes this whole discipline worth investigating from several perspectives. However, on the challenging side, it is also quite difficult to extract useful and

D. Schwizer, M. Burch, *Data Excellence in Sports*, Management for Professionals,
https://doi.org/10.1007/978-3-032-10993-4_1

valuable information for any kind of related person, for example, to improve profit-increasing strategies.

Although various sensors measure and record vast amounts of data, which means supporting data generation and data handling processes, it becomes more and more challenging to link data sources with the goal of obtaining knowledge from them to prevent negative issues, predict unknown events, or just find patterns and correlations in the data. For example, focusing on improving one's own playing and winning strategies or finding problems in the e-ticketing system might be such challenges. This process requires efficient algorithms (Garey & Johnson, 1979) that preprocess, manipulate, transform, or cluster the data to find the right decisions for sportsmen, managers, trainers, spectators, betting agencies, etc. However, no matter how much data on certain sports activities exist, researchers need profound knowledge about how to link all the powerful concepts to uncover any meaningful information that could help to improve one or several aspects in the field of sports. But not only the knowledge about the data generation aspects is of particular interest in the field of sports digitalization, but also the perspective of the people involved in the sports events plays a crucial role, to set the found data insights in the context of each individual niche involved in a sports event. All of these facts might bring new future jobs in the fields of sports management, for example, a chief experience officer who is responsible for data, customers, and supporters/fans at the same time. This person might work for a sports organization or only a specific sports club. Such a role already exists in other domains, for example, in aviation.

In summary, this whole process creates some kind of process pipeline, starting with the preparation of the event (before), the event itself (during), and what happens when the event is over (after) (see Fig. 1.1). People related to a sports event have different roles and step in during these phases to different extents, participating in various ways, linked or unlinked to each other, generating different amounts of profit, typically in the form of money and fame. But indirectly, they might profit in the form of data, which are transformed to money later on, depending on the explicit value the data have in each specific sports event and for each specific person or person group involved in this money-making process. As an example, we might consider an advertisement that might make more money if

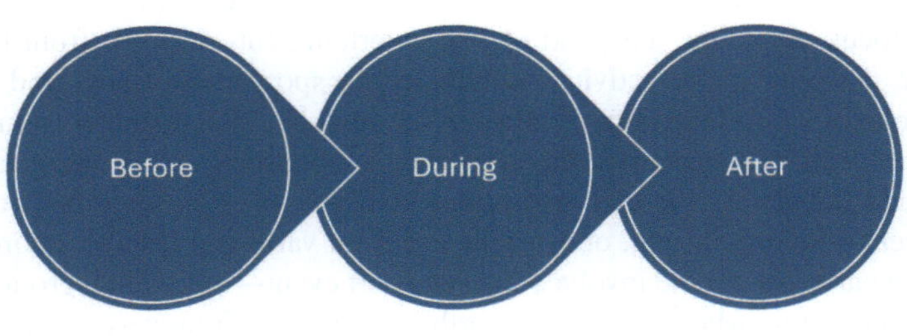

Fig. 1.1 We identified three sports event phases: before, during, and after an event. These phases correspond to the training, competition, and rehabilitation that can be regarded as a cyclic process, over and over again. Figure created by the authors

it is located in most people's fields of view that could be measured by modern eye tracking systems (Burch et al., 2025). However, the generated eye movement data (Duchowski, 2017; Holmqvist et al., 2011) must first be analyzed (Burch, 2022) to find any insight to improve the advertisement position for example. This transformation from data to money can be found anywhere in sports, but typically at different importance levels.

Before storing and analyzing valuable data, a fact that is made possible by digitalization, it must first be recorded, at ever faster rates and at ever finer granularity leading to big data. In addition to standard sports data, recorded by sensors, video cameras, or other tracking systems, we find that eye tracking is a suitable technology to augment and enrich existing data sources, as it can bring into play new features of visual attention that we were not aware of by analyzing traditional sports data. With eye tracking, we are able to measure the point of gaze of sportsmen but even spectators of sports events to, for example, place advertisements exactly in the field of view of many people. However, for the sportsmen themselves, it might give data analysts the opportunity to understand playing strategies with a finer granularity in time and space, which could help trainers improve those strategies. Negatively, the eye movement data come in a spatiotemporal form which brings new challenges for data analytics, in particular, if the data have to be analyzed in real time, for example, during a sports event to react to the opponent's playing strategy.

In addition to eye tracking, modern virtual (VR), augmented (AR), or mixed reality (MR) concepts can be applied to enrich the experience of spectators or sportsmen, for example, for training sessions or just for entertainment purposes in environments and situations in which a real sports event does not seem possible. Various advanced research fields can be combined to achieve the goal of analyzing sports data recorded in a fast and efficient way, for example, machine and deep learning, interactive visualization and visual analytics, or even more advanced technologies such as immersive analytics (Marriott et al., 2018), integrating VR, AR, and MR into the data analysis process. However, no matter how powerful these fields are, human users with their perceptual abilities (Healey & Enns, 2012; Ware, 2004, 2008) to quickly recognize patterns, for example, using human-computer interaction (HCI), play a crucial role in the decision-making stages to finally identify data patterns (Burch & Dannehl, 2025). A popular example for exploiting sports data might be found in a book or a movie called Moneyball, focusing on finding the optimal team members in a baseball match (Surendra & Denton, 2009).

1.1 The Many Facets of Sports

The field of sports has a long tradition and changed a lot during its evolution, mostly due to the fact that the glory of winning, joy, and entertainment has attracted more and more people from all over the world. However, digitalization and broadcasting technologies played an important role in this increase in interest. In the early days, only seven sports were said to have been actively practiced. This was the case with

Fig. 1.2 The Olympic Games are one of the oldest and most popular sports events combining various sports activities over a longer time period and including athletes from all over the world

the first appearance of the Olympic Games, which also involved only a few athletes from a few nations (Jablonsky, 2018) starting in Greece (see Fig. 1.2 for the variety of sports activities during the Olympic Games visualized as a word cloud). Those seven sports were, as found in the literature, equestrian, running, long jump, javelin, shot put, boxing, and pankratium (Dervenis, 2007). Today, people have the choice of several hundred sports played around the world in several national and international federations (Wood, 2025), bringing some kind of competition between sports into play. However, each sport has its own rules, sometimes very similar, and is practiced in various ways. This includes indoor vs. outdoor, individual vs. group vs. team sports, recreational vs. professional sports, or sports that last for a fixed amount of time, e.g., soccer, basketball, handball, etc., while other sports end with a reached point limit, e.g., volleyball or tennis. Some others include a finish line to cross, like skiing, cycling, or running. Moreover, sports events can have different durations, from 90 minutes of a soccer match split into two halves to the Olympic Games that last several days (Haggis & Vasilache, 2019) divided into several events and competitions. These might be classified as a typical multisport and multicultural event; see also the Pan American Games or the European Games. The Olympic Games also include individual, group, and team sports in one large event over a longer time span, which is a general difference from more classic sports events that typically only last for a few hours. Sports events may even be pieces of a bigger longer event, for example, a match day of a soccer league season.

There is even a difference between countries and regions in the world with respect to sports and how it is practiced. For example, a slightly different rule set might apply to the same sports depending on certain environmental circumstances.

One example is that another player can fixate the ball with the hands in penalty situations in countries like the Faroe Islands due to a lot of wind that would otherwise make the execution of a penalty impossible in such situations. Another example is an experiment to allow for ten changes in Major League Soccer in the United States (Maurer, 2021). The differences between countries with respect to sports can also have various other reasons, such as money, traditions, or regional aspects. Sports exist in a variety of forms, sometimes distinguished in four components: the organizational one, the technological one, the symbolic one, and the educational one (Xiao et al., 2017). The definition of sports depends on many aspects, but in general one says (Loy, 1968) that sports might be comparable to a game focusing on entertainment, joy, or social activities, as well as space and time to build a natural limit (Caillois, 2001; Huizinga, 1955). Sports and games both share the uncertainty effect that generates some form of excitement; otherwise it could be boring to participate. Both are based on rules and build some kind of competition between people or groups, parties, and teams of people while at the same time demanding winning strategies, experiences, and skills (Loy, 1968). The differences between sports and games could be found in the physical strengths that are required more in sports than in games, typically gained by a training process to reach a certain level of strength and skill.

From a digitalization and data science perspective, all of these variations in the field of sports make data recording challenging. In addition, data analyses as well after recording or even during a running sports event are challenging, especially when real-time data are being processed, expecting to give insight into data patterns that are valuable information for trainers or sportsmen to react with the intention of improving their own strategy of playing. However, such data analyses are typically expensive, including professional data analytics companies with employees educated in various related fields such as computer and data science (Ahmad et al., 2022), statistics (Kaptein & van den Heuvel, 2022), machine and deep learning (Wichert & Sa-Couto, 2021), visualization (Munzner, 2014), or visual analytics (Chen et al., 2012), to mention a few of a much longer list. However, only a clever combination of all these fields, in an interdisciplinary way, can guarantee that we can successfully use the sports data generated in the digitalization era. Furthermore, data scientists must ensure that the measured and recorded data they provide to the coaching staff are understood by them as well and really serve the desired analysis purposes, while they match the tasks at hand to be solved. The many facets in the field of sports additionally create a spectrum of variations which data analytics disciplines have to deal with. These typically include domain experts from the field of sports to be able to extract important data patterns from the data, match them with certain effects, correlations, or strategic rules related to a sports event; therefore, knowledge and insights are generated at a domain-synergetic level.

Sports can be practiced in an individual style, for example, jogging on one's own on the many paths in a forest, in a group style, for example, doing the same sports together, in a group, but not as strongly connected as in a team, in which all actors must follow certain common strategies or tactics to win a game. Sports could be performed outdoors or indoors, which actually makes a difference for data recording, but even for spectators and the entire organization since the spatial component of such a sports event is not as limited as it would be in an indoor activity. In addition, sports could be different depending on the fact that they are performed before, during, or after a sport event, corresponding to training, real competition, and rehabilitation phases. These make a difference for data recording and data analytics. In the training and rehabilitation phases, there are not that many other people involved, such as spectators, journalists, sponsors, etc., as in the real competition in which sportsmen are trying to give their best to reach their goals. All of these aspects need to include different technologies from the field of digitalization and data science to support the field of sports at its best.

1.2 From Ancient Times to the Digital Age

Although sports have been practiced since the old days at least of the Olympic Games in Olympia, Greece in 776 BC, some sports activities remained the same, while still many others came as new ones into the field, showing that sports as a common human activity has won a lot of interest since then. Today we can count an amazing number of more than 8000 different sports (Liponski, 2003). However, some of those activities are rather practiced in niche communities, and for the nonexpert it is hard to accept those as real sports, for example, traditional games in which physical activities are rather mental activities. Still, both sports and games have to follow certain structures, rules, norms, schemata, or routines to make them a successful and fair activity. What all sports have in common is the fact that people are involved as the major actors following a certain task, trying to reach a goal by typically acting physically. Sports can be practiced individually or even simultaneously with many people, in many cases as a team, following a common goal by improving one's own winning strategy. Sports are mainly a competition event, generating a clear winner who receives a medal or another kind of trophy after the competition has ended, such as in Formula One races (Lampprecht et al., 2019), but in some sports, even a draw is imaginable, for example, in a soccer or ice hockey match. Some competitions even do not allow for draws, even if it was possible. A popular example in this respect is the Swiss ice hockey league in which a draw is avoided by an extra time and even by a penalty shootout, in case there is still a draw after the extra time. Such end results might be particularly important and have an impact on the offers of betting agencies (Li et al., 2024) that increasingly enter the sports market, to not only earn money but also invest money, for example, as a sponsorship for interested sports organizations.

There are several definitions in the literature about what a sport is and what it stands for McLean et al. (2021). Sports are considered some kind of leisure, focusing on amusing and entertaining humans. It is also regarded as a competition, linked to some form of physical activity, causing mainly some kind of joy to spectators and to participants. However, the enjoyment differs between those two groups of people involved. Sports are also defined as "an activity engaged in for relaxation and amusement" (Company, 1996). Sports are typically regarded as a complex

Fig. 1.3 Checking a possible offside in a soccer match by using modern technologies, like calibrated lines and video data. Picture taken by one of the authors in the first round of the German soccer cup (Elversberg vs. Leverkusen)

system of activities with people in the focus of some kind of competition based on physical athleticism. To allow a smooth sports event, athletes have to follow well-defined rules, creating a fair competition, typically involving some kind of referee or several referees who are responsible for checking the correct application of those rules. Even verification of such rules has undergone changes in the digital world, for example, the well-known video assistant referee in soccer or goal line technology (GLT) (see Fig. 1.3 for an offside check of the VAR with a calibrated line). Therefore, modern equipment and technologies will play an important role in the field of sports in many respects.

Depending on the type of sport and the rules to be checked, there are several technologies involved which are only possible due to the impact of the digital age. Table 1.1 summarizes some of those examples, for some sports types, as well as the approximate year of the first use in sports. More and more sports activities are integrating such technologies due to the fact that a much more fair competition with more precise decisions of the referee or the jury can be guaranteed. However, at the cost of losing many spectacular scenes or incorrect decisions that would otherwise build much space for many discussions, a sporting event is interesting and exciting for spectators, fans, supporters, and participants. Moreover, many of those technologies are still to be improved to produce faster decisions, for example, the video assistant referee (VAR) system in soccer is said to take too long at the moment, leading to many frustrated spectators and soccer players, and consequently, a more AI-supported technique would be beneficial (Held et al., 2024). In particular, for soccer players it may be a bad idea to interrupt the game all the time for a few minutes, since this can have a negative impact on the muscles, as well as on the flow in the match. These negative aspects show that the digital age brings benefits to sports, and in some scenarios, most of them are a first attempt to improve fairness in sports, but at the cost of leaving many doubts about their real positive consequences. However, even if the real purpose of a digital technology in sports is doubtful, it at least generates a new kind of data that can be analyzed, which is beneficial for data science. With such data, we can also determine how efficient and effective a technology really is.

Table 1.1 Example technologies in sports, an approximate year of first usage, and in which competition it was officially used. Those technologies have not been used before digitalization made its way into the field of sports

Sports	Technology	Year	Competition
Skiing	Inert. meas. unit (IMU) (Supej & Holmberg, 2021)	1942	U.S. Navy
Ice Hockey	In-net camera (Mackie, 2020)	1970	NHL
Baseball	High-tech batting cage (Komura et al., 2002)	1972	Training in CA
Formula One	Transponders (Brunner, 2002)	1974	Silverstone GB
Volleyball	Boundary line technology (White, 2016)	1974	NERVA & PVL
Tennis	Hawk-Eye line-calling (Mecheri et al., 2016)	2001	TV coverage cricket
Cricket	Hot spot infrared imaging (Sangwan, 2014)	2006	The Gabba
Lacrosse	GPS monitoring (Aughey, 2011)	2006	USA Lacrosse
Austr. Football	Smart ball (Hibbins & Ruddell, 2009)	2009	AFL
Soccer	Goal-line technology (Spagnolo et al., 2013)	2012	FIFA Club World Cup
Soccer	Video-assistant referee (Shollo & Xiao, 2019)	2012	KNVB Eredivisie
Basketball	Instant replay (Tingle, 2020)	2014	German BBL
Rugby	Hawk-Eye spotter system (Uzor et al., 2023)	2015	Rugby WC
Handball	Headset communication (Dodt & Memmert, 2023)	2016	NHV Netherlands

The modern digital age has changed and also improved various points in sports (Konzag & Schütz, 2024), but still sports remained more or less the main event, even if more and more surrounding people or institutions participate in this whole event, mainly to get some benefits in terms of money and fame. This might only be true for professional sports; however, in leisure sports such as public running events we might find counterexamples for this effect. But in professional sports, sponsors, marketing experts, or journalists play a more and more crucial role, the higher the level of professionalization of a sports event. Digitalization is also one reason why sports are becoming more and more commercialized. People can now consume sports content anywhere in the world and access it quickly due to the increasingly faster and more reliable World Wide Web. This is enabled by all the technologies involved, including modern devices and sensors, as well as concepts of data and computer science. In general, digitalization has made tremendous changes in the world of sports and its evolution, not only the good ones but also negative issues have to be mentioned, such as overcommercialization, saturation of interests, excess supply of sports events, and many more.

In general, digitalization could be described as the use of digital technologies based on digitized data. Digitalization is said to have a positive effect on productivity and also efficiency, while at the same time the costs and the number of people involved are reduced (Xiao et al., 2017). Previously, manual activities of humans are based on hardware and software components in the digital age. In addition, the field of sports, as many others, has been influenced by digitalization, for example, storing and displaying scores, analyzing events during a football match like VAR and GLT, or applying data science concepts to find patterns and anomalies in any kind of sports data, at different levels of temporal granularity (D'Urso et al., 2023). We could argue that digitalization has brought much more structure to the field of sports, particularly through the World Wide Web. The web makes it possible to quickly access any desired information from nearly any location in the world, making sports a more widely distributed activity.

Digitalization has also brought about changes in the sports domain that continue to this day (Smith & Stewart, 2010). In modern times, we find different ways in sports to reach consumers, such as fans or the sports industry with long-standing traditions (Krzanich, 2016) but even other industries involved in sports events such as the food, advertising, or the sports clothing industry. This change affects more than just industrial sectors. It includes the development, implementation, and delivery of software solutions for sports data, as well as new hardware technologies that can keep up with the advancing digitalization of sports. It also extends to e-sports as a new way for people to participate in sports. In addition, academic research has been involved in the area of sports digitalization, for example, in educating people with the goal of finding experts in data analytics, data monitoring, data measurement, and data handling. Not only sports data analytics but also more and more available online services build much room for research, for example, to produce more reliable and fast solutions to e-ticketing systems that also produce valuable data worth analyzing. In general, many digital processes typically produce large amounts of data, while examining such data can lead to useful insights. This can be beneficial to all the actors or institutions involved. However, successful work in these fields of sports science (D'Urso et al., 2023) and sports analytics (Chartier, 2025) demands knowledge and experience in many subdomains among sports and digitalization. Further fields focusing on this interdisciplinary aspect may be sports informatics, sports psychology, sports economics, sports health, or sports management, to mention a few (Baca et al., 2022; Link & Lames, 2009).

1.3 The Role of Data Analytics in Sports

Digitalization brings many opportunities into the field of sports. Regardless of which kind of technology is used, in most cases, data are generated. Just measuring and storing such data does not make any sense since the valuable data patterns would be unused, and hence, a great chance for improvements, based on those found patterns and anomalies, would be lost. Data analytics and data science take over a prominent role in the field of sports in modern times (D'Urso et al., 2025), due to the ever-increasing role of digitalization with all technologies, devices, instruments, sensors, systems, and tools involved (Konzag & Schütz, 2024). Data handling and data storage are definitely crucial stages in the entire data analysis process. This is related to the three Ps of sport event data management: prepare, perform, and progress. However, there are even more concepts related to sports data analytics, including transforming, processing, clustering, mining, or simulating artificial data. They mainly focus on removing the data flood, identifying valuable patterns, or creating data based on data generation models. In addition, research fields such as statistics, visual analytics, human-computer interaction, and the like are the main ingredients, including efficient algorithms. In addition, interactive visualizations exploit the perceptual abilities of human users (Healey & Enns, 2012) with the goal of building synergy effects between the machine and the human to quickly and reliably find insights and create knowledge (Keim et al., 2012). A famous quote by Leo Cerne or Albert Einstein brings this idea to the point: “The computer is incredibly fast, accurate, and stupid. Man is incredibly slow, inaccurate, and brilliant. The marriage of the two is a force beyond calculation.”

The role of data analytics is the fast processing of data, while human users are important decision-makers to guide the entire data analytics process. An important ingredient in this whole knowledge generation process is the experience level of the human users, and in the best case they are familiar with or even an expert in data science and sports science. The challenging problem with data science comes from the fact that each dataset has its own characteristics and structure, that is, it is based on one or several data types and stems from a certain scenario and environment with its own conditions. Data structures have to be identified first to ensure smooth and error-free analysis and reading of the data, which are prerequisites for a correct interpretation of the data. Moreover, data can come in several files that require some kind of linking procedure, trying to combine and extract the most valuable features of all the datasets to support the identification of certain patterns or anomalies in such datasets. In the field of data science we would denote several data sources as heterogeneous data (Pal et al., 2020) which brings various challenges to the data analytics process, not only the linking. In addition, the size of the data makes a difference for each analytics process. For example, in the sense of big data analytics (Polimeno et al., 2025) we are confronted by aspects such as velocity, volume, variety, and veracity. Those are especially problematic if we have to deal with real-time analyses, i.e., requiring a quick response to the current situation at hand, a scenario that often occurs in the sports domain. An example would be not only VAR decisions that require quick analyses but also semi-automatic decisions involving human sports domain experts. A big challenge in general is the time-varying nature of data which is obvious in the field of sports, since most sports events evolve over time, meaning they have a certain duration in which various things can happen which are worth analyzing and reacting on. As one negative issue, also in sports, we can find challenges in data privacy and ethics (see Fig. 1.4) that make the use and analysis of such data more and more limited, a fact that finally does not help to improve certain problems in sports and can therefore be regarded as one of the future challenges in this domain.

No matter what kind of data analytics technique is chosen, those have to be selected with care, typically focusing on user tasks that must be solved. Those tasks can occur in various forms, such as search tasks, correlation tasks, counting tasks, estimation tasks, or pattern matching tasks, just to mention a few. Those tasks are mainly based on previously generated hypotheses such as “team A scored more goals than team B,” which falls into the category of a counting task. A more complex hypothesis might state that “each time the measured value X increases, the measured

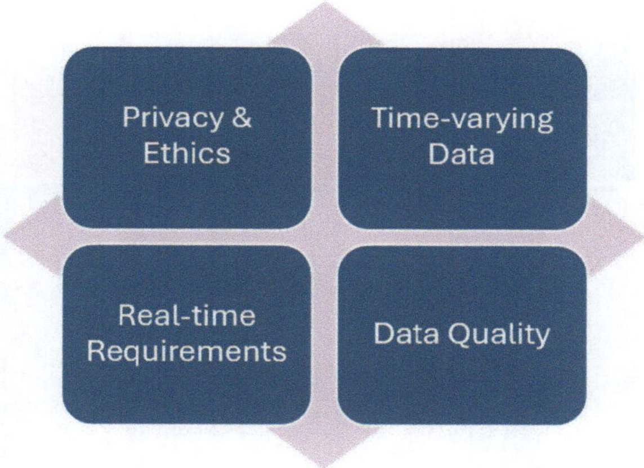

Fig. 1.4 The sports data analytics process combines automated processing with human expertise while addressing key challenges in data quality, privacy and real-time requirements, and many more. Figure created by the authors

value Y decreases," which would fall into the category of a correlation task. Hypotheses can be built, confirmed, rejected, or even refined, typically resulting in new hypotheses (Keim et al., 2012), which is a job of visual analytics. The powerful idea behind this concept is that algorithmic approaches and visual ones are combined step by step to closer and closer come to a solution to a task, hopefully helping to confirm or reject hypotheses. The user in the loop is responsible in visual analytics to guide this entire insight detection, knowledge generation, or decision-making process; however, data are still the core ingredient, and without a reliable dataset we cannot really find suitable solutions to given tasks at hand. In some situations, a pure algorithmic solution is preferred, for example, in cases in which human knowledge and experience cannot directly flow into the pattern detection stage, maybe in a real-time scenario in which a quick solution is required to hint at a problem to react on rapidly.

Data science is in general useful for many research fields, in particular, if those generate vast amounts of data—data that have varying properties such as quantitative, ordered, or categorical data in the primitive case or relational, hierarchical, spatiotemporal, textual, or multivariate data in a more complex scenario.

The goal of data science is to apply powerful concepts like machine learning, deep learning, data mining, clustering, and many more to detect patterns, knowledge, and meaning from given datasets and data sources. Those might come as big data, even be stored on various data files or data bases as heterogeneous data, or showing a temporal behavior, being real-time datasets for example. Data might even be conflicting, error-prone, noisy, and full of measurement gaps; hence data science concepts must even be able to clean such data, close missing gaps if possible, and the like. Statistical approaches might be used as data science concepts to derive aggregated and summarized values about datasets that might hint at trends or anomalies. In addition, interactive visualization or visual analytics are disciplines that include human users with their perceptual and cognitive strengths to find data patterns (see Fig. 1.5 for an example of an interactive visualization of time-varying

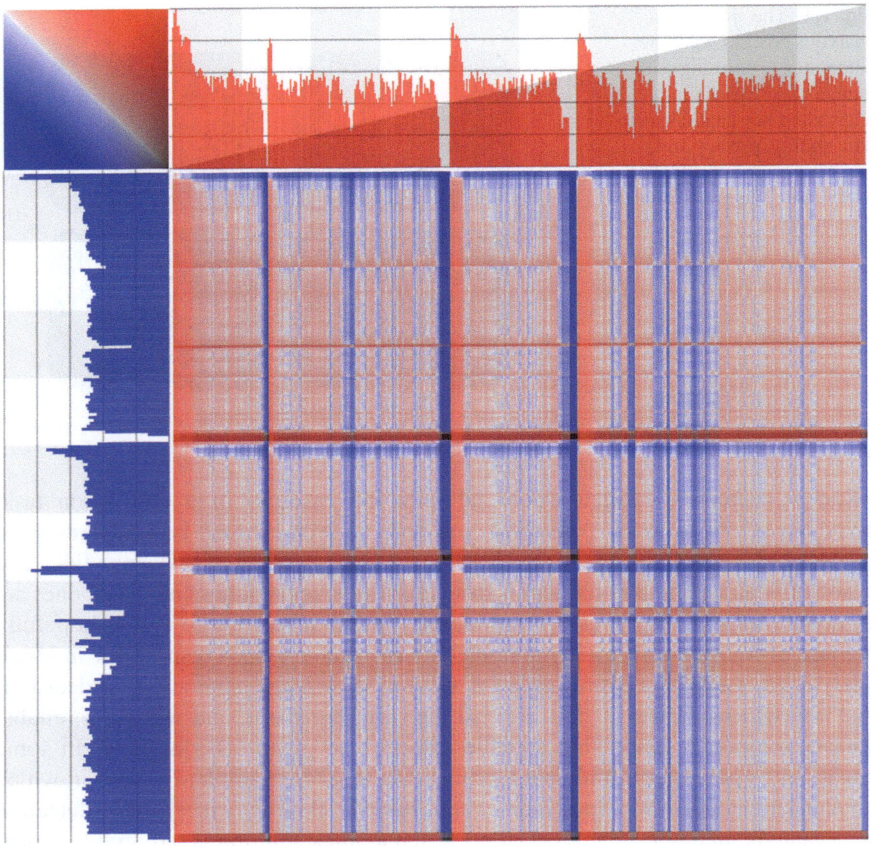

Fig. 1.5 Time-varying performance measures for two cyclists from the Tour de France in a matrix comparison visualization (Beck et al., 2016). Permission to use this image given by the authors. Figure provided by Fabian Beck

sports data). However, visual approaches are typically slower than pure algorithmic approaches, but with the level of human user experience, we could guide the entire data pattern identification process. Even novel research fields such as virtual, augmented, or mixed reality can play a role in the data exploration process, typically falling into the research field of immersive analytics (Marriott et al., 2018).

In particular, for the field of sports, we can find all the aforementioned aspects that make it an interesting research field to discuss. Data science attempts to use analytical, statistical, and visual techniques and technologies to explore data from the digital world that is measured and recorded by sensors, cameras, or any kind of tracking system, mostly with the goal of improving certain aspects related to sports, for example, focusing on a team's winning strategy, a sponsor's money making process, a marketing company's selling procedure, or a journalist's reporting

Fig. 1.6 The book structure progresses from trends and challenges through foundational concepts to practical applications and future developments in sports data management. Figure created by the authors

efficiency. Such data analyses might even be useful to help find a good sports team organization and to manage it to take the best out of it, for example, by trying to invest money efficiently into new players and the like. Not only traditional sports might benefit from data science but also new types of sports, for example, e-sports, or new services like e-ticketing to sell tickets easier, earlier, faster, and more reliably for an event. Most of the sports data come from physical equipment and devices that can measure and record the data very accurately in real time, generating a wealth of data worth analyzing. The results of the analysis are typically shown on high-tech displays to directly inform or report to sportsmen, just like a monitoring system that gives instant feedback to performances, i.e., sportsmen these days are able to monitor themselves without the help of an extra expert in data science.

This book takes a look at the many aspects of the field of sports with the ultimate goal to categorize the data-related aspects, in particular, in light of sports events and involved people and person groups, bringing new challenges and opportunities for data analytics. The book is organized as follows (see Fig. 1.6): First, we start by introducing sports from the perspective of trends in sport management in Chap. 2. Then we take into account the challenges of data and its management in sport organizations in Chap. 3. A sports data management framework is discussed in Chap. 4. Best practices in sports data management are described in Chap. 5, and we conclude the book by focusing on challenges, limitations, and future directions in Chap. 6.

References

Ahmad, N. B., Hamid, A., & Ahmed, V. (2022). Data science: Hype and reality. *Computer, 55*(2), 95–101.

Aughey, R. J. (2011). Applications of GPS technologies to field sports. *International Journal of Sports Physiology and Performance, 6*(3), 295–310.

Baca, A., Dabnichki, P., Hu, C., Kornfeind, P., & Exel, J. (2022). Ubiquitous computing in sports and physical activity—recent trends and developments. *Sensors, 22*(21), 8370.
Batistic, S., & van der Laken, P. (2019). History, evolution and future of big data and analytics: A bibliometric analysis of its relationship to performance in organizations. *British Journal of Management, 2*(30), 229–251.
Beck, F., Burch, M., & Weiskopf, D. (2016). A matrix-based visual comparison of time series sports data. In M. Guthe, M. B. Hullin, M. Stamminger & T. Weinkauf (Eds.), *Proceedings of the 21st International Symposium on Vision, Modeling, and Visualization, VMV*. Eurographics Association.
Brunner, G. L. (2002). *TAG Heuer – Die Beherrschung der Zeit*. Editions Assouline.
Burch, M. (2022). *Eye tracking and visual analytics*. River Publishers.
Burch, M., & Dannehl, S. (2025). Analyzing player types in football. In *Proceedings of the International Convention on Information and Communication Technology, Electronics and Microelectronics, MIPRO*.
Burch, M., Kurzhals, K., & Weiskopf, D. (2025). Eye tracking studies in visualization: Phases, guidelines, and checklist. In *Proceedings of the Symposium on Eye Tracking Research and Applications, ETRA*.
Caillois, R. (2001). *Man, play, and games*. University of Illinois Press.
Chartier, T. (2025). Sports analytics double take: The need for multiple perspectives on data. *The American Mathematical Monthly, 132*(1), 63–76.
Chen, C., Hou, H., Hu, Z., & Liu, S. (2012). An Illuminated Path: The Impact of the Work of Jim Thomas. In J. Dill, R. A. Earnshaw, D. J. Kasik, J. A. Vince & P. C. Wong, (Eds.), *Expanding the frontiers of visual analytics and visualization* (pp. 9–30). Springer.
Company, H. M. (1996). *Roget's II the new thesaurus* (3rd ed.). Houghton Mifflin Harcourt.
Dervenis, K. (2007). The martial arts of ancient Greece: Modern fighting techniques from the age of Alexander.
Dodt, M., & Memmert, D. (2023). The handball referee's personality through the lens of players and coaches. *German Journal of Exercise and Sport Research, 54*, 462–475.
Duchowski, A. T. (2017). *Eye tracking methodology: Theory and practice* (3rd ed.). Springer.
D'Urso, P., Gallo, M., & Zuccolotto, P. (2025). Editorial: Special issue on sports data science. *Computational Statistics, 40*(4), 1683–1688.
D'Urso, P., Giovanni, L. D., & Swartz, T. B. (2023). Editorial: Big data and data science in sport. *Annals of Operations Research, 325*(1), 1–7.
Garey, M. R., & Johnson, D. S. (1979). *Computers and Intractability: A Guide to the Theory of NP-Completeness*. W. H. Freeman.
Haggis, D., & Vasilache, S. (2019). The Olympic Games as a multicultural environment and their relationship with social media. In G. Meiselwitz (Ed.), *Proceedings of the 11th International Conference on Social Computing and Social Media. Design, Human Behavior and Analytics*, volume 11578 of Lecture notes in computer science (pp. 506–523). Springer.
Healey, C. G., & Enns, J. T. (2012). Attention and visual memory in visualization and computer graphics. *IEEE Transaction on Visualization and Computer Graphics, 18*(7), 1170–1188.
Held, J., Itani, H., Cioppa, A., Giancola, S., Ghanem, B., & Droogenbroeck, M. V. (2024). X-VARS: Introducing explainability in football refereeing with multi-modal large language models. In *Proceedings of the IEEE/CVF Conference on Computer Vision and Pattern Recognition, CVPR* (pp. 3267–3279). IEEE.
Hibbins, G., & Ruddell, T. (2009). A code of our own: Celebrating 150 years of the rules of Australian Football. *The Yorker, 39*.
Holmqvist, K., Nyström, M., Andersson, R., Dewhurst, R., Halszka, J., & van de Weijer, J. (2011). *Eye tracking: A comprehensive guide to methods and measures*. Oxford University Press.
Huizinga, J. (1955). Homo Ludens: A study of the play-element in culture.
Jablonsky, J. (2018). Ranking of countries in sporting events using two-stage data envelopment analysis models: A case of Summer Olympic Games 2016. *Central European Journal of Operations Research, 26*(4), 951–966.

Kaptein, M., & van den Heuvel, E. R. (2022). *Statistics for data scientists—an introduction to probability, statistics, and data analysis*. Undergraduate topics in computer science. Springer.

Keim, D. A., Zhang, L., Krstajic, M., & Simon, S. (2012). Solving problems with visual analytics: Challenges and applications. *Journal of Multimedia Processing and Technologies, 3*(1), 1–11.

Komura, T., Kuroda, A., & Shinagawa, Y. (2002). NiceMeetVR: Facing professional baseball pitchers in the virtual batting cage. In G. B. Lamont, H. Haddad, G. A. Papadopoulos & B. Panda (Eds.), *Proceedings of the ACM Symposium on Applied Computing (SAC)* (pp. 1060–1065). ACM.

Konzag, H., & Schütz, N. S. (2024). Sports digitalization – realizing the potential value of tracking technologies in professional sports organizations. In T. X. Bui (Ed.), *Proceedings of the 57th Hawaii International Conference on System Sciences, HICSS* (pp. 1508–1517). ScholarSpace.

Krzanich, B. (2016). Digitization is upon us—the biggest change in sports in over 100 years. *The Cauldron*.

Lampprecht, T., Salb, D., Mauser, M., van de Wetering, H., Burch, M., & Kloos, U. (2019). Visual analysis of formula one races. In E. Banissi et al. (Ed.), *Proceedings of the 23rd International Conference on Information Visualisation, IV* (pp. 94–99). IEEE.

Li, Y., Hsieh, C., & Fan, S. (2024). A social selection mechanism for sports betting market. *Decision Support Systems, 178*, 114119.

Link, D., & Lames, M. (2009). Sport informatics—historical roots, interdisciplinarity and future developments. *International Journal of Computer Science in Sport, 8*(2), 68–87.

Liponski, W. (2003). *World sports encyclopedia*. Motorbooks International.

Loy, J. W. (1968). The nature of sport: A definitional effort. *Quest, 10*(1), 1–15.

Mackie, J. (2020). Retrieved August 25, 2025, from https://vancouversun.com/news/local-news/the-history-of-the-vancouver-canucks-through-a-photographers-lens

Marcenko, I., & Nikiforova, A. (2021). Digitalization in sports to connect child's sport clubs, parents and kids: Simple solution for tackling social and psychological issues. In S. S. Cherfi, A. Perini & S. Nurcan (Eds.), *Proceedings of the 15th International Conference on Research Challenges in Information Science, RCIS*, volume 415 of Lecture notes in business information processing (pp. 595–601). Springer.

Marriott, K., Schreiber, F., Dwyer, T., Klein, K., Riche, N. H., Itoh, T., Stuerzlinger, W., & Thomas, B. H., editors (2018). *Immersive analytics*, volume 11190 of Lecture notes in computer science. Springer.

Maurer, P. (2021). How U.S. soccer experimented with 10 changes to the game before launching MLS.

McLean, S., Kerherve, H. A., Stevens, N., & Salmon, P. M. (2021). A systems analysis critique of sport-science research. *International Journal of Sports Physiology and Performance, 16*(10), 1385–1392.

Mecheri, S., Rioult, F., Mantel, B., Kauffmann, F., & Benguigui, N. (2016). The serve impact in tennis: First large-scale study of big hawk-eye data. *Statistical Analysis and Data Mining, 9*(5), 310–325.

Munzner, T. (2014). *Visualization analysis and design*. A.K. Peters visualization series. A K Peters.

Pal, G., Atkinson, K., & Li, G. (2020). Managing heterogeneous data on a big data platform: A multi-criteria decision making model for data-intensive science. In W. Lee, L. Chen, Y. Moon, J. Bourgeois, M. Bennis, Y. Li, Y. Ha, H. Kwon & A. Cuzzocrea (Eds.), *Proceedings of the IEEE International Conference on Big Data and Smart Computing, BigComp* (pp. 229–239). IEEE.

Polimeno, A., Mignone, P., Braghin, C., Anisetti, M., Ceci, M., Malerba, D., and Ardagna, C. A. (2025). Balancing protection and quality in big data analytics pipelines. *Big Data, 13*(2), 127–143.

Sangwan, S. (2014). Hot spot technique in cricket. *International Journal of Enhanced Research in Educational Development, 2*(5), 46–49.

Shollo, A., & Xiao, X. (2019). Back to the future: De-sequencing time with video assistant referee technology. In *Proceedings of the 40th International Conference on Information Systems (ICIS)*.

Smith, A. C., & Stewart, B. (2010). The special features of sport: A critical revisit. *Sport Management Review, 13*(1), 1–13.

Spagnolo, P., Leo, M., Mazzeo, P. L., Nitti, M., Stella, E., & Distante, A. (2013). Non-invasive soccer goal line technology: A real case study. In *Proceedings of the IEEE Conference on Computer Vision and Pattern Recognition Workshops* (pp. 1011–1018).

Supej, M., & Holmberg, H.-C. (2021). Monitoring the performance of alpine skiers with inertial motion units: Practical and methodological considerations. *Journal of Science in Sport and Exercise, 3*, 249–256.

Surendra, N. C., & Denton, J. W. (2009). Designing IS curricula for practical relevance: Applying baseball's "Moneyball" theory. *Journal of Information Systems Education, 20*(1), 77–86.

Tingle, J. K. (2020). Instant replay in the National Basketball Association. In M. Armenteros, A. J. Benitez & M. A. Betancor (Eds.), *The use of video technologies in refereeing football and other sports* (pp 119–137). Routledge.

Uzor, T. N., Ikwuka, D. C., & Ujuagu, N. A. (2023). Hawkeye technological innovation: Challenges and intervention strategies in sports. *Journal of Modern Educational Research, 2*, 3.

Ware, C. (2004). *Information visualization: Perception for design*. Morgan Kaufmann.

Ware, C. (2008). *Visual thinking: For design*. Morgan Kaufmann Series in Interactive Technologies, Paperback.

White, K. (2016). In and out line monitoring system for volleyball.

Wichert, A., & Sa-Couto, L. (2021). *Machine learning—a journey to deep learning—with exercises and answers*. World Scientific.

Wood, R. (2025). Topend sports – sports science, fitness testing & event analysis. *Topend Sports Website, first published January 2001*. Retrieved August 25, 2025, from https://www.topendsports.com/index.htm

Xiao, X., Hedman, J., Tan, F. T. C., Tan, C., Clemmensen, T., Lim, E. T. K., Henningsson, S., Mukkamala, R. R., Vatrapu, R., & van Hillegersberg, J. (2017). Sports digitalization: A review and a research agenda. In Y. J. Kim, R. Agarwal & J. K. Lee (Eds.), *Proceedings of the International Conference on Information Systems – Transforming Society with Digital Innovation, ICIS*. Association for Information Systems.

Trends in Sports Management

2

In this chapter, we will discuss some trends in the field of sports management (Bilohur et al., 2022). We first look into digitalization aspects (see Sect. 2.1) with expanding data volumes, diversification of data types, importance of data quality, complexity of data analysis, as well as interdisciplinary cooperation. Also professionalization plays a crucial role in this domain (see Sect. 2.2) including the increasing professionalism of data analysis, specialized services and software, the growing importance of data standards, a costly data infrastructure, as well as ethics and data protection. Individualization aspects (see Sect. 2.3) focus on new opportunities for personalization, data as a basis for individual performance diagnostics, an improved injury management, development of custom products and services, and a contribution to personal responsibility and motivation. Commercialization (see Sect. 2.4) includes utilizing data as new revenue sources, optimizing marketing and sponsorship through data analysis, improving fan engagement, enabling new business models, and increasing transparency and regulation. Finally, sustainability (see Sect. 2.5) takes into account data analysis as a way to promote sustainable decisions, uses technologies to enable resource-saving solutions, focuses on data-based communication to strengthen environmental awareness, and looks at transparency and traceability, reaching a sustainable development that is becoming a competitive factor.

2.1 Digitalization

Discussing the term digitalization (Konzag & Schütz, 2024) in the context of sports demands for perspectives on the produced data and how the data rates increase over time (Roecker & Schöllhorn, 2022) (see Sect. 2.1.1), how the data are measured and recorded and which different data types (see Sect. 2.1.2) it creates, of which quality the recorded data are (see Sect. 2.1.3), and how reliable the data analyses are, based on existing data sources. However, with increasing amounts of data, large number of

D. Schwizer, M. Burch, *Data Excellence in Sports*, Management for Professionals,
https://doi.org/10.1007/978-3-032-10993-4_2

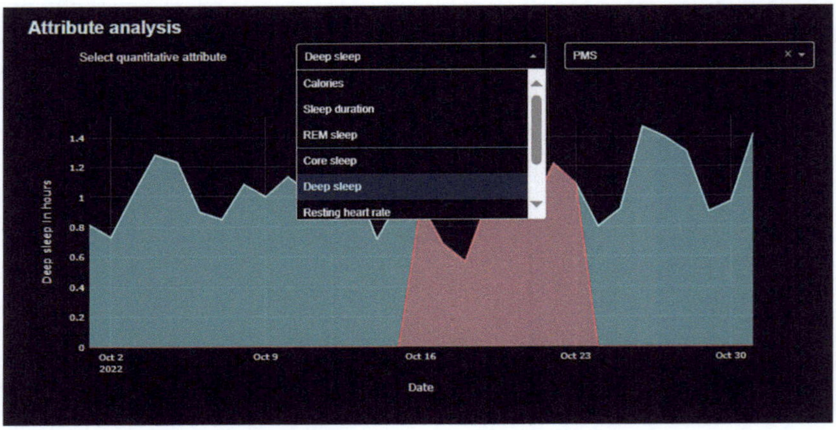

Fig. 2.1 A dashboard showing visualizations of personal data related to sports activities (Zacheo et al., 2023). Image created with the permission of the paper authors

data types, and higher tracking rates, it becomes more and more complex to analyze the data (see Sect. 2.1.4) and to find rules, patterns, correlations, or anomalies, i.e., insights and knowledge in it. The analysis cannot be done by algorithms alone, and also domain experts have to be involved in some kind of interdisciplinary style (see Sect. 2.1.5), typically ending in semiautomatic solutions to the problems at hand. Such solutions are mainly guided by graphical user interfaces in the form of dashboards (see Fig. 2.1 for an example dashboard from a sports-related visualization project) that consist of various views and perspectives on the data (Sect. 4.4.5), equipped with a multitude of interaction techniques, also known as multiple coordinated views (Roberts, 2003). They focus on the strengths of the perceptual abilities of the visual systems of humans that allow rapid recognition of patterns (Ware, 2004, 2008).

2.1.1 Data Volume Explosion

As digitalization advances, the amount of data collected in sports increases exponentially (see Fig. 2.2 for a chart showing an estimation of the data in zetabytes over the years). This observation is in line with the general explosion in data in computer and data science that has been monitored in the past years, with a change from analog to digital storage (Mabry, 2011). This data explosion offers sports organizations both new opportunities and new challenges (Roecker & Schöllhorn, 2022). On the one hand, data-driven insights can lead to better decision-making, enhanced performance, and personalized athlete training. On the other hand, there is a risk that organizations become overwhelmed by the sheer volume of data they are able to dispose of.

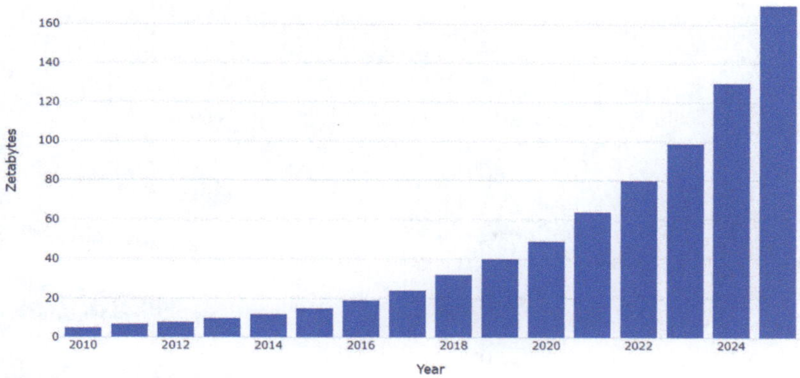

Fig. 2.2 There are estimations about the data generated every year. We can see a continuous increase in the global data, also including sports data (Mabry, 2011). Image created by the authors with Plotly Express

The increase in the complexity of the data requires specialized knowledge that often exceeds the internal capabilities of many sports organizations. In modern days we are confronted by big data (Clissa et al., 2024) issues including the five V's volume, velocity, variety, veracity, and value that are hard to tackle and often lead to missing solutions to tasks at hand. This gap is driving the need for new roles and expertise within a sports organization. Such roles can be played by different specialists. These include data scientists (Mildenberger et al., 2023), analysts, and engineers. It is utterly important that they are capable of handling and transforming data into actionable insights. Without these specialized skills, sports organizations may have difficulty using data intentionally. Like this, there are no strategic benefits to the organization.

Moreover, managing large-scale data requires effective storage solutions and robust data management frameworks. It is a shift toward holistic data management. Furthermore, this ensures that the data are easily accessible to relevant stakeholders. Especially for protagonists without a data science background, such as athletes, coaches, or medical personnel, visualization of data (Munzner, 2014) is important. Visualizations help them to understand and apply the insights generated from the data. The users on the training ground or in the management sphere are the ones to transfer the insights into actions in the daily training and work routine. Easily accessible and clear visuals enable stakeholders from all over the sports organization to benefit most from all the data analyzed by specialists. They recognize trends, create effective strategies, and work on tangible performance improvements—be they on the pitch or on the executive floor.

Faced with the evolving data landscape, sports organizations that take professional data management seriously and invest in appropriate practices are better positioned to take advantage of the flood of data and turn it into a competitive advantage in both the sporting and management spheres.

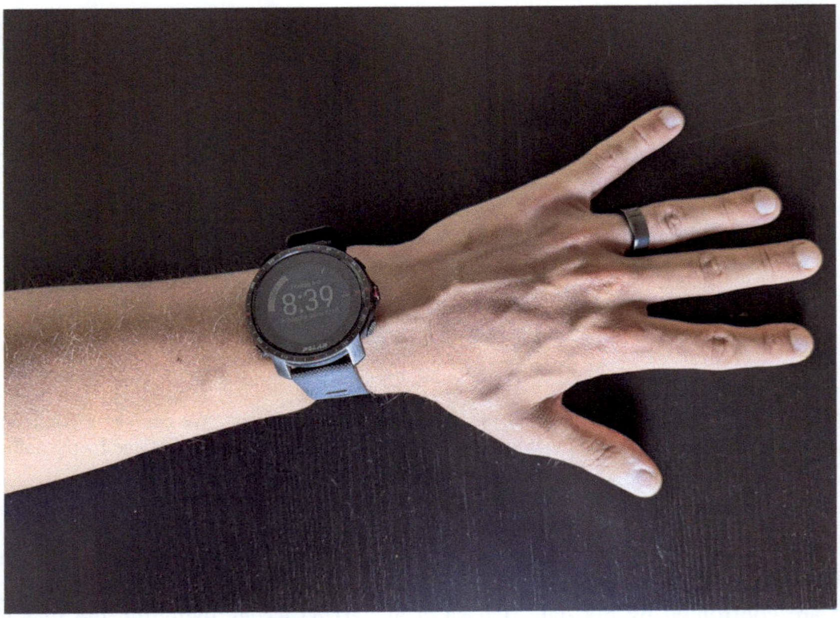

Fig. 2.3 One example of a wearable in form of a watch (Polar, Grit X Pro, 2.1.0) and a finger ring (Oura, Third generation heritage black, 3.2.2). Permission to show the picture given by Alexander van Schie

2.1.2 Diversification of Data Types

There exists a wide array of data collection technologies (Shi & Zou, 2024), such as cameras, sensors, wearables, and many other devices (see Fig. 2.3 for an example of a wearable). They enable sports organizations to gather diverse and detailed information as never before. Data include both quantitative and qualitative components, typically coming as a combination of many data sources of several data types denoted heterogeneous data (Baca et al., 2020) (see Sect. 3.3.1 for more details on heterogeneous data). Typical qualitative data include movement patterns or player positions. Subjective data can also be considered, for example, data collected by athletes themselves (Saw et al., 2016). Examples of subjective data include perceived exertion or self-reported well-being. These partly new types of data provide sports organizations with a more holistic view of sporting and business performance and thus allow more nuanced strategies in training and management. However, this new wave of data comes with significant new data management challenges because different types and data sources require specific methods in all phases of the data management process, from data collection to integration and interpretation (see Sect. 4.4.2 for more details about different types of data in the field of data science and visualization).

To maximize the benefit of different types of data, sports organizations need qualified teams that bring together a number of different knowledge and abilities (Roecker & Schöllhorn, 2022). Data management in sports organizations goes beyond simply processing numbers. In general, it is necessary to include the competencies of a variety of different experts such as data analysts, sports scientists, software developers, nutrition specialists, medical personnel, and coaches (see Sect. 4.5.3 for more details on domain experts and their roles). The perspective of each specialist helps to analyze the data in the right context and to ensure that the data are being analyzed purposefully. Like this, the insights are valuable for practice, and athletes, coaches, and managers really benefit from it. This interdisciplinary approach enables cross-functional communication and close collaboration that includes various perspectives on the data problems to be solved. It is essential to get useful and actionable insights from raw data.

However, in many cases, sports organizations do not have all of these specialists in-house all the time. There is also a way to collaborate with certain specialists on a project basis (Wäsche et al., 2017). Like this, sports organizations approach selected data management challenges during a certain period of time and do not employ all the specialists, since many sports organizations cannot afford this. Such a focused collaboration can also add substantial value to sports organizations without integrating all the specialists into the own organization. This has the advantage that sports organizations remain flexible and cost-effective even if they have to give up on maximizing all potential in sports data management. Discussions between specialists and end users, as well as the management team, ensure that the knowledge of every specialist is effectively integrated into the data management process. Insights should always be context-specific and relevant to those applying them in their daily work.

2.1.3 Importance Gain in Data Quality

Due to the explosion of data and the diversification of data types (Song et al., 2021), it is particularly important for sports organizations to ensure high data quality. This must take into account concepts including accuracy, completeness, timeliness, consistency, validity, and uniqueness (see Fig. 2.4 for an overview of relevant concepts in the data quality domain). The sheer quantity and variety of data alone only represent real added value if overall quality is ensured. This section looks at why data quality is so important for sports organizations in the age of digitalization.

First, it is about avoiding data waste. An analysis can only be as good and meaningful as the data available for it is adequate. The principle of "garbage in, garbage out" (Geiger et al., 2021) applies here. This means that poor data quality always results in poor analyses. In contrast, good data quality is not automatically a guarantee that it will always result in a meaningful analysis. Poor data quality has negative consequences. For example, it leads to incorrect decisions being made during training. This in turn can be the cause of over training or under training. This

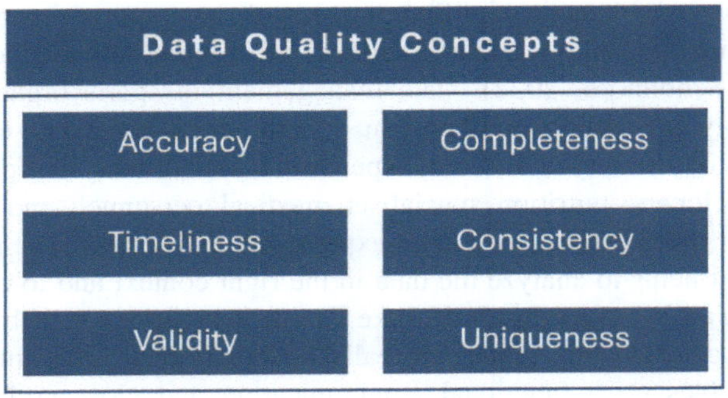

Fig. 2.4 General data quality concepts also play a crucial role in the field of sports including accuracy, completeness, timeliness, consistency, validity, and uniqueness. Figure created by the authors inspired by DQLabs

is why it is important to always provide the pure data with a plausibility check and to incorporate the years of experience of the trainers and the medical staff (McCall et al., 2016).

Another problem with poor data quality is incorrect performance analysis. These increase the risk of wrong conclusions about the performance of individual athletes or entire teams. Poor data quality has a potentially negative impact on the preparation of competition. Tactical decisions during the competition can also be affected. The risk of injury is also incorrectly assessed. Incorrect health data, for example, have a negative impact on prevention and rehabilitation (van Mechelen et al., 1992). Measures are less effective and, therefore, suboptimal. Therefore, it is crucial that incorrect diagnoses can still be corrected retrospectively in the database. Finally, poor data quality leads to wrong decisions being made about young talent and transfer (Morgulev et al., 2018). This means that the development or current status of athletes is not adequately mapped, and the wrong basis for decisions can be created when putting together teams or signing and promoting new players.

Sport is also characterized by the fact that even small details make a big difference (Mackenzie & Cushion, 2013). Even small deviations in data quality have a major impact. This is particularly the case with tactical decisions. In particular, heterogeneous systems and data silos pose major challenges for sports organizations (Morgulev et al., 2018). Different departments in a sports organization, such as medicine, scouting, finance, and sponsorship, often use incompatible software systems. This leads to challenges in data integration.

In some cases, individual data are still manually entered. This process step proves to be particularly error-prone. This may involve training records, nutrition monitoring, or medical reports. In addition, there are often inconsistent measurement methods and definitions. Different trainers and coaches record similar facts differently (Robertson et al., 2017). This leads to additional inconsistencies, especially when there are changes in the coaching and support staff. Sometimes technical errors in the data collection itself also play a role (Hoppe et al., 2018).

These can be defective sensors, incorrect device calibration, or general transmission problems that lead to inaccurate data. Clear guidelines and central data standards are of great importance (Roecker & Schöllhorn, 2022). They allow data work processes to be standardized independently of individuals. To do this, employees of the sports organization must be trained to become aware of the need to ensure data quality (Batini & Scannapieco, 2016). This will improve the data quality in general.

It is clear from these challenges that great attention should be paid to data quality management. High data quality is ensured by not viewing it as a one-time project, but as a continuous process that must also be taken into account in daily operations (Batini & Scannapieco, 2016). Investments in high-quality data are complex and often expensive. However, they pay off in the long term and increase the reliability of analyses. This enables well-founded decisions to be made in the sporting and economic fields. High data quality is an indispensable basis for successful data management in professional sports organizations. Only high-quality data hold potential for future competitive advantages and success.

2.1.4 Increased Complexity of Data Analysis

After explaining the importance of high-quality data, this section looks at why the analysis of these data is becoming increasingly complex due to the trend toward digitalization and the more and more advanced algorithmic concepts to find patterns and anomalies in such data (see Sect. 4.4.4 for more details on algorithms and Sect. 4.7.3 for scalability issues when applying algorithms), even in real time (see Fig. 2.5 for a repertoire of prominent algorithms like clustering, dimensionality reduction, and data mining). In principle, the increase in data volumes and diversity provide a good foundation and new opportunities for in-depth research. However, at the same time, more advanced methods and additional, often highly specialized expertise are required for well-founded evaluations and insights (Roecker & Schöllhorn, 2022). This section explores why data analysis is becoming increasingly complex as an important part of data management in sports organizations and what the consequences are.

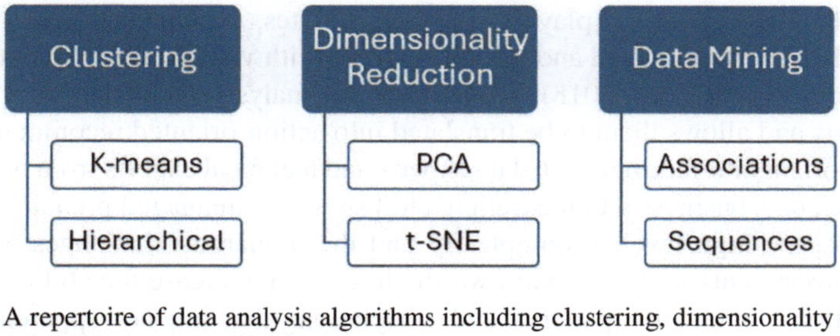

Fig. 2.5 A repertoire of data analysis algorithms including clustering, dimensionality reduction, and data mining. Figure created by the authors

The reasons for the increasing complexity are made up of different aspects, which are not equally pronounced in all sports organizations. Different data formats pose challenges (Morgulev et al., 2018). They make it difficult to integrate and analyze different types of data. Basically, one can differentiate between the following data types: structured, such as tables with performance data or results, unstructured, for example, in the form of text comments or video recordings, and semi-structured data, for example, in the form of tracking data. These different data formats require different tools, approaches, and methods (Morgulev et al., 2018). Complexity also results from increasing interdependencies and correlations. Modern analyses examine complex relationships and interactions between different datasets rather than focusing on isolated variables. An example of this would be the fact that both the training load (Gabbett, 2016) and the quality of sleep affect the probability of injury.

Examining entire time series data also tends to increase the complexity of data analysis. When looking at performance development over an entire season, special statistical methods are required to identify and correctly interpret trends, seasonal fluctuations, and outliers. In addition, there is an increasing amount of spatial data. These play a particularly important role in team sports (Memmert et al., 2017). The analysis of these spatial data (e.g., running routes, tactical formations, etc.) requires special algorithms and visualization techniques.

Many sports organizations also collect subjective data (Saw et al., 2016). Considering and analyzing subjective data (such as well-being) and combining it with objective measures require methods that adequately account for the uncertainty and variability of these data. The increasing complexity of data analysis has several implications for sports organizations. The complexity requires the use of specialists, as data analysis can generally no longer be performed using standard tools or pure business or sports management knowledge alone. Experts are needed who have specific knowledge of statistics, machine learning, data visualization, and sport or its economic sector (see also Sect. 2.1.5).

In addition, the complexity of data analysis requires modern tools and technologies. Powerful software, cloud computing resources, and special algorithms are required to process and analyze large, diverse, and complex datasets (see also Sect. 2.2.2). Furthermore, while the complexity of the data analysis must be taken into account in the analysis step, it is also crucial to translate the findings back into the language of users (players, coaches, athletes, management, etc.) after the analysis has been completed and to support them with visualizations oriented to the target group (Perin et al., 2018). This makes the analyses understandable even for nonexperts and allows them to be translated into action-oriented recommendations. This important interface between data experts and technical experts from other fields (sports science, business administration, etc.) should be managed proactively.

Despite the high level of complexity and the numerous challenges associated with it, investments in this area are worthwhile. They increase the ability of sports organizations to identify patterns and correlations that are not apparent at first glance. These would not be discovered with a simpler type of data analysis and would not be incorporated into the measures taken. In sport, even small variations

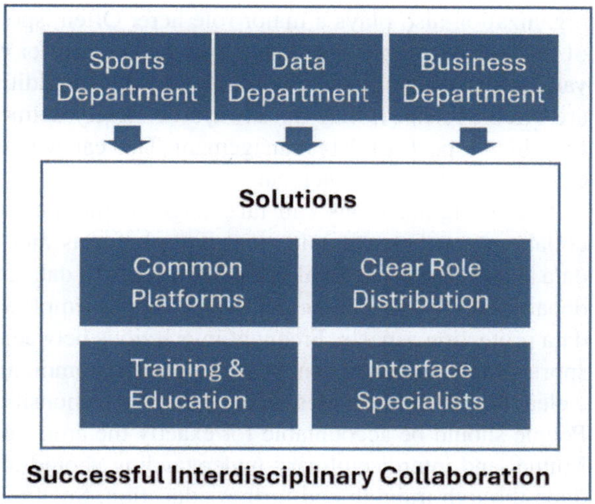

Fig. 2.6 Successful interdisciplinary cooperation in sports data management requires overcoming departmental barriers through common platforms, clear roles, and specialized interface positions. Figure created by the authors

can make the difference between success and failure—both in sporting and in economic terms. The increasing complexity of data and its analysis not only presents sports organizations with a major challenge but also offers opportunities. The recipe for success in data management lies in the ability to combine the appropriate expertise and suitable technologies in such a way that the right conclusions can be drawn in the form of actionable results.

2.1.5 Importance of Interdisciplinary Cooperation

The growing complexity of data analysis increasingly requires close collaboration between different disciplines and highly specialized experts within and outside of sports organizations (see Fig. 2.6 for the steps and stages required to be successful in interdisciplinary cooperation). This is unavoidable because isolated data analysis in data silos within individual departments does not take advantage of the full potential of knowledge and, therefore, does not allow optimal decisions to be made. This section discusses why interdisciplinary collaboration in data management is important for sports organizations to leverage the maximum value from their datasets.

However, interdisciplinary collaboration requires the ability to overcome barriers. They sometimes inhibit effective cooperation. These challenges include aspects such as the array of specialized languages and ways of thinking. Experts in various domains often employ unique terminologies and can approach particular problems in a distinctive way. There is a risk of silo mentality. Individual departments optimize the results for themselves and do not always focus on the result at the whole organizational level (Bayle & Clausen, 2025). Insights are not sufficiently shared, and knowledge remains limited to a specific area. Communication within a sports organization also plays a major role here. Often, sports organizations are unaware of the lack of established channels and processes for clear communication between various departments when it comes to data. In addition, roles and responsibilities are often unclear. It may not always be clearly defined who is exactly responsible for which aspects of data management. This can lead to irritation, neglect, or loss of efficiency in data management.

Sports organizations can take targeted measures to promote interdisciplinary collaboration. For example, common platforms and tools prevent the creation of data silos at the procedural level. The access to data and the analyses from different departments and disciplines should be kept as simple as possible, without neglecting data protection aspects. Frequent interactions between the various departments of a sports organization are beneficial for general communication. It is important to have a clear distribution of roles. In addition, the responsibilities should also be clarified. People should be accountable for exactly the areas for which they are responsible. Mutual and interdisciplinary understanding should also be promoted. This can be done through training and further education. Such measures also provide valuable information on the mindsets and methods of other disciplines that may go beyond sports. Finally, specialists play a central role at the interface between different departments and disciplines. They act as mediators and facilitate the exchange between the players involved. However, such profiles are rare on the labor market and correspondingly are cost intensive.

Interdisciplinary collaboration plays a central role in professional management of data in sports organizations (Burns & Collins, 2023). Only by bringing together different specialist areas can a deeper understanding of cross-departmental processes within the organization be reached. On this basis, jointly supported decisions can be made that have a lasting impact on both the sporting and economic areas.

2.2 Professionalization

We discuss trends in sports from the perspective of professionalization. This means that we consider data analyses (Sect. 2.2.1) as a way to find reliable insights and knowledge in the data by applying specialized software and services (Sect. 2.2.2). Such software must be compatible with the problems at hand, scalable, and well-performing. This also includes data standards (Sect. 2.2.3) that become important due to the variety of data sources and types that are available, making such applications costly endeavors due to complex data infrastructures (Sect. 2.2.4). Finally, ethics and data protection (Sect. 2.2.5) play vital roles these days, sometimes even slowing or hindering the execution of data analysis processes.

2.2.1 Increase of Data Analysis Professionality

In the previous sections, we have established that data analysis is complex and requires interdisciplinary collaboration. In this section, we will look at why data

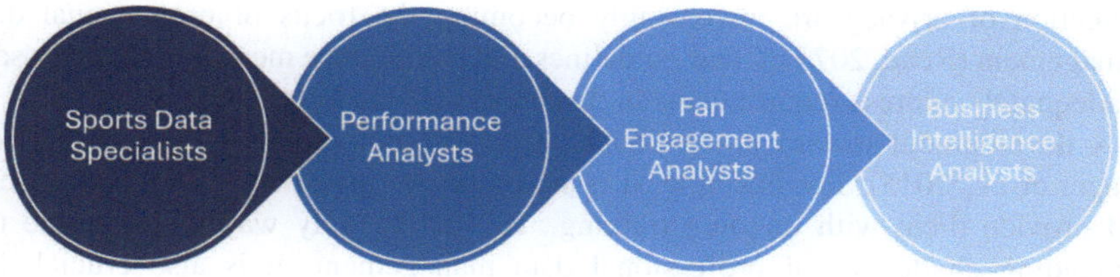

Fig. 2.7 An increase of professionalization in data analysis including sports data specialists, performance analysts, fan engagement analysts, and business intelligence analysts. Figure created by the authors based on Olaniyan et al. (2024)

management should be increasingly professionalized in sports management (see Fig. 2.7 introducing new roles such as sports data specialists, performance analysts, fan engagement analysts, and business intelligence analysts) (Olaniyan et al., 2024). This is a core task for sports organizations with their own standards, methods, and functions. This section also examines the question of how the increasing professionalization of data analysis in sport manifests itself and what consequences this has for sports organizations.

The increasing professionalization can be seen, among other things, in the role designations of specialists in sports organizations. New roles and specializations are emerging. Whereas in the past, sports scientists were simply employed who perhaps worked with data from time to time, today comparable positions are often held by data specialists in sport. Specific designations often conceal the unique training and skills of employees.

Furthermore, the professionalization of data management in sports organizations can also be seen in the establishment of standards and best practices (Bai & Bai, 2021). These increase the comparability of results and evaluations and improve the overall quality of data analysis. These standards can include various elements of data management, such as data collection, processing, analysis, and communication. The increasing professionalization is also reflected in the use of advanced methods and technologies. Sports organizations are increasingly relying on statistical modeling, machine learning, artificial intelligence, and big data technologies to find answers to complex questions and to make approximate forecasts to anticipate and better manage certain developments in the economic or sporting areas of the organization (Hecksteden, 2025). This requires not only a high degree of professionalism but also a great deal of experience.

In addition, validity and reliability play an increasingly important role in this domain (Francis et al., 2025). Professional data analysis is characterized by the fact that great importance is placed on the validity (what is being measured actually?) and reliability (are the results reproducible?) of the data and methods used. This requires strict quality controls and transparent documentation. Finally, professionalization is also reflected in the growing importance of ethical aspects and data protection. This is important in sports organizations because athlete and fan data are particularly sensitive areas. This is why ethical issues and the protection of privacy are increasingly becoming the focus of professional data management (Read, 2023). Clear guidelines and compliance measures are necessary to adequately address requirements in this area (see also Sect. 2.2.5).

A development toward professionalization is accompanied by various effects (Nagel et al., 2015). For example, it is necessary to invest in specialized experts and provide them with ongoing training. This is the only way to overcome the demanding challenges of professional data management. It is also crucial that these specialists are provided with the necessary infrastructure and modern tools. Modern work with data in sports organizations requires suitable technical equipment (Rosen & Smith, 2020). This includes high-performance hardware and suitable software and secure database systems (see also Sects. 2.2.2 and 2.2.4). Collaboration between different specialists as an expression of professionalization only works if there are clear procedures and responsibilities for data management processes. This applies to various phases of data processing, such as the formulation of questions, data collection, the use of various analysis methods, and the interpretation and communication of results. It must be clear who bears the main responsibility for each of these steps.

Furthermore, a central component of professional data management in sports organizations is not only providing descriptive statistics but also generating prescriptive and predictive findings. These influence strategic planning and decision-making at all levels of the sports organization. To this end, it is important that not only data specialists deal with the professionalization of data management but also an organizational-wide data-driven culture is established (see also Sect. 3.5). Thus, it will become a natural process that planning and decision-making at all levels of the sports organization and in various areas, especially sporting and economic areas, are based on figures, data, and facts rather than exclusively on intuition or experience (Schelling & Robertson, 2020). In conclusion, it can be said that the professionalization of data analysis represents a paradigm shift in sports management. Sports organizations that recognize this trend in good time and make appropriate investments will be able to make well-founded decisions and optimize their performance in both sports and economic terms. This creates the basis for sustainable and organization-specific competitive advantages. Therefore, it is imperative that sports organizations address the professionalization of their data management (Postma, 2023).

2.2.2 Specialized Software and Services

The increasing professionalization of data management in sports organizations is largely driven by the development and availability of specialized software and services (see Fig. 2.8 for an example of such a tool for running activity over a longer period). These tools and services offer functionalities that go beyond generic data analysis tools and in many cases are specifically tailored to the needs of sports organizations. This section examines the question of what new opportunities arise

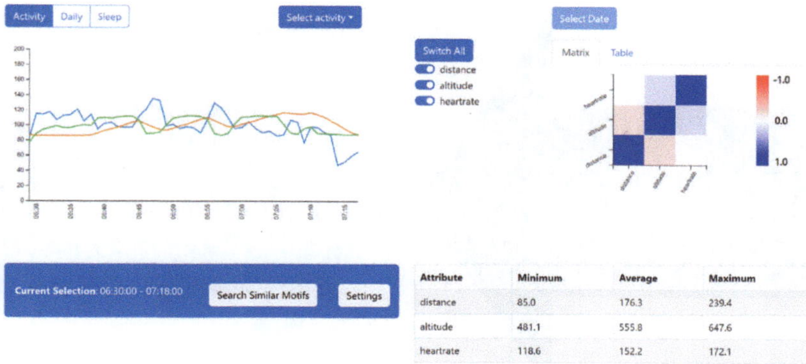

Fig. 2.8 Analysis tools are important to find insights in sports data: Here we see a simple interactive dashboard to monitor a running activity in different modes and from the perspectives of several running-related metrics. Permission to use this image by Alexander van Schie

for sports organizations using specialized software and data management services and to what extent they contribute to professionalization.

Movement analysis is particularly important in team sports (Parker et al., 2024). Special software provides insight into different aspects. They range from running routes to acceleration and interaction between players. This would hardly be possible with conventional methods. Specialized software, on the other hand, often integrates complex algorithms for pattern recognition, spatial analyses, and visualization of movement data.

Another example of specialized software is programs that enable holistic athlete management. In such programs, training and performance data, as well as health data and subjective assessments, can be recorded centrally. This enables a comprehensive integrated analysis of the athletes. Specific scouting software should also be mentioned, which automatically collects and processes large amounts of player data from various sources and creates comparable profiles. This enables an increase in efficiency in the scouting process. By automating substeps and routine tasks, both time and resources can be saved. The freed capacities can, in turn, be used for more complex data management steps.

The use of suitable software makes it much easier to create visualizations. This improves communication with the respective target groups, who make important decisions based on the analyzed data. Customized dashboards serve as an important support element here (Juliano et al., 2023). This increases the effectiveness of data-based decisions. New forms of collaboration between different specialists are also made possible as data exchange and processing are facilitated (Davis et al., 2024). External partners, such as consulting firms, also benefit from this.

Cloud-based solutions are increasingly being used for actual data analysis tools in the narrower sense (Davis et al., 2024). These create flexible analysis capacities and limit the necessary initial investment in expensive hardware. This benefits small- and medium-sized sports organizations in particular. It also gives these sports

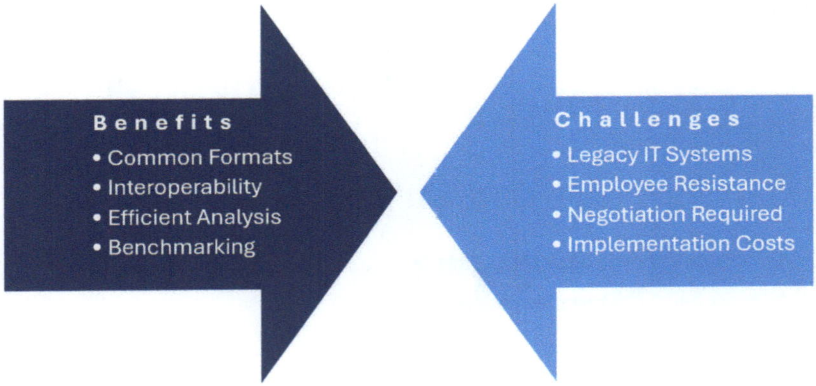

Fig. 2.9 Data standards in sports management balance implementation challenges against long-term benefits in efficiency, interoperability, and data quality. Figure created by the authors

organizations access to tools that would otherwise have been difficult or costly to acquire. Small- and medium-sized sports organizations can also benefit from the fact that software providers and experienced organizations often offer training courses and workshops on their tools (Barça Innovation Hub, 2025). This allows employees to get to know the applications and optimize their use. In addition, data management skills have also been improved.

2.2.3 Growing Importance of Data Standards

In the previous sections, we noted that data analysis in sports organizations is becoming increasingly professional (see Sect. 2.2.1) and that more diverse data can be analyzed thanks to specialized software and services (Link, 2018). This section now focuses on the growing importance of data standards in sports management (see Fig. 2.9 for some of the most relevant points). Not only do the sports organizations themselves play an important role here, but also the associations, leagues, and sports umbrella organizations. They are important players when it comes to creating uniform standards for the effective use of data and ensuring the full potential of data analysis available in sport. This section focuses on the question of why data standards are becoming increasingly important in sports management and what benefits this brings for sports organizations.

Several reasons lead to the importance of uniform data standards. First, they create common formats that allow one to seamlessly integrate data from different sources. Like this, one can ensure that everyone involved works with the same terminology and structure. In addition, this is an important factor to ensure interoperability. Moreover, this makes it easier to merge these data. Data can also be standardized during processing. Therefore, standardized recording processes help generate overall reliable and consistent data. The aim of uniform standards is to ensure interoperability not only between different actors but also between their applications.

The exchange of data for benchmarking analyses, research projects, or the development of joint initiatives across department boundaries is significantly facilitated using uniform data standards (Krüger et al., 2023). In addition, standardized data enable more efficient and scalable analysis processes. This is because data analysts do not have to make individual adjustments for each data source. Finally, it increases not only the efficiency but also the comparability of data, as the standards create a basis for objective comparisons and benchmarking. An example of such a uniform metric in sport is the standardized definitions of "expected goals" in soccer. They make it possible to compare teams in different contexts.

Although the introduction of data standards is desirable to increase efficiency, it also brings with it numerous challenges. Different sports organizations work with different IT landscapes. Many sports organizations use a variety of historically grown and different systems, which can be difficult to adapt to new standards (Blobel et al., 2021). It can also be difficult to establish new standards in a sports organization, as employees are often critical of change and the transition to new standards can be time-consuming. Furthermore, data standards in sport must first be negotiated, as there are often no comprehensively established data standards that are accepted by all. Various interest groups must collaborate to develop and implement such standards. Furthermore, implementing data standards can require initial investments in system technology or at least adjustments to existing infrastructure. This triggers costs and is resource intensive.

In summary, it can be said that data standards are becoming increasingly important in sport (Link, 2018). They enable the effective use of the potential of data in sports management. Although the implementation of data standards in sport presents challenges, the long-term benefits in terms of data quality, efficiency, and interoperability clearly outweigh them and make a significant contribution to the continued professionalization of data management in sport and sports organizations.

2.2.4 Costs of Data Infrastructure Setup

In the previous sections, we have seen that data analysis in sports organizations is becoming increasingly professionalized, with specialized software and services, opening up new possibilities and increasing the importance of data standards. All of this involves investment. Setting up a good data infrastructure is expensive (see Fig. 2.10 for relevant points when it comes to data infrastructure costs). Costs are a particular challenge for sports organizations, especially smaller or less well-positioned ones. This section therefore examines which cost factors are relevant when setting up a data infrastructure in sports organizations and why the magnitude of these should not be neglected. Particular attention is paid to the various cost factors. These essentially include hardware, software, personnel, implementation, maintenance, and staff training.

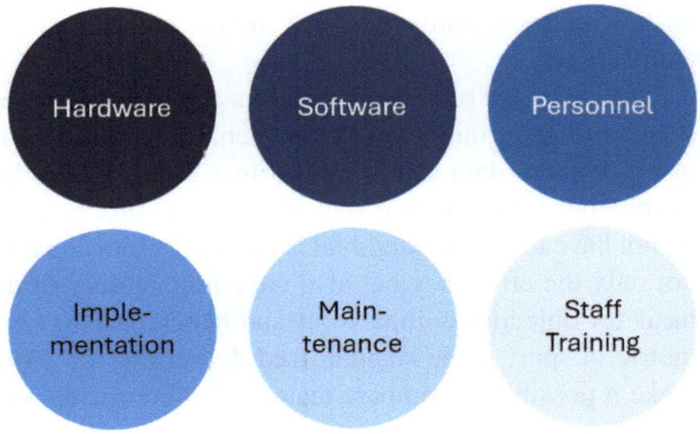

Fig. 2.10 Data infrastructure costs in sports organizations encompass six key areas from initial hardware and software investments to ongoing maintenance and staff training requirements. Figure created by the authors

The collection, storage, and processing of large amounts of data require powerful hardware (Johansen et al., 2020). This includes servers for databases and analyses, network infrastructure for data transmission, and, in some cases, special hardware for data acquisition, such as high-performance camera systems in video analysis. In addition to hardware, specialized software solutions are also key concepts. These include database systems, data integration tools, analysis platforms (e.g., for statistics, machine learning, or business intelligence), tools for visualization and visual analytics, as well as specialized software solutions for certain sports—such as programs for analyzing movement sequences. An illustrative example of such specialized systems is the investment of Formula 1 teams in simulation software that processes and analyzes large amounts of sensor data in real time to optimize racing strategies (Nimmala & Nimmala, 2023).

Special hardware and software alone do not make a sports organization a pioneer in data analysis. A modern data infrastructure requires qualified specialists to set up, use, and maintain it. Relevant roles include data engineers, database administrators, IT security experts, and cloud specialists. As these are highly specialized professionals with sound training and ideally extensive practical experience, they are expensive and represent a significant cost factor.

A data infrastructure is not a static entity. Rather, it requires ongoing maintenance. This is essential to ensure smooth operation and data security. In practice, this often results in costs through software subscriptions, support contracts, or the use of internal IT resources. System failures must be avoided at all costs. They can result in both economic and sporting disadvantages. Furthermore, the data infrastructure is constantly evolving. This is why continued training and further education are necessary for employees. This applies, for example, not only to trainers and analysts but also to business administration staff. They must be trained in new tools and applications to optimally integrate the systems into their work processes (Houtmeyers et al., 2021). Certain software providers also offer training for precisely this purpose.

Fig. 2.11 Ethical data management requires addressing core principles and challenges through systematic solutions built on trust and compliance. Figure created by the authors

2.2.5 Ethics and Data Protection

Professional data management in sports organizations also includes responsible handling of data (Krüger et al., 2023). It goes far beyond simple collection and analysis of figures, data, and facts. Ethical considerations should therefore be a mandatory component of holistic data management. This also includes consistent compliance with data protection regulations. Many of the data related to athletes and consumers must be handled sensitively and transparently. This helps maintain the trust of these key stakeholders. Compliance with ethical principles (see Fig. 2.11 for important ethical principles in research and business) and the implementation of appropriate data protection measures are therefore essential for sports organizations.

The ethical aspects of data management in sports organizations go beyond mere compliance with legal requirements. Different principles of data use must also be upheld. For example, athletes and fans must be informed transparently about the use of their data. Only in this way they can give their consent. Sports organizations have a responsibility in this regard. It is therefore important that the players concerned consent to the use of their data. This is particularly problematic in the case of athletes, as they are subject to a certain systemic pressure: If a soccer player wants to be part of a team, for example, he can hardly avoid the data analysis of the respective club.

Furthermore, discrimination and stigmatization must be avoided at all costs. This applies in particular to data management based on historical data series. Their analysis can unintentionally reproduce prejudices or lead to discriminatory decisions (Zhang & Li, 2022). An example of this would be data analysis around talent management (e.g., in selection and promotion).

Finally, it is also important that sports organizations guarantee the rights of data subjects (Tataru & Tataru, 2020). This includes, for example, the possibility of obtaining information about the stored data, correcting incorrect data records, or even requesting the deletion of data. However, the latter is particularly problematic in the area of athletes in that sports organizations tend to be interested in an analysis over a longer period. They will therefore hardly be willing to voluntarily refrain from storing interesting data. The storage of fan data is somewhat less problematic. For example, a fan can unsubscribe at any time from a newsletter list for which he or she once registered. The above shows that the ethical and legal aspects of data management must be considered from the outset and cannot be implemented retrospectively (Hagg et al., 2021). Ethical considerations should be an integral part of professional data management and should be given strategic consideration. Clear guidelines, employee training, and clear processes and responsibilities help to guarantee responsible and ethical data handling. Compliance with legal requirements is only the minimum objective.

2.3 Individualization

Athletes are the central players in the field of sports. The recorded data create new opportunities for personalization (Sect. 2.3.1) including individual content and target groups. It is also the basis for individual performance diagnostics (Sect. 2.3.2) at different levels of granularity and focusing on various physiological metrics related to the body. It allows better injury management (Sect. 2.3.3), for example, using imaging techniques, biomechanical analyses, or even clinical tests. Customized products and services (Sect. 2.3.4) can also be developed based on data and their insights. In addition, data can contribute to personal responsibility (Sect. 2.3.5) and motivation.

2.3.1 New Opportunities for Personalization

Data play an important role in personalization strategies in sport. It provides the basis for individualizing content and tailoring it to the respective target groups. Personalization affects not only the performance of athletes (i.e., the sports sector) but also the fan experience and thus the commercial activities of sports organizations. This section answers the question of how data enable personalization in sport and what benefits this brings to athletes, fans, and sports organizations themselves.

Personalization is likely to become increasingly important in competitive sports (Nassis et al., 2020). This is particularly related to individual training and personalized medical care (see Fig. 2.12). Dynamic adaptation plays an important role here. Data about athletes allow for individualized support. Training plans can be adapted to the current training status of the athletes. Individual requirements can be

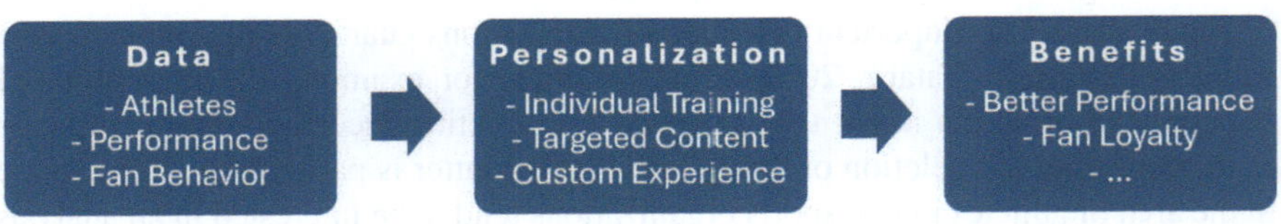

Fig. 2.12 Data-driven personalization transforms athlete and fan data into customized experiences that improve performance and loyalty along with other key metrics. Figure created by the authors

considered appropriately. Individually designed training plans make an important contribution to systematic performance development (Halson, 2014). They also improve preventive aspects of training and competition. Consistent individualization can lead to a more consistent performance, which is in the interest of both the individual athlete and the entire sports organization.

Data create new optimization opportunities not only in training but also in the medical and therapeutic field. This allows rehabilitation measures after injuries to be even better tailored to the needs of the individual athlete. Furthermore, therapy progress also becomes visible in the data. Ideally, the recovery process is accelerated. This is an important factor in competitive sports. In addition, data exchange between various specialists also allows holistic and coordinated treatment. An aspect should be crystal clear here: The individualization of training and therapy is a dynamic process. It must be reviewed and adjusted regularly, as the needs of athletes also change constantly.

In addition, personalization also becomes increasingly important in the commercial sector of a sports organization (Pashaie et al., 2024). Fan engagement can be promoted by creating customized content for audiences (Mahmoud, 2024). Data help to better align content, channels, and audiences. Insights into fans' media usage behavior also help reach fans in a targeted and tailored manner. This creates added value for both fans and sports organizations. Fans are shown more relevant content, while sports organizations can increase the effectiveness of their communication measures.

However, the sports organization must provide the necessary technological infrastructure. Powerful computers and systems are a prerequisite for collecting and processing the necessary data. This includes elements such as sensors, wearables, databases, analysis platforms, and customer relationship management (CRM) systems. And finally, there are also ethical and data protection aspects to consider (see Sect. 3.1.3). Personalization in sport is always associated with challenges and requirements in this area. The privacy of athletes and fans must be protected and respected in a credible and transparent manner. Transparent data processing creates the basis for trust and an increased chance of obtaining consent for data processing from affected stakeholders.

2.3.2 Individual Performance Diagnostics

In sports, individual performance diagnostics (see Fig. 2.13) are an essential basis for achieving the desired personalization (see Sect. 2.3.1). Data make it possible to analyze and understand the performance of athletes at a detailed level, which forms the basis for tailored measures. This section explores the extent to which data form the basis for individual performance diagnostics in sports and the benefits for athletes and sports organizations.

Data contribute a great deal to various aspects of individual performance diagnostics (Bourdon et al., 2017). These include objectification of performance measurement, the identification of strengths and weaknesses, monitoring of per-

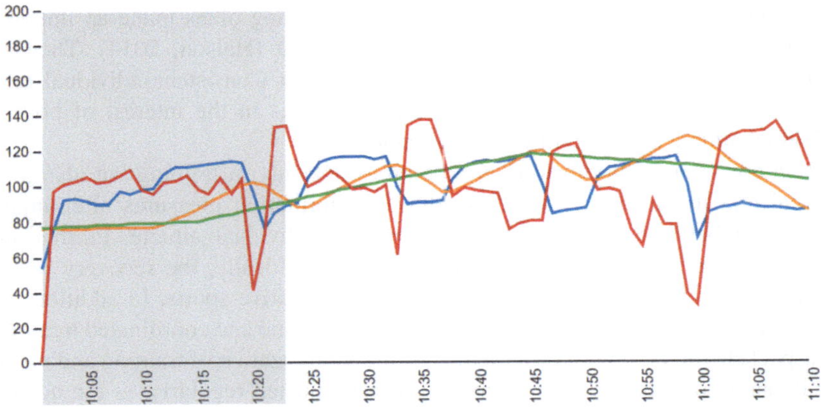

Fig. 2.13 Individual performance diagnostics including the heart rate metric over time under different conditions (like running uphill or in flat land for example). A time period is currently selected to apply further analyses. Permission to use this image by Alexander van Schie

formance development, and early detection of risks. On the one hand, data offer the opportunity to objectively measure athlete performance instead of simply relying on subjective assessments. On the other hand, it should be emphasized that both objective and subjective evaluations (see Sect. 4.6) represent the optimal combination for many questions in performance diagnostics. In general, the quantifiable component element based on the data enables a more precise and well-founded assessment of the level of performance.

Data also make it possible to identify the individual strengths and weaknesses of athletes. This forms the basis for targeted training measures and individually tailored performance optimization. In swimming, movement data can be analyzed in this way to uncover weaknesses in a technique (Kon et al., 2015). Specific exercises can then be used to adapt training to optimally improve the performance of the athlete. However, not only the optimization of training exercises but also the overall development of performance data can be monitored using individual performance diagnostics. This allows progress or setbacks to be documented over a longer period. These data are therefore an important basis for long-term training planning and adjusting goals. For example, an athletics coach on a basketball team can record the development of his players' jumping height to track how effective training is throughout the season and which regeneration measures help restore full performance as quickly as possible (Yoon et al., 2019).

Finally, individual performance diagnostics can also be used to identify risks at an early stage (Gabbett, 2016). This applies both to health risks and to the danger of a decrease in performance due to overtraining or injury. Therefore, these are preventive measures to ensure long-term performance. An example of this is monitoring of heart rate variability and sleep quality to detect signs of overtraining early and thus prevent performance losses or injuries. Individual performance diagnostics are used not only for training management and injury prevention but can also have a positive effect on the motivation and willingness of athletes to perform. Objectifiable performance data and good communication of this data via visualizations (Ware, 2004, 2008) enable athletes to recognize that their training and individual measures are effective. In the ideal case, this leads to higher motivation and a positive self-reinforcing cycle (Ryan & Deci, 2000). Such a positive dynamic usually results in a further increase in performance. Like this, athletes are encouraged to consistently pursue their long-term goals even during difficult periods of training.

In addition, data for individual performance diagnostics also play a role for athletes who are not yet in their own sports organization. In this way, data can help to discover athletes with great potential and to strive to sign them up. Data therefore help to assess the suitability of potential new recruits and provide an objective basis to make the right transfer decisions. This minimizes the risk of incorrect purchases. However, this point is not equally relevant for all sports organizations but mainly affects team sports. If the athlete in question is signed, the data help promote talent or new additions in the best possible way.

Effective individual performance diagnostics are based on several basic requirements that are necessary for this. For example, a sports organization depends on qualified personnel who can understand performance diagnostics in a meaningful way. This requires both expertise in data analysis and sports science (see Sect. 4.5.3) and knowledge about the respective sports. In addition, the necessary infrastructure must be provided. Only in this way are adequate recording, processing, and analysis of the data ensured. And finally, ethical considerations (see Sect. 2.2.5) must also be considered, for example, to ensure the privacy of individual athletes' data. In conclusion, it can be summarized that data form the basis for objective, precise, and effective individual performance diagnostics in sports. However, individual performance diagnostics not only optimize the performance of athletes but also help sports organizations in various other areas such as scouting, talent identification, and training planning.

2.3.3 Improved Injury Management

Injury management is of vital importance in sports organizations. Athletes are employed to perform. This employment status is especially true for team sports. Therefore, it is important to avoid injuries whenever possible or, in the event of an injury, to allow the athletes to return as quickly as possible. Data contribute to ensuring precisely this. Data-driven management enables precise diagnoses (Gruetzemacher et al., 2016). In addition, rehabilitation measures can be individualized. The following section discusses how the use of data allows better injury management, from which athletes and sports organizations benefit equally.

If an athlete sustains an injury, various analytical methods facilitate diagnosis. These include imaging techniques, biomechanical analyses, and clinical functional tests (see Fig. 2.14). These methods provide relevant data and create a good basis

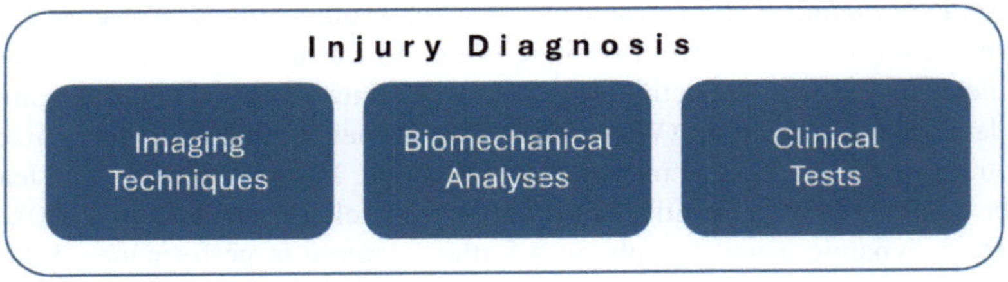

Fig. 2.14 Injury diagnosis: Imaging techniques, biomechanical analyses, and clinical tests are some of the crucial points that must be considered for an impactful diagnosis. Figure created by the authors

for accurate diagnoses. This also allows the severity of a specific injury to be determined. The appropriate treatment is initiated on this basis. This in turn also generates data. Based on these data, a decision can also be made as to when a return to competition is possible. In competitive sport, there is a risk of returning too early and therefore also the risk of relapses or subsequent injuries. This is neither in the interests of the individual athlete nor in the interests of the sports organization.

There are also other aspects of injury management. Data make it possible to identify systematic problems in training. For example, analyses at team level can help uncover training or coaching problems that lead to an increased risk of injury (Windt & Gabbett, 2017). This provides indications of the necessary adjustments to the training methods or the organizational framework to prevent injuries. The recurring incidence of muscle injuries in a team can be an indication of an excessive training load. Data can be used to optimally manage training load and recovery times. This enables improvement in medical care and optimization of treatment results. Especially in large sports organizations and for longer periods of time, the systematic collection of data on the healing process of athletes with a specific injury under different treatment approaches makes it possible to compare the effectiveness of different methods.

Data-supported injury management is a challenging task for a sports organization. To ensure professional injury management, interdisciplinary collaboration is necessary within a sports organization (Wiese-Bjornstal, 2010). The departments involved must optimally coordinate their individual measures to ensure optimal care. Therefore, it is crucial that the various departmental specialists have access to an integrated data system in which the parties involved can exchange important information about the athlete's treatments and health status. This allows for optimal coordination of individual measures. Coordinated care creates a solid medical foundation to adapt therapies and achieve the fastest possible recovery. The optimal time for a return to competition can also be determined more precisely (Creighton et al., 2010). This reduces the risk of setbacks. In addition, overall medical care within the sports organization is continuously optimized.

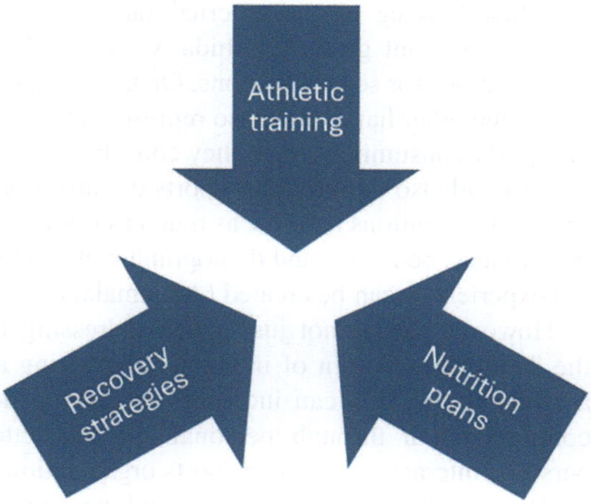

Fig. 2.15 Data help to tailor athletic training, nutrition plans, and recovery strategies. Figure created by the authors

2.3.4 Customized Products and Services

Data not only contribute to the personalization of training and treatment measures in the medical field but also allow the development of custom products and services for different target groups in sport. This requires a deep understanding of the needs and preferences of target groups as a basis for developing successful and targeted offers. This section focuses on the key question of how data enable the development of such tailored products and services in sport and what opportunities this opens for both the sports organizations themselves and their target groups. One can differentiate between the internal and external target groups.

The athletes themselves are arguably the most important internal target group of any sports organization. Data-driven approaches allow individualization of training, nutrition, and recovery (see Fig. 2.15). This individualization should help maximize the chances of success. Coaches play an important role in this process. They translate the data into practicable training units and plans and continuously check to what extent further individual adjustments are necessary when implementing them in daily practice (Sousa, 2019). As a rule, they do not only rely exclusively on the available data but also contribute their personal experience to the training design. A key success factor here is communication between coaches, athletes, and other stakeholders.

As already explained above (see Sect. 2.3.3), personalized information contributes to better medical care. Data enable doctors and other medical personnel to provide a comprehensive overview of the health status and risks of injuries of athletes or entire teams (Fuller et al., 2018). This allows more precise diagnoses to be made, resulting in individualized care and optimal rehabilitation. Not only does the treatment of existing medical problems play a role here, but also the prevention of injuries and the minimization of injury risks through targeted load management.

When looking at the external target groups of a sports organization, fans are an important group (Yoshida & James, 2010). They are important to sports organizations for several reasons. On the one hand, they support athletes and teams, but on the other hand, they also represent an economic factor as a consuming target group. By consuming sports, they contribute significantly to the revenue of sports in general and also of individual sports organizations. Therefore, it is in the interest of sports organizations to know as much as possible about their fans. This includes fan preferences, behavior, and demographic characteristics. On this basis, personalized fan experiences can be created (Annamalai et al., 2021).

However, this is not just about addressing fans individually. It also refers to the data-driven design of integrated marketing and communication campaigns on a larger scale. This can increase the effectiveness of these measures. Individual communication through personalized newsletters can also contribute to more personal interaction between sports organizations and fans.

The development of personalized products and services presents numerous challenges for sports organizations (Woratschek et al., 2014). It is challenging to collect meaningful data in the respective areas and utilize it with targeted analyses. Furthermore, it requires a powerful infrastructure. This allows data specialists to capture relevant information and make it available for personalized analysis.

Data create new opportunities for personalized offerings to fans and personalized support for athletes. This generates an opportunity for sports organizations to differentiate their offerings and address specific target groups with appropriate measures. These contribute to the sporting and economic success of the sports organization.

2.3.5 Personal Responsibility and Motivation

Data and analysis give athletes the opportunity to better understand their own performance (Malcata & Hopkins, 2014) and track their training progress. This promotes personal responsibility and motivation (see Fig. 2.16 for one of Pele's famous quotes). The trend toward individualization not only means that data enables the adaptation of training and support measures for athletes but also plays a fundamental role in the personal responsibility and motivation of individual athletes. The digitalization of sport is transforming the role of the athlete from a passive recipient of instructions to an active codesigner of their own development. The intelligent and targeted use of data is making a significant contribution to this transformation. This section explores how data can promote athletes' personal responsibility and motivation by providing transparent insights into their performance development.

As a rule, individualization is not simply a matter of passively receiving training data and programs or medical support measures, but rather the athletes themselves actively contribute to ensuring a rich and balanced database (Seshadri et al., 2019). This is because the data do not only consist exclusively of quantitative components but also contain qualitative data.

"Success is no accident. It is hard work, perseverance, learning, studying, sacrifice and most of all, love of what you are doing or learning to do."

Pele, soccer player

Fig. 2.16 Motivation is very important when doing sports, no matter in which kind of sports. A quote by Pele, a famous former soccer player, indicates that the right motivation in sports can lead to success

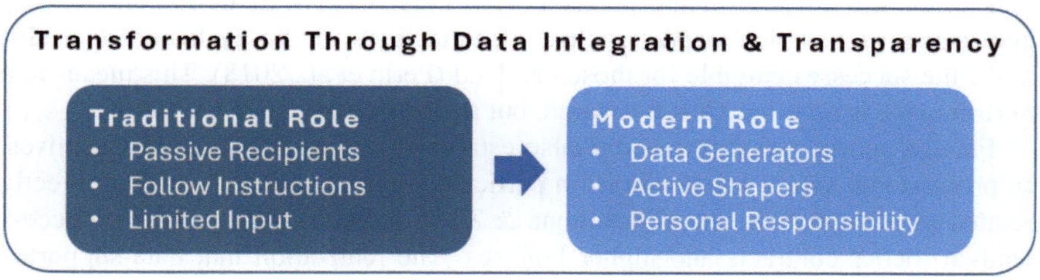

Fig. 2.17 Modern sports data management transforms athletes from passive recipients to active data partners who shape their own performance development through qualitative feedback and personal responsibility. Figure created by the authors

Qualitative sets go beyond objective measurements. It is also possible to request feedback from athletes on training content and effects. Through regular feedback on specific exercises, training intensity, or the effects of recovery measures, athletes provide important qualitative data that allow them to fine-tune the programs. In addition, recording the mental state is also of great importance. This involves recording data on concentration ability, mental fatigue, or similar factors and completing the existing picture.

These active contributions of athletes also change their role in general data management within sports organizations (see Fig. 2.17). Athletes do not remain passive recipients of information but become data generators and data curators who, together with the appropriate specialists, maximize the benefits of data management for themselves and the entire sports organization (Kellmann et al., 2018). Athletes not only serve as objects for data collection but are also an integral part of the entire data management process. This creates a better understanding of the links between training, performance, and recovery. Finally, it also strengthens personal responsibility.

An important aspect here is transparency. If data collection and use are understandable to the athlete and primarily serve athletic development, willingness to cooperate increases. The data clearly show how stress, training, and recovery affect performance and which interrelationships should be considered. Thus, effective measures can be identified and pursued. In this way, athletes can actively participate in the data process and contribute their opinions and experiences, further refining and individualizing the process.

When athletes take responsibility for data-based collaboration, the results can be further improved. In this way, athletes are no longer simply recipients of instructions but actively shape their performance. This is possible because athletes are better informed and can be more conscious about how they structure their daily lives. This results in a proactive rather than passive attitude.

If they succeed in positively shaping their own development through data-based load and training management, this can generate further motivation. Individual progress is visible, even if it is often only slight in competitive sports. However, it is often still evident in the precisely collected data, be it in strength values, endurance, or technical aspects. Clear visualizations of the evaluated data also make the successes tangible for those involved (Perin et al., 2018). This means that performance is no longer just measured, but actively shaped.

Finally, sports organizations can also establish performance-related incentives. In professional sports organizations in particular, sporting success is often directly related to economic success (Di Simone & Zanardi, 2021). More sporting success leads to better contracts and higher bonuses. The realization that data-supported improvements in the sporting area also improve the economic situation of a sports organization can increase additional motivation not only among athletes but also among people working economically for a sports organization.

In conclusion, it can be said that the data are changing the role of the athlete in modern sports management. It creates opportunities to provide athletes with more precise and individualized support. It also promotes personal responsibility and increases motivation by making athletes active partners in their own performance development. The transparent and trusting provision and the joint interpretation of the data create a new scope for creativity, which makes a significant contribution to exploiting the full potential of athletes.

2.4 Commercialization

The term commercialization includes several ideas, for example, how data generate new sources of revenue (Sect. 2.4.1) or how data analysis optimizes marketing and sponsorship (Sect. 2.4.2). Moreover, we see an improvement in fan engagement (Sect. 2.4.3) that is also caused by using and analyzing the right type of data. New business models (Sect. 2.4.4) can also be envisioned by including data, which was not possible many years ago. Finally, we also see an increasing importance for transparency (Sect. 2.4.5) and regulation.

2.4.1 New Sources of Revenue

Data and professional handling of them can be a decisive success factor for sports organizations (Bai & Bai, 2021). If data are used in a targeted manner, it can directly influence both sports and economic success (Scelles et al., 2017). In addition to the analysis of performance data for the sporting sector, the question of how data

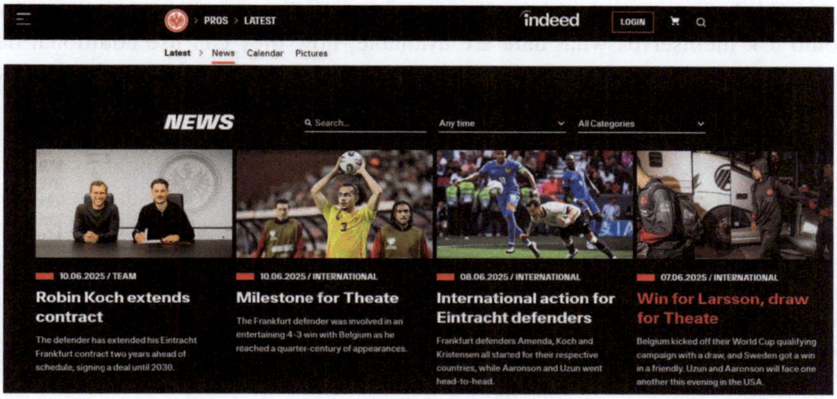

Fig. 2.18 A central interface for Eintracht Frankfurt's services including ticketing, content, e-commerce, and fan interaction. Permission to use the picture given by the club (©Eintracht Frankfurt)

can be used to tap into new sources of economic revenue is increasingly coming to the fore. The professionalization of sport increases the need for specialists to carry out complex management tasks (Nagel et al., 2015). This requires investments in organization and infrastructure, investments that in turn require new business models, and income streams. This is the only way to create economic foundations that will secure sporting operations in the future. Data can become a key lever here: It helps create personalized offers, for example, in ticketing, merchandising, or the design of digital platforms.

Platform strategies such as those of Eintracht Frankfurt show where data-driven monetization can lead: With the "Eintracht Digital Platform," a central interface was created on which ticketing, content, e-commerce, and fan interaction are merged (see Fig. 2.18). The aim is to use digital user behavior to draw conclusions about commercial potential, for example, through individual offer logic in the fan store or data-based partner offers (EintrachtTech GmbH, 2022).

It is crucial that the use of data is strategically embedded and fits the context of the respective sports organization. There is no strategy that can be applied to several sports organizations. Instead, solutions must always be tailored to the specific organization and situation. The Danish club FC Midtjylland shows how far data-driven business models can go: The owners founded "Smartodds," a sports betting company whose analyses are not only used for sporting purposes but whose profits are in turn invested in the club as well (Anderson & Sally, 2013).

Another example is provided by the City Football Group (including Manchester City), which has specifically built data expertise in-house to commercialize its global fan relationships. More than 100 million fans worldwide provide interaction data that are used for product development, sponsorship involvement, and customer relationship management (CRM)—an example of scalable data-based strategies with a global reach (City Football Group, 2022).

In addition to opportunities, there are also challenges. Sports organizations should ask themselves what data are available, how they can use additional data sources, what resources are required to analyze them, and which specific use cases have economic potential (Bai & Bai, 2021). At the same time, it is important to anticipate possible resistance—from fans or data protection authorities, for example.

The ethical handling of sensitive customer and fan data is essential to gain and maintain trust in the long term (Read, 2023). The sensitivity to data-driven business models is likely to increase further in the future, among fans, the media, and political institutions. Organizations are therefore advised to build internal expertise at the interface of data analysis and business model development (Watanabe et al., 2021). Such investments in data expertise pay off in the long term if they are embedded in well-thought-out strategies.

2.4.2 Sponsorship Optimization

Sponsorship partnerships represent an economically important source of income for numerous sports organizations (Cornwell & Kwon, 2020). Data-driven management of sponsorship partnerships is therefore a key aspect for sports organizations. To make this clear, one should stress that the focus is less on the acquisition of new sponsors, but on the development of existing partnerships and their activation (Schwizer, 2021). Like this, the goal is to achieve collaborations that work in the long run.

Ideally, most sponsorship partnerships in the world of sports last a long time (Urriolagoitia & Planellas, 2007). Therefore, continuous success evaluation is important. This reveals potential for improvement. Data-based key performance indicators (KPIs) are values that show the effectiveness of sponsorship activities (see Fig. 2.19). These allow the various measures to be reviewed and improved over time. Furthermore, this strengthens the negotiating position of sports organizations with their sponsorship partners. Eye-tracking analyses (Burch, 2022) are an important element in measuring the impact of sponsorship. Based on data, the position, duration, and graphic design of advertising measures in stadiums or on digital channels can be optimized, thus achieving greater effectiveness (Breuer & Rumpf, 2015).

With the increasing relevance of digital media channels, the spectrum of sponsorship activation is also expanding. Digital campaigns—for example, in the form of interactive social media campaigns, in-app branding, or gamified fan campaigns—can be measured in detail and optimized in a targeted manner. This creates new sources of income (see Sect. 2.4.1) while at the same time increasing the verifiability of the communication effect. The systematic evaluation of all these dimensions requires suitable data management structures within the sports organization. Sponsorship optimization is therefore not just a marketing task, but an interdisciplinary challenge that brings together technological, economic, and communicative perspectives (Schweizer, 2015).

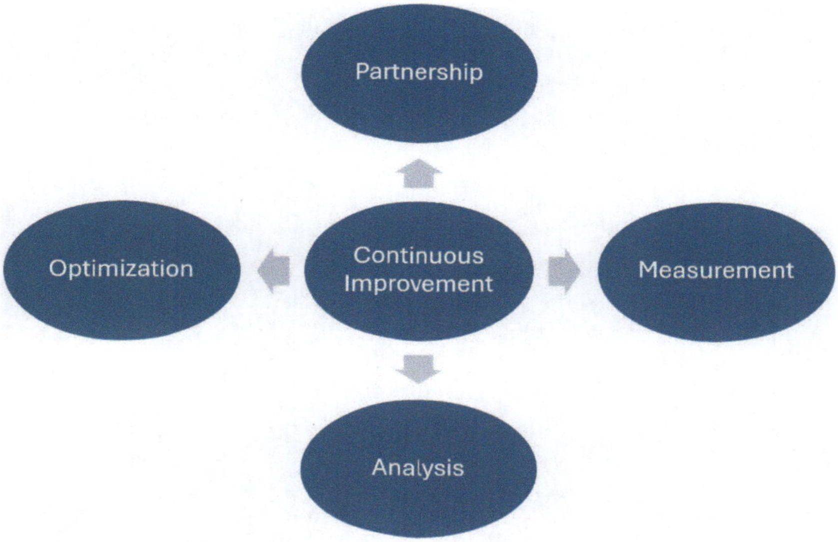

Fig. 2.19 Data-driven sponsorship management creates a continuous cycle of measurement, analysis, and optimization to maximize partnership value and revenue potential. Figure created by the authors

For sports organizations, data-driven analysis-based sponsorship optimization offers considerable potential. Those who not only enter partnerships but also actively manage them increase the loyalty of existing sponsors, improve internal argumentation skills, and increase monetization in the medium term (Schweizer, 2015). The prerequisites for this are systematic data processes, a holistic understanding of communication impact, and the willingness to develop sponsorship iteratively.

2.4.3 Data-Driven Fan Engagement

This section focuses on the question of how data-based approaches can contribute to sustainably increasing fan loyalty, fan experience, and fan value in sports organizations—and what opportunities and risks arise from this. Fans are a key economic resource for sports organizations (Sponsors, 2025), be it directly through attendance at the stadium (see Fig. 2.20), the purchase of promotional items or the use of catering services, or indirectly through media reach and associated sponsorship and media revenues. Data-based strategies allow sports organizations to understand the behavior, needs, and preferences of their fans in a differentiated manner and to take targeted action based on this (Yiapanas, 2025).

The ability to personalize the content and offers is key. By specifically analyzing data, target groups can be segmented and individually addressed. Like this, not

Fig. 2.20 Fans are a key economic resource for sports organizations. Picture taken by one of the book authors during the 2015 UEFA Champions League Final between Juventus Turin and FC Barcelona in Berlin, Germany

only can the relevance of the messages be improved, but also the loyalty of the fans (Bühler & Nufer, 2020). Borussia Dortmund uses a data warehouse approach to compile fan preferences from various sources and create personalized newsletters or ticket offers (Bühler & Nufer, 2020). The stadium experience can also be optimized based on data, for example, using visual stimuli within the sports venue in a targeted way (Hüttermann et al., 2018).

Applied to the experience of the fans, this means that digital advertising messages or navigation aids in the stadium, for example, can be placed and improved specifically. These possibilities offer advantages not only for sponsors but also for the design of a pleasant and efficient stadium visit.

Another field of application is the evaluation of the fan value using the so-called fan lifetime value (Lewis, 2024). This attempts to determine the economic significance of a fan throughout the relationship period. This allows differentiated strategies to be developed for various fan environments (Bühler & Nufer, 2020). However, there is a danger that fans are classified primarily according to their economic benefit. In the worst case, this can lead to alienation. Transparent communication about the use of data is therefore essential. However, data-based fan engagement also contains challenges. In addition to data protection issues, there is also the question of when fans perceive the measures as overly commercialized (Winell, 2023). Too much personalization can also cause rejection, especially among traditional target groups. Sports organizations should therefore design their data strategies so that they are context-specific and geared toward individual fan groups.

In summary, data-based fan engagement offers potential for differentiation and, therefore, also for targeted value creation (Yiapanas, 2025). Data can help create individual added value, improve communication processes, and personalize experiences. This opens up new revenue models (see Sect. 2.4.1). However, it is important to find a good balance between the economic interests of the sports organization and the expectations of the fans.

2.4.4 Subscription-Based Models

As part of the digital transformation, subscription-based business models are becoming increasingly relevant in professional sport (Vindicia, 2024). They enable sports organizations to build direct revenue streams in which digital content and membership offers are systematically monetized. This development is based on the increasing availability of fan data, which makes it possible to tailor offers to the needs and interests of the respective target groups.

A subscription model is particularly valuable when it succeeds in offering the fan recognizable and emotionally charged added value. This is typically achieved through exclusive access to content that provides a look behind the scenes of the organization or in-depth information on specific topics (Kim, 2021). Such offerings deliberately differentiate themselves from traditional sports reporting by creating proximity to the organization and activating the fans' personal connection. In this way, they detect the central emotional dimensions of being a fan—such as belonging, recognition, or participation—and translate these into a commercial offer (see Fig. 2.21).

Data management plays a dual role in the strategic design of such subscription offerings: On the one hand, fan data are used to collect preferences and usage behavior to curate relevant content, play it out in a targeted manner, and gradually develop it further. However, continuous interaction with subscribers creates a separate database, which in turn can be considered an intangible asset (CapTech,

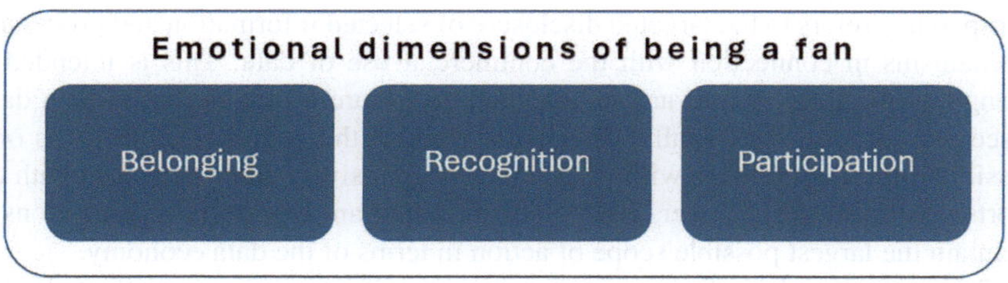

Fig. 2.21 Emotional dimensions of being a fan include belonging, recognition, and participation. Figure created by the authors

2023). The use of these data for product individualization ties in with the role of individualization in the management of the data previously discussed in Sect. 2.3. It also complements the personalization logic of the data-based offers discussed in Sect. 2.4.3, in that not only the offer itself but also the structure of the offer (e.g., subscription packages) can be personalized.

From the perspective of sports organizations, the strategic benefits of such models lie in several areas: First, they allow the establishment of stable and predictable revenue streams that exist independently of match operations or media rights. Second, they strengthen the emotional relationship between the fan and the organization through recurring and exclusive points of contact (Mastromartino & Zhang, 2020). Third, media-related content can be commercialized in this way, which better justifies the sometimes high production costs. Fourth, separate digital communication channels are created that complement existing media partnerships without directly competing with them. These considerations are also related to the topic of data-based value creation discussed in Sect. 2.4.2 and the concepts of intangible assets introduced in Sect. 2.4.1.

At the same time, subscription models are not without their challenges. One key hurdle is the need for a sufficiently large and activatable fan base—often supraregional or international—to make the model economically viable. The willingness of fans to pay is also not a static factor: It competes with other expenditures in the sports context, such as stadium visits, merchandise, or third-party platforms with free access. In addition, the long-term attractiveness of the offer strongly depends on the available content.

In general, subscription-based business models represent a potentially attractive model for data-savvy sports organizations to economize on proximity, identification, and exclusivity, provided they have the necessary resources, digital expertise, and strategic clarity in their positioning.

2.4.5 Commercial Transparency

Data-based management not only leads to new opportunities for revenue models but also fuels the expectations of greater transparency (Hutchins & Rowe, 2023). The responsible handling of data for commercialization purposes is becoming increasingly important (Vieira De Almeida, 2025). In this context, commercial transparency refers to the targeted disclosure of selected information and processing mechanisms in connection with the commercial use of data. This is intended to strengthen the trust of relevant stakeholders to ensure a reliable basis for a data-based way of working. Finally, data-based work in the commercial sector is only possible if these groups are willing to actively or passively share their data with the sports organization (Falconer, 2025). This is important for sports organizations to maintain the largest possible scope of action in terms of the data economy.

The strategic value of proactive transparency has a preventive effect. If data processing is not transparent, this leads to mistrust and uncertainty among relevant stakeholders (Costa et al., 2025) (see Fig. 2.22). In extreme cases, they no longer

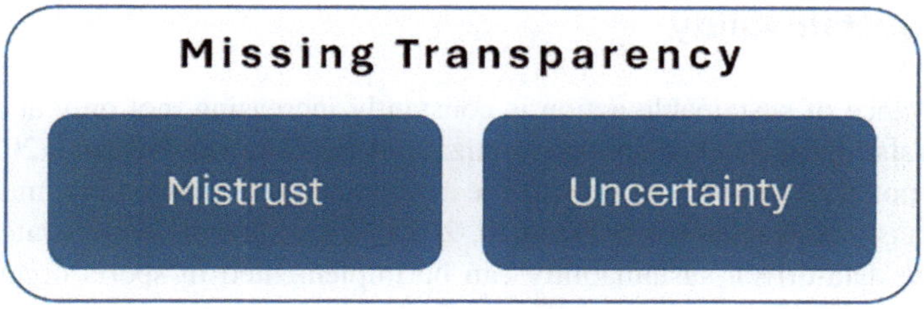

Fig. 2.22 Missing transparency can lead to mistrust and uncertainty. Figure created by the authors

agree to share their data or restrict its use. This weakens the database and jeopardizes potential data-based revenue models, for example, in personalization of selected offers or in sponsorship activation and individual member communication.

Sports organizations face the challenge of finding a healthy balance between commercial optimization and credible transparency (Costa et al., 2025). Data should certainly be used in such a way that new revenue opportunities arise. However, these practices must be presented to the outside world in such a transparent manner that the purpose, benefits, and limits are clearly demonstrated. This includes not only complying with applicable data protection guidelines but also voluntarily revealing selected aspects, for example, by creating options for opt-in (Martin & Murphy, 2017).

The greater the economic weight of a data-based instrument, the more relevant the issue of transparency becomes. If, for example, ticket prices are optimized through algorithmic analyses, it should be clear to what extent such pricing is fair, rule-based, and interest-oriented. The same applies to the commercial use of fan data by third-party partners: Especially in a situation in which fans are already heavily involved financially through admission prices, merchandising, or media subscriptions, there is a growing need for comprehensible and meaningful data practices.

One possible way for sports organizations is to link the economic goals of data usage with the individual value proposition of stakeholders. If, for example, more relevant content is created through data-based analyses, sponsorship can be better activated or events can be planned more efficiently, it can be communicated that the economic added value not only benefits the organization itself but also the fan, the sponsor, or the community. In this way, trust can be maintained and added value expanded at the same time—without breaking into overregulated or defensive data management.

Ultimately, commercial transparency remains a field of ongoing negotiation. The requirements vary depending on the context, legal form, and business model. Accordingly, it is not a question of full disclosure, but of clever management of communicative openness, with the aim of combining data-based commercialization potential with legitimacy and acceptance.

2.5 Sustainability

The relevance of sustainable action is constantly increasing, not only at a societal level but also for individual sports organizations (CSR in Deutschland, 2024). Data have the potential to promote sustainable action and, at the same time, make meaningful decisions (Venkatesh & Prasanth, 2025). This section demonstrates various ways how data-driven sustainability can be implemented in sports organizations. First, sustainable infrastructures (Sect. 2.5.1) promote conscious management of sustainability aspects. In this sense, not only is the ecological sphere touched, but also the economic and social one. Furthermore, circular resource management (Sect. 2.5.2) contributes to the sustainable use of human and financial resources. In addition, the next section focuses on different components of social sustainability (Sect. 2.5.3). These include participation, accessibility, and equal opportunities. In conclusion, responsible financial management (Sect. 2.5.4) and value-based data management (Sect. 2.5.5) are important topics for the functioning of a sports organization. All these perspectives demonstrate how sports organizations can find ways to promote data-driven sustainability.

2.5.1 Sustainable Infrastructure

Professional sports organizations are under some pressure to deal with ecological, economic, and social sustainability issues due to the social debate on sustainability (Boros et al., 2024). The key question here is how data management can contribute to solving these problems. Data open new opportunities: One can make decisions that are more profitability-based on the one hand or more sustainability-oriented on the other. Sustainable thinking can contribute to bringing these two aspects closer to each other.

In this context, the term sustainable infrastructure refers to the use of data to make processes and decisions within a sports organization more ecologically, economically, and socially compatible (McCullough et al., 2020a) (see Fig. 2.23). It is not primarily about technical infrastructure issues, but about the strategic ability to use resources more consciously, reduce emissions, improve social impact, and ensure economic stability based on data-based findings.

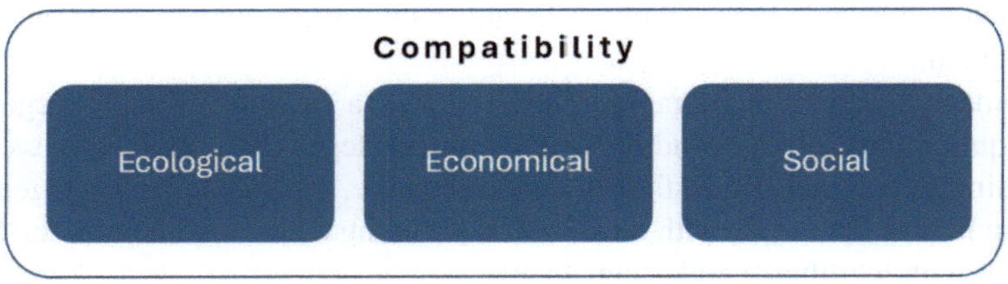

Fig. 2.23 Processes and decisions must be ecologically, economically, and socially compatible. Figure created by the authors

A central field of application is the analysis and optimization of ecological impacts in the context of events (Xuan et al., 2025). Data on energy consumption, fan mobility, and the use of materials, for example, in catering, can be evaluated to identify more resource-efficient alternatives. In addition, data-based sustainability management offers potential beyond match operations, for example, in the selection of suppliers, the design of merchandising products, or the management of logistics processes. The planning of match times in terms of energy consumption, consumer behavior, or travel behavior could also be data-informed in the future, for example, in cooperation with leagues or cities.

Data also allow simulations of behavioral scenarios that can be used to assess the impact of sustainability measures in advance (Wicker, 2021). For example, one could analyze how the wait time after a match affects whether fans use public transport. On this basis, mobility offers can be improved. A proactive approach to these challenges strengthens the social responsibility of the sports organization and its strategic positioning in public discourse (Lagoudaki, 2025).

In general, the topic of promoting sustainability remains complex. This is also due to the fact that the degree of sustainability often cannot be clearly measured based on isolated data. The interactions between ecological, economic, and social factors are too diverse. Even an ecologically advantageous measure can be economically expensive or socially problematic. Data are a means of recognizing such conflicting goals and making them visible. However, the management must decide how to resolve the conflicting objectives. One quality of management is to holistically evaluate these conflicting objectives and to consciously decide on a strategy (Engert et al., 2016).

Credibility is an important aspect. A sports organization should not only pursue data-based sustainability measures but these should also be comprehensible and communicated to the outside world (McCullough et al., 2020b). This strengthens the trust of stakeholders. The decisive factor here is not the symbolic visibility of individual measures, but their actual effectiveness and the ability to communicate this based on evidence. Only those who show how and why certain decisions were made can prevent sustainable commitment from being perceived as greenwashing.

Data-based sustainability in sports organizations therefore means not only using new tools but also establishing new forms of thinking, decision-making, and communication with the aim of harmonizing sporting performance, economic viability, and social responsibility in a future-oriented way.

2.5.2 Circular Resource Management

The idea of a circular economy is also becoming increasingly important in the context of professional sports organizations (Gerke et al., 2024). Circular resource management aims to use physical resources in a way that is not linear, in the sense of "take, make, waste," but to keep them in circulation as long as possible, enable multiple uses, and recycle them in an environmentally friendly way at the end of their life cycle (Geissdoerfer et al., 2017). This applies in particular to the use of materials, logistics, and supply in the event context but can also be extended to other areas.

Sports organizations cannot escape their social responsibility in terms of sustainability (Ferkins & Shilbury, 2015). In addition to match operations, events, training infrastructure, merchandising, and catering represent significant impact factors. Prudent resource management can contribute to environmental sustainability in all these areas—for example, through reusable packaging, recyclable fan merchandise, or a conscious selection of regional and durable materials.

Data management plays a central role here. On the one hand, best practices can be derived by evaluating existing data. An example is how to plan the catering quantities based on empirical values. However, continuous monitoring can uncover potential efficiency and reduce waste. Circular resource management is therefore not just a static measure, but an iterative learning process in which decisions are based on reliable forecasts and historical comparisons (Garcia-Saravia Ortiz-de Montellano et al., 2023).

The targeted deployment of human resources can also be supported by data management (Nowicka et al., 2024). In areas such as stadium management or event organization, for example, it is possible to simulate how many employees must be effectively scheduled for different numbers of spectators—a measure that conserves resources both economically and ecologically. In many sports, the number of spectators has increased in recent years, besides COVID-19 times.

However, the implementation of the corresponding measures is associated with challenges. There is often a lack of internal expertise to systematically transfer the concept of the circular economy to sports organizations. External expertise is required, which in turn needs additional resources. At the same time, there is a risk that individual measures will be perceived as greenwashing. This is especially true if the measures are implemented in isolation and symbolically. Therefore, the credibility of circular resource management depends in large part on the seriousness and transparency of its implementation.

There is also potential for synergies, particularly in circular thinking. Measures that promote ecological sustainability can, if cleverly designed, also make economic sense. If less is wasted, not only efficiency and impact but also public acceptance increases. Circular resource management is therefore not only an ecological necessity but also a strategic opportunity for sports organizations to position themselves as responsible and future-oriented players (Gerke et al., 2024).

2.5.3 Social Inclusion

It should be noted that social inclusion is gaining strategic relevance in sport (Deutscher Olympischer Sportbund (DOSB), 2024), also after digitalization. Although diversity and equal opportunities have been seen more as sociopolitical concerns for years, sports organizations are increasingly recognizing that targeted measures to promote social inclusion can also contribute to long-term legitimacy, acceptance, and performance of the organization. Data management can be used as

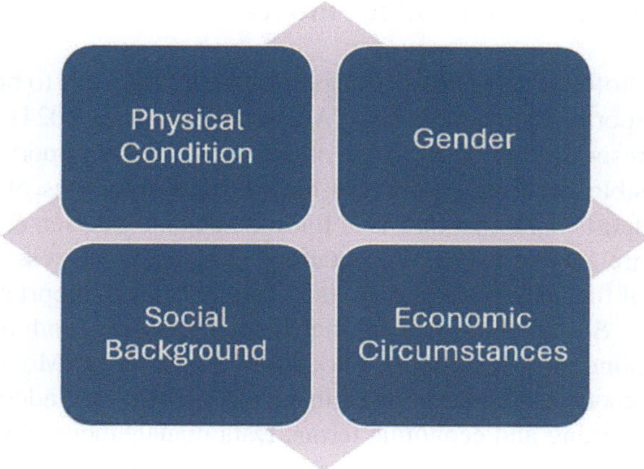

Fig. 2.24 Social inclusion must consider several barriers like physical condition, gender, social background, or economic circumstances. Figure created by the authors

a support tool to systematically record social participation, monitor developments, and manage them in a targeted manner (Venkatesh & Prasanth, 2025).

Various aspects can be summarized under social inclusion. These include equal access to sports facilities and the practice of physical activity, regardless of physical condition, gender, social background, or economic circumstances (see Fig. 2.24). Social inclusion is therefore extremely diverse and is related to various support measures within a sports organization (Grandisson et al., 2019).

In youth sports, data management contributes to equitably distributing scarce resources. Like this, the occupancy plans for the sports facilities are optimized. This leads to optimal training opportunities for as many children as possible, even in areas with poor infrastructure or socially disadvantaged population groups. Such resources are often managed at the local authority level. Data-based needs analyses form the basis for fair planning.

Another aspect is the handling of medical and training-related data. Many studies, diagnoses, and recommendations in high-performance sports are still uniquely based on male datasets (Zimmel & Bischoff, 2023). However, a modern, data-driven sports organization should recognize gender-specific differences and actively work to collect and systematically use data specific to women. Only in this way can preventive measures, training management, and medical care be tailored to individuals and target groups.

Data-based approaches should be seen as supporting tools; they can facilitate social inclusion but do not enable automated justice (Lambert & Denison, 2022). In contrast, the exclusive focus on measurable key figures can also lead to phenomena being over- or misinterpreted. Inclusion in practice is created through attitude, structures, and cultural openness, not through monitoring and reporting alone. In addition to data-based management, credible inclusion work therefore requires, above all, consistent anchoring in the daily life of the organization. Only when both levels interact can the data fully develop its potential to promote social participation.

2.5.4 Responsible Finance

Professional sports organizations must find ways to balance economic pressure and sporting competitiveness (Adam & Bachmaier, 2024). In this context, the concept of responsible finance is becoming increasingly important. This refers to the responsible handling of data on the financial resources of a sports organization. Many sports organizations have limited budgets (Nielsen & Storm, 2017). However, they are subject to high expectations of sporting success. Management and monitoring of financial resources are therefore of central importance.

Sustainable financial management requires both a high degree of budget discipline and an effective allocation of resources (Moon et al., 2022). The available resources should be used in such a way that the added value is maximized in both sporting and economic terms. Data management can play an important supporting role in this area because it allows more accurate forecasts and a transparent basis for decision-making. This makes it possible to learn from past financial decisions and derive options for future action.

Concrete financial decisions can be made in a more targeted manner using data. In professional sport, for example, transfer decisions can be backed by data by simulating sporting potential, injury risks, market values, and indirect financial effects (Islam & Nahid, 2024). In club and popular sports, on the other hand, membership fees and fee models can be data-informed, with the aim of enabling both economic viability and social participation (see also Sect. 2.5.3).

Typical financial risks in sports organizations, such as lack of sporting success, can be better anticipated and mitigated through data-based control (Ranjith et al., 2024). Sporting success has a direct influence on spectator interest, ticket sales, merchandising, and the attractiveness of sponsors (Nielsen, 2025). Responsible finance is therefore closely linked to sporting control: Both data streams—sporting and economic—must be correlated to make informed decisions. The linking of these systems creates transparency and allows the identification of key variables for economic stability.

A central field of application for data-based management lies in the allocation of funds within the organization. Limited budgets in sports organizations lead to correspondingly tough distribution battles between different areas (Swiss Olympic, 2024). The effectiveness of investments in individual departments can be better verified and thus legitimized through data tracking. This is important because there is often a tension in sports organizations between short-term sporting success and long-term economic stability (Martín-Magdalena et al., 2024).

In addition, a data-based approach also opens the possibility of recording qualitative aspects of the impact of expenditure. The question of whether certain funding has achieved the desired effect—be it in the sporting, social, or structural area—can only be answered if relevant data are continuously recorded, linked, and evaluated. This demonstrates the potential of a learning system that systematically draws conclusions for the future from feedback effects.

Added value is created when financial data and impact data are combined over time. For example, it can be made visible whether certain investments (such as in medical care or athletic development) not only show short-term effects but also contribute to performance and competitiveness in the medium term. However, this requires professional data management that can bring together structured and comparable data from different areas.

Proper implementation of data-supported responsible finance is a major challenge. This requires not only the suitable infrastructure but also the appropriate skills and abilities of the personnel to deal with financial data. At the same time, a purely numbers-driven approach is not expedient: The impact of investments cannot always be precisely quantified. Decisions in the sports context therefore always require consideration, experience, and contextual knowledge (Wilson & Kiely, 2023).

Responsible finance in data-based sports management therefore does not mean automating decisions but rather making them more fact-based, comprehensible, and learning-oriented. Those who specifically link financial data with other management data can not only manage more efficiently but also invest more specifically in future viability, thus ensuring the long-term economic foundation of the sports organization.

2.5.5 Value of Data-Driven Approaches

Data-based sustainability is not yet standard practice for many sports organizations (Moon et al., 2022). Sustainability offers considerable potential, particularly in professional sports management. Organizations that already have strong data skills, for example, in the areas of performance analysis, ticketing, or fan interactions, can also use these skills specifically for sustainability issues. This is because the data make the impact of certain measures visible. This creates a basis for strategic decisions. Such framework conditions can have a positive influence on employee motivation. In this sense, the data-based approach can be seen as an effective tool for successful sustainability management in sports organizations.

Even if the traditional focus on sporting and economic success is understandable, sustainability is still perceived as an external issue in many sports organizations. However, sustainability has long been the center of social expectations. Furthermore, it is increasingly becoming a decisive differentiation factor also for sports organizations. This is also because the data help to objectively evaluate the effectiveness of the measures taken. They represent the ground for further development of sustainability measures in a targeted manner. This enables sports organizations to make their decisions based on objective criteria.

Examples of this can be found in all three aspects of sustainability. In the ecological area, for example, the CO_2 savings potential can be identified by analyzing the use of materials in stadium catering, and alternative products can be used more effectively. In the social sphere, data can help answer how many children are reached by youth programs with a certain budget and how this reach can be improved. Data-based planning is also valuable in the economic sector, for example, when it comes to better forecasting staffing requirements for home games, avoiding overcapacity, and efficiently using resources.

In addition to internal benefits, the data-driven sustainability approach also has external potential. Credibility is crucial here. Sustainability communication that is based on real progress and can be transparently documented using data has an authentic effect and strengthens trust. This benefits sponsors, for whom credible image transfer is becoming increasingly important. Data-based sustainability reports—for example, in the annual report or on digital platforms—offer the opportunity to make your own positioning visible. However, practice also shows that if an attempt is made to simply simulate sustainability, for example, through selective reporting or cosmetic measures, there is a risk of greenwashing (Traberg et al., 2025). Uncovering such strategies can lead to considerable reputational damage—not only in terms of public perception but also in relation to partners and fans.

For data to be effective in the context of sustainability, certain requirements must be met. Sports organizations often lack reliable data sources or focus on individual areas. In such cases, it can make sense to initially set a focus—for example, on ecological issues or social initiatives—and to record and improve these in a targeted, data-based manner. The gradual expansion of data-based sustainability management can also take place with external support, for example, through specialized consulting or cooperation with research.

Not every aspect of sustainability must be quantified. Rather, it is about consciously deciding where data create added value, be it at a strategic, communicative, or operational level. Sports organizations that follow this approach do both: They position themselves as responsible players and as sustainable brands. Therefore, such a data-based approach is not a panacea but is an effective way to transform sustainability from an abstract claim into a concrete strength.

References

Adam, S., & Bachmaier, B. (2024). Interlinking financial stability regulation and governance in German professional soccer: Contribution and implications. *Frontiers in Sports and Active Living, 6*, 1486759.

Anderson, C., & Sally, D. (2013). *The numbers game: Why everything you know about football is wrong*. Penguin Books.

Annamalai, B., Yoshida, M., Varshney, S., Pathak, A. A., & Venugopal, P. (2021). Social media content strategy for sport clubs to drive fan engagement. *Journal of Retailing and Consumer Services, 62*, 102648.

Baca, A., Dabnichki, P., Heller, M., & Kornfeind, P. (2020). Quantification of wearable sensor technology in sports—a systematic review. *IEEE Sensors Journal, 20*(17), 9646–9656.

Bai, Z., & Bai, X. (2021). Sports big data: Management, analysis, applications, and challenges. *Complexity, 2021*, 6676297.

Barça Innovation Hub. (2025). Introduction to sports analytics. Online course, Accessed July 9, 2025.

Batini, C., & Scannapieco, M. (2016). *Data and information quality: Dimensions, principles and techniques*. Springer.

Bayle, E., & Clausen, J. (2025). A conceptual model to understand and assess international sport federations' organizational performance. *Journal of Global Sport Management, 10*(4), 487–513.
Bühler, A., & Nufer, G. (2020). *Marketing im sport* (5th ed.). Schäffer-Poeschel
Bilohur, V., Skrypchenko, I., & Nepsha, O. (2022). The concept of sports management as a factor of effective sports activities. *Humanities Studies, 12*(89), 60–70.
Blobel, T., Rumo, M., & Lames, M. (2021). Sports information systems: A systematic review. *International Journal of Computer Science in Sport, 20*(1), 1–25.
Boros, A., Tőzsér, D., & Géczi, G. (2024). The predominance of sustainability perspectives in sports—a bibliometric analysis. *Sports Research International, 1*(1), 30–44.
Bourdon, P. C., Cardinale, M., Murray, A., Gastin, P., Kellmann, M., Varley, M. C., Cable, N. T., et al. (2017). Monitoring athlete training loads: Consensus statement. *International Journal of Sports Physiology and Performance, 12*(Suppl 2), 161–170.
Breuer, C., & Rumpf, C. (2015). The impact of color and animation on sports viewers' attention to televised sponsorship signage. *Journal of Sport Management, 29*(2), 170–183.
Burch, M. (2022). *Eye tracking and visual analytics*. River Publishers.
Burns, A., & Collins, D. (2023). Interdisciplinary practice in performance sport: A scoping review of evidence of collaboration. *European Journal of Sport Science, 23*(9), 1877–1891.
CapTech. (2023). The power of fan data: Using fan data to win the engagement game. Retrieved August 25, 2025, from https://www.captechconsulting.com/articles/the-power-of-fan-data-using-fan-data-to-win-the-engagement-game
City Football Group. (2022). Annual review: Digital growth and fan monetization. Retrieved June 5, 2025, from https://www.mancity.com/news/club/manchester-city-2022-23-annual-report-63835619
Clissa, L., Lassnig, M., & Rinaldi, L. (2024). How big is big data? A comprehensive survey of data production, storage, and streaming in science and industry. *Frontiers Big Data, 6*, 1271639.
Cornwell, T. B., & Kwon, Y. (2020). Sponsorship-linked marketing: Research surpluses and shortages. *Journal of the Academy of Marketing Science, 48*(4), 607–629.
Costa, S., Silva, A. J., Dias, T., Marinho, D. A., Batalha, N. M., Roque, R., Afonso, C., Aminova, M., & Ferraz, R. (2025). Integrity and transparency in sports: A survey review. *The Open Sports Sciences Journal, 18*, e1875399X353976.
Creighton, D. W., Shrier, I., Shultz, R., Meeuwisse, W. H., & Matheson, G. O. (2010). Return-to-play in sport: A decision-based model. *Clinical Journal of Sport Medicine, 20*(5), 379–385.
CSR in Deutschland. (2024). Nachhaltigkeit im Sport: Wie kann das gelingen? https://www.csr-in-deutschland.de/DE/CSR-Allgemein/CSR-in-der-Praxis/Branchen/Sport/sport-artikel.html
Davis, J., Bransen, L., Devos, L., Jaspers, A., Meert, W., Robberechts, P., Van Haaren, J., & Van Roy, M. (2024). Methodology and evaluation in sports analytics: Challenges, approaches, and lessons learned. *Machine Learning, 113*, 6977–7010.
Deutscher Olympischer Sportbund (DOSB). (2024). Monitoring 2024: Umsetzung der Inklusion im und durch Sport.
Di Simone, L., & Zanardi, D. (2021). On the relationship between sport and financial performances: An empirical investigation. *Managerial Finance, 47*(6), 812–824.
EintrachtTech GmbH. (2022). Innovation durch Integration: Die digitale Plattformstrategie der Eintracht Frankfurt Fußball AG. Retrieved June 5, 2025, from https://klub.eintracht.de/eintrachttech/digitales-oekosystem
Engert, S., Rauter, R., & Baumgartner, R. J. (2016). Exploring the integration of corporate sustainability into strategic management: A literature review. *Journal of Cleaner Production, 112*, 2833–2850.
Falconer, M. (2025). The transformative role of data collaboration in sports fan engagement: An interview with Sportradar's Mike Falconer.
Ferkins, L., & Shilbury, D. (2015). Social responsibility in sports: A call for a systematic approach. *Journal of Legal Aspects of Sport, 25*(2), 183–200.
Francis, J. W., Kyte, J. L., Bateman, M., & Nicholls, S. B. (2025). The landscape of validity and reliability practices from applied performance analysts: Establishing a best practice framework. *International Journal of Sports Science & Coaching, 20*(3), 1014–1036.

Fuller, C. W., Taylor, A., & Raftery, M. (2018). Epidemiology of concussion in men's elite rugby-7s (Sevens World Series) and rugby-15s (Rugby World Cup, Junior World Championship and Rugby Trophy, Pacific Nations Cup and English Premiership). *British Journal of Sports Medicine, 52*(8), 478–485.

Gabbett, T. J. (2016). The training-injury prevention paradox: Should athletes be training smarter and harder? *British Journal of Sports Medicine, 50*(5), 273–280.

Garcia-Saravia Ortiz-de Montellano, C., Ghannadzadeh, A., & van der Meer, Y. (2023). The circular pathway: A new educational methodology for exploratory circular value chain redesign. *Frontiers in Sustainability, 4*, 1197659.

Geiger, R. S., Cope, D., Ip, J., Lotosh, M., Shah, A., Weng, J., & Tang, R. (2021). "Garbage in, garbage out" revisited: What do machine learning application papers report about human-labeled training data? *Quantitative Science Studies, 2*(3), 795–827.

Geissdoerfer, M., Savaget, P., Bocken, N. M. P., & Hultink, E. J. (2017). The circular economy—a new sustainability paradigm? *Journal of Cleaner Production, 143*, 757–768.

Gerke, A., Fehrer, J., Benson-Rea, M., & McCullough, B. P. (2024). A typology of circular sport business models: Enabling sustainable value co-creation in the sport industry. *Journal of Sport Management, 38*(4), 225–239.

Grandisson, M., Tétreault, S., & Freeman, A. (2019). Strategies to foster inclusion through sports: A scoping review. *Inclusion, 7*(4), 220–234.

Gruetzemacher, R., Gupta, A., & Wilkerson, G. B. (2016). Sports Injury Prevention Screen (SIPS): Design and Architecture of an Internet of Things (IoT) Based Analytics Health App. In *Proceedings of CONF-IRM, The International Conference on Information Resources Management: Digital Emancipation in a Networked Society* (p. 18).

Hagg, A., Asteroth, A., Rasche, C., Bach, K., & Pfeiffer, M. (2021). *Künstliche Intelligenz für den Spitzensport im Spannungsfeld zwischen Big und Small Data (KISs-BiS)*. Number 2021/03 in Schriftenreihe des Bundesinstituts für Sportwissenschaft. Sportverlag Strauß.

Halson, S. L. (2014). Monitoring training load to understand fatigue in athletes. *Sports Medicine, 44*(Suppl 2), 139–147.

Hecksteden, A. (2025). Künstliche Intelligenz als neuer Teamplayer im Spitzensport. *Deutsche Zeitschrift für Sportmedizin, 76*(4).

Hoppe, M. W., Baumgart, C., Polglaze, T., & Freiwald, J. (2018). Validity and reliability of GPS and LPS for measuring distances covered and sprint mechanical properties in team sports. *PLoS ONE, 13*(2), e0192708.

Houtmeyers, K. C., Jaspers, A., & Figueiredo, P. (2021). Managing the training process in elite sports: From descriptive to prescriptive data analytics. *International Journal of Sports Physiology and Performance, 16*(11), 1719–1723.

Hüttermann, S., Noël, B., & Memmert, D. (2018). Eye tracking in high-performance sports: Evaluation of its application in expert athletes. *International Journal of Computer Science in Sport, 17*(2), 182–203.

Hutchins, B., & Rowe, D. (2023). Data as capital and ethical implications in digital sport business models. *Convergence: The International Journal of Research into New Media Technologies, 29*(6), 1637–1654.

Islam, K. T., & Nahid, M. H. (2024). Applications & implications of data-driven analytics in the football player valuation. In *SHS Web of Conferences* (Vol. 204, pp. 04006).

Johansen, H. D., Johansen, D., Kupka, T., Riegler, M. A., & Halvorsen, P. (2020). Scalable infrastructure for efficient real-time sports analytics. *Proceedings of the ACM on Interactive, Mobile, Wearable and Ubiquitous Technologies, 4*(3), 1–26.

Juliano, E., Thakkar, C., Taber, C., Raval, M. S., Kaya, T., & Senbel, S. (2023). A dynamic online dashboard for tracking the performance of division 1 basketball athletic performance. In *International Sports Analytics Conference and Exhibition (ISACE) Preconference Workshop*, Singapore.

Kellmann, M., Bertollo, M., Bosquet, L., Brink, M., Coutts, A. J., Duffield, R., & Meeusen, R. (2018). Recovery and performance in sport: Consensus statement. *International Journal of Sports Physiology and Performance, 13*(2), 240–245.

Kim, H. S. (2021). *The role of year-round fan engagement: A new approach to sport fan behavior*. PhD thesis, University of Mississippi.

Kon, Y., Omae, Y., Sakai, K., Takahashi, H., Akiduki, T., Miyaji, C., Sakurai, Y., Ezaki, N., & Nakai, K. (2015). Toward classification of swimming style by using underwater wireless accelerometer data. In K. Mase, M. Langheinrich, D. Gatica-Perez, H. Gellersen, T. Choudhury & K. Yatani (Eds.), *Proceedings of the ACM International Joint Conference on Pervasive and Ubiquitous Computing and Proceedings of the ACM International Symposium on Wearable Computers, UbiComp/ISWC Adjunct* (pp. 85–88). ACM.

Konzag, H., & Schütz, N. S. (2024). Sports digitalization – realizing the potential value of tracking technologies in professional sports organizations. In T. X. Bui (Ed.), *Proceedings of the 57th Hawaii International Conference on System Sciences, HICSS* (pp. 1508–1517). ScholarSpace.

Krüger, M., Biniossek, C., Stocker, M., & Betz, D. (2023). Perspectives and potentials of open data for the sports sciences. *Zeitschrift für Sportpsychologie, 30*(4), 173–184.

Lagoudaki, G. (2025). Evaluating the impact of a corporate social responsibility strategy on sports organizations. *Systems, 13*(5), 321.

Lambert, C., & Denison, J. (2022). Quantification, big data, and biometrics in sport. R. In Giulianotti & D. Malcolm (Eds.), *Sociology of sport: A global subdiscipline in review* (pp. 259–273). Emerald Publishing Limited.

Lewis, M. (2024). Fan lifetime value. In *Fandom analytics*. Springer.

Link, D. (2018). Sports Analytics. Wie aus (kommerziellen) Sportdaten neue Möglichkeiten für die Sportwissenschaft entstehen. *German Journal of Exercise and Sport Research, 48*(1), 13–25.

Mabry, P. L. (2011). Making sense of the data explosion. *American Journal of Preventive Medicine, 40*(5), 159–161.

Mackenzie, R., & Cushion, C. (2013). Performance analysis in football: A critical review and implications for future research. *Journal of Sports Sciences, 31*(6), 639–676.

Mahmoud, A. B. (2024). Digital marketing analytics in sports. In *Sports analytics: Data-driven sports and decision intelligence* (pp. 55–74). Springer.

Malcata, R. M., & Hopkins, W. G. (2014). Variability of competitive performance of elite athletes: A systematic review. *Sports Medicine, 44*(12), 1763–1774.

Martin, K. D., & Murphy, P. E. (2017). The role of data privacy in marketing. *Journal of the Academy of Marketing Science, 45*(2), 135–155.

Martín-Magdalena, J., los Ríos-Sastre, S. D., Redondo, R., & Alaminos, D. (2024). Effectiveness of UEFA's regulation for European football financial stability: Evidence from the Spanish league. *Heliyon, 10*(7), e151821.

Mastromartino, B., & Zhang, J. J. (2020). Affective outcomes of membership in a sport fan community. *Frontiers in Psychology, 11*, 881.

McCall, A., Davison, M., Andersen, T. E., et al. (2016). Injury prevention strategies at the FIFA 2014 World Cup: Perceptions and practices of the physicians from the 32 participating national teams. *British Journal of Sports Medicine, 50*(11), 687–693.

McCullough, B. P., Orr, M., & Kellison, T. B. (2020a). Sport ecology: Conceptualizing an emerging subdiscipline within sport management. *Journal of Sport Management, 34*(5), 393–406.

McCullough, B. P., Pelcher, J., & Trendafilova, S. (2020b). An exploratory analysis of the environmental sustainability performance signaling communications among north American sport organizations. *Sustainability, 12*(5), 1950.

Memmert, D., Lemmink, K. A. P. M., & Sampaio, J. (2017). Current approaches to tactical performance analyses in soccer using position data. *Sports Medicine, 47*(1), 1–10.

Mildenberger, T., Braschler, M., Ruckstuhl, A., Vorburger, R. S., & Stockinger, K. (2023). The role of data scientists in modern enterprises—experience from data science education. *SIGMOD Record, 52*(2), 48–52.

Moon, P., Bayle, E., & François, A. (2022). Assessing international sport federations' sustainability practices: Toward integrating sustainability in their main sports events. *Frontiers in Sports and Active Living, 3*, 752085.

Morgulev, E., Azar, O. H., & Lidor, R. (2018). Sports analytics and the big-data era. *International Journal of Data Science and Analytics, 5*(4), 213–222.

Munzner, T. (2014). *Visualization analysis and design*. A.K. Peters visualization series. A K Peters.
Nagel, S., Schlesinger, T., Bayle, E., & Giauque, D. (2015). Professionalisation of sport federations—a multi-level framework for analysing forms, causes and consequences. *European Sport Management Quarterly, 15*(4), 407–433.
Nassis, G. P., Massey, A., Jacobsen, P., Brito, J., Randers, M. B., Castagna, C., et al. (2020). Elite football of 2030 will not be the same as that of 2020: Preparing players, coaches, and support staff for the evolution. *British Journal of Sports Medicine, 54*(7), 369–370.
Nielsen. (2025). 2025 Global Sports Report. Retrieved August 25, 2025, from https://www.nielsen.com/insights/2025/global-sports-report-2025/
Nielsen, K., & Storm, R. K. (2017). Profit maximization, win optimization and soft budget constraints in professional team sports. In K. Nielsen, U. Wagner & R. K. Storm (Eds.), *When sport meets business: Capabilities, challenges, critiques* (pp. 153–166). Sage.
Nimmala, R., & Nimmala, J. (2023). Racing into the data age: Harnessing sensor intelligence, advanced analytics, and Kafka's real-time stream in Formula 1. *International Journal of Artificial Intelligence and Machine Learning, 3*(1), 70–80.
Nowicka, J., Pauliuchuk, Y., Ciekanowski, Z., Fa lda, B., & Sikora, K. (2024). The use of data analytics in human resource management. *European Research Studies Journal, 27*(2), 203–215.
Olaniyan, O., Dehe, B., Bamford, D., & Ward, S. (2024). Enhancing on-pitch learning capabilities with data analytics and technologies in elite sports. *European Sport Management Quarterly, 24(6)*, 1195–1214.
Parker, S., Duthie, G., & Robertson, S. (2024). A framework for player movement analysis in team sports. *Frontiers in Sports and Active Living, 6*, 1375513.
Pashaie, S., Golmohammadi, H., & Zakhirani, E. (2024). Digital transformation in sports marketing: The impact of artificial intelligence on personalization and customer engagement. *International Journal of Innovation in Management, Economics and Social Sciences, 4*(4), 42–58.
Perin, C., Vuillemot, R., & Fekete, J.-D. (2018). SoccerStories: A kick-off for visual soccer analysis. *IEEE Transactions on Visualization and Computer Graphics, 24*(1), 22–31.
Postma, M. (2023). *Best practices for big data management in the sports industry* (pp. 1–8). TScIT 39, University of Twente. Accessed July 10, 2025.
Ranjith, P., Baranidharan, K., Sabitha, K., & Deepika, V. (2024). An examination of the utilization of sports in the realm of financial analytics. *International Journal of Research Publication and Reviews, 5*(7), 1743–1750.
Read, D. (2023). Data as capital and ethical implications in digital sport business models. *Convergence: The International Journal of Research into New Media Technologies, 29*(6), 1618–1633.
Roberts, J. C. (2003). Guest editor's introduction: Special issue on coordinated and multiple views in exploratory visualization. *Information Visualization, 2*(4), 199–200.
Robertson, S., Bartlett, J. D., & Gastin, P. B. (2017). Red, amber, or green? Athlete monitoring in team sport: The need for decision-support systems. *International Journal of Sports Physiology and Performance, 12*(Suppl 2), 73–79.
Roecker, K., & Schöllhorn, W. I. (2022). Big data and artificial intelligence in sports: A systematic review. *International Journal of Environmental Research and Public Health, 19*(6), 3456.
Rosen, S., & Smith, M. (2020). Big data in sports: The role of technology in modern sports analytics. *International Journal of Computer Science in Sport, 19*(1), 1–14.
Ryan, R. M., & Deci, E. L. (2000). Self-determination theory and the facilitation of intrinsic motivation, social development, and well-being. *American Psychologist, 55*(1), 68–78.
Saw, A. E., Main, L. C., & Gastin, P. B. (2016). Monitoring the athlete training response: Subjective self-reported measures trump commonly used objective measures: A systematic review. *British Journal of Sports Medicine, 50*(5), 281–291.
Scelles, N., Durand, C., Bonnal, L., Goyeau, D., & Andreff, W. (2017). Determinants of professional sports firm values in the United States and Europe: A comparison between sports over the period 2004–2013. *International Journal of Sport Finance, 12*(4), 324–346.

Schelling, X., & Robertson, S. (2020). A development framework for decision support systems in high-performance sport. *International Journal of Computer Science in Sport, 19*(1), 1–23.

Schweizer, N. (2015). *Improving Sponsorship Performance – Three Papers on Sponsorship Portfolio Management, Outsourcing and Inefficiencies*. PhD thesis, University of Zurich.

Schwizer, D. (2021). *Aktivierung im Sportsponsoring: Gestaltung strategischer Partnerschaften aus Sponsorenperspektive*. Springer Fachmedien Wiesbaden.

Seshadri, D. R., Li, R. T., Voos, J. E., Rowbottom, J. R., Alfes, C. M., Zorman, C. A., & Drummond, C. K. (2019). Wearable sensors for monitoring the physiological and biochemical profile of the athlete. *NPJ Digital Medicine, 2*, 72.

Shi, X., & Zou, H. (2024). Data collection and analysis based on sensor technology in sports training. *Scalable Computing: Practice and Experience, 25*(5), 4399–4406.

Song, Y., Liu, T., & Jia, W. (2021). Data diversification revisited: Why does it work? In I. Farkas, P. Masulli, S. Otte & S. Wermter (Eds.), *Proceedings of the 30th International Conference on Artificial Neural Networks, ICANN*, volume 12893 of Lecture notes in computer science (pp. 521–533). Springer.

Sousa, T. (2019). The role of a strength and conditioning coach. In M. N. Doral & J. Karlsson (Eds.), *The sports medicine physician* (pp. 107–119). Springer.

Sponsors. (2025). Global Sports Report 2025: Neue Formate, neue Fans, neue Chancen. Retrieved August 12, 2025, from https://spobis.com/article/global-sports-report-2025-neue-formate-neue-fans-neue-chancen

Swiss Olympic. (2024). Verbandsbefragung 2024: Studien & Fakten. Retrieved August 25, 2025, from https://swissolympic.ch/verbaende/fuehrungsinstrumente/studien-fakten

Tataru, S. R., & Tataru, I. T. (2020). Privacy & data protection in sport industry. *Sport and Society, 0*.

Traberg, J., Orr, M., & Horbel, C. (2025). What will a greenwashing ban entail for the sport industry? *Managing Sport and Leisure*, 1–9.

Urriolagoitia, L., & Planellas, M. (2007). Sponsorship relationships as strategic alliances: A life cycle model approach. *Business Horizons, 50*(2), 157–166.

van Mechelen, W., Hlobil, H., & Kemper, W. (1992). Incidence, severity, aetiology and prevention of sports injuries: A review of concepts. *Sports Medicine, 14*(2), 82–99.

Venkatesh, R., & Prasanth, V. V. (2025). Smart operations in sports management: Transforming physical-sports culture in the society 5.0 era. *Retos 68*, 258–271.

Vieira De Almeida. (2025). Avoiding the offside trap: The legal challenges of data monetisation in sports. Retrieved August 25, 2025, from https://www.vda.pt/en/publications/insights/avoiding-the-offside-trap-the-legal-challenges-of-data-monetisation-in-sports/25957/

Vindicia. (2024). Accelerate growth off the sports field with digital subscription success. Retrieved August 25, 2025, from https://www.vindicia.com/sites/default/files/whitepapers/accelerate-sports-white-paper.pdf

Ware, C. (2004). *Information visualization: Perception for design*. Morgan Kaufmann.

Ware, C. (2008). *Visual thinking: For design*. Morgan Kaufmann Series in Interactive Technologies, Paperback.

Watanabe, N. M., Shapiro, S., & Drayer, J. (2021). Big data and analytics in sport management. *Journal of Sport Management, 35*(3), 197–201.

Wicker, P. (2021). Intentions of environmentally friendly behavior among sports club members: An empirical test of the theory of planned behavior across genders and sports. *Frontiers in Sports and Active Living, 3*, 657183.

Wiese-Bjornstal, D. M. (2010). Psychology and socioculture affect injury risk, response, and recovery in high-intensity athletes: A consensus statement. *Scandinavian Journal of Medicine & Science in Sports, 20*(Suppl 2), 103–111.

Wilson, P., & Kiely, J. (2023). Developing decision-making expertise in professional sports staff: What we can learn from the good judgement project. *Sports Medicine - Open, 9*(1), 100.

Windt, J., & Gabbett, T. J. (2017). How do training and competition workloads relate to injury? The workload–injury aetiology model. *British Journal of Sports Medicine, 51*(5), 428–435.

Winell, E. (2023). How are fans affected by the commercialization of elite sports? A review of the literature and a research agenda. *Sport, Business and Management: An International Journal, 13*(2), 123–145.

Woratschek, H., Horbel, C., & Popp, B. (2014). The sport value framework—a new fundamental logic for analyses in sport management. *European Sport Management Quarterly, 14*(1), 6–24.

Wäsche, H., Dickson, G., Woll, A., & Brandes, U. (2017). Social network analysis in sport research: An emerging paradigm. *European Journal for Sport and Society, 14*(2), 138–165.

Xuan, S., kai Zhou, Z., Zhou, J.-X., Xia, Q.-F., Qin, Y.-N., & Wu, J.-P. (2025). The impact of sporting events on carbon emissions and the emission reduction measures: A systematic review from 2019 to 2024. *Polish Journal of Environmental Studies, 34*(3).

Yiapanas, G. (2025). The application of big data analytics in sports as a tool for personalized fan experience, operations efficiency, and fan engagement strategy. *Business and Management Theory and Practice, 2*(1), 3075.

Yoon, Y., Hwang, H., Choi, Y., Joo, M., Oh, H., Park, I., Lee, K., & Hwang, J. (2019). Analyzing basketball movements and pass relationships using realtime object tracking techniques based on deep learning. *IEEE Access, 7*, 56564–56576.

Yoshida, M., & James, J. D. (2010). Customer satisfaction with game and service experiences: Antecedents and consequences. *Journal of Sport Management, 24*(3), 338–361.

Zacheo, G., Buzimkic, A., Roi, A. L., van Schie, A., Staudt, Y., & Burch, M. (2023). FitYou: A personalized dashboard for health data. In R. Malina, K. Zhang, W. Zeng & G. Wallner (Eds.), *Proceedings of the 16th International Symposium on Visual Information Communication and Interaction, VINCI* (pp. 4:1–4:5). ACM.

Zhang, J., & Li, J. (2022). Mitigating bias and error in machine learning to protect sports data. *Journal of Healthcare Engineering, 2022*(1), 4777010.

Zimmel, H., & Bischoff, L. L. (2023). Der Gender Data Gap und geschlechtsspezifische physiologische Unterschiede im Sport. *Sportorthopädie-Sporttraumatologie*.

Data Challenges in Sports Organizations 3

In this chapter, we examine data challenges in sports organizations considering data access (Sect. 3.1) as fragmented data systems, focusing on ownership and access rights, looking at data protection and security requirements, discussing data literacy, and describing real-time data processing. Data quality (Sect. 3.2) is affected by incorrect data collection, incomplete data, different measurement methods, the subjectivity of the data, and data cleansing. Data integration (Sect. 3.3) plays a vital role in the evaluation of heterogeneous data sources, semantic data alignment, large amounts of data as in the field of big data, data security, and a lack of standards. Data analytics skills (Sect. 3.4) are required to explore the lack of data literacy, the lack of specialized data scientists, the complexity of the data and analysis methods, the communication and interpretation of the results, as well as the cultural change. Finally, we are in a data-driven culture (Sect. 3.5) that is resistant to change, lacks trust in data, trains for cultural heritage, needs incentives, and sees the importance of leadership to drive cultural change.

3.1 Data Access

The professional handling of data requires that sports organizations have not only data but also targeted access to them (Postma, 2023). Data access is more than a technical issue; it is about responsibilities, rights and roles, quality, security, and speed (see Fig. 3.1). Today, in professional sports organizations, access to data is a decisive factor in the quality of decisions and the continued development of sporting and economic processes.

This section shows how the topic of data access needs to be viewed in a differentiated way along five thematic focal points. It begins with Sect. 3.1.1, which describes the challenge of fragmented data systems. In many sports organizations, data are available in isolated individual systems. This fragmentation makes network analysis difficult and can lead to untapped potential. Section 3.1.2 discusses the

D. Schwizer, M. Burch, *Data Excellence in Sports*, Management for Professionals,
https://doi.org/10.1007/978-3-032-10993-4_3

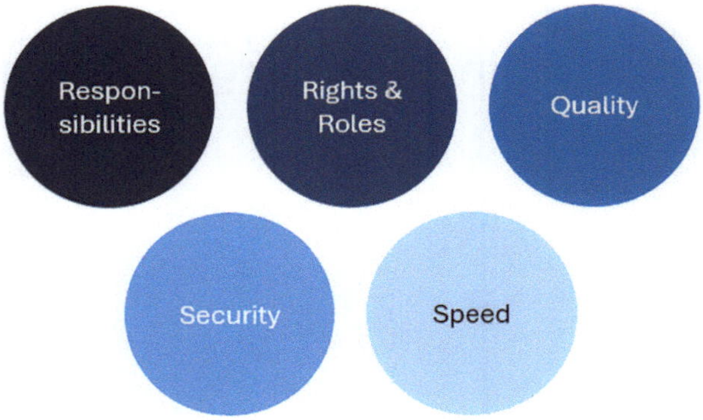

Fig. 3.1 Data access is also related to responsibilities, rights and roles, quality, security, and speed. Figure created by the authors

question of who really owns the data and who is allowed to access them. Clearly defined access options and responsibilities are key to avoid frictional losses and ensure efficient and legally compliant data access. Section 3.1.3 focuses on the protection of sensitive data. Medical and performance-related information requires not only legally compliant security standards but also conscious handling in terms of ethically responsible data management. Section 3.1.4 shows that the best access to data is of little use if employees do not have the necessary data knowledge. Data literacy is understood as a combination of individual skills and organizational structures. It is a prerequisite for being able to use data in a meaningful way. Section 3.1.5 concludes with the processing of real-time data. Where decisions must be made immediately, for example, during a game or in organizational processes in real time, it is not only access to data that is crucial but also the ability to interpret these data immediately and remain capable of acting. Thus, in professional sports, a practice-oriented introduction to the complexity of data access is offered. It shows that data only add value if they can be used at the right time, in the right form, and by the right people, in a responsible, targeted, and networked way.

3.1.1 Fragmented Data Systems

In sports organizations, it is often the case that different departments use different tools. As a result, data are stored on different systems that have no direct connection to each other. This leads to the so-called data silos (Yue et al., 2025). This is problematic because the sports organization no longer has a complete overview of its organizational data. As a result, data are not used efficiently, or important links and correlations are not or are only insufficiently visible. This affects data from all possible areas of a sports organization, such as training, performance, medical, and marketing data (see Table 3.1).

Fragmentation usually arises from historically grown structures (Jacobsen, 2023). Data are playing a more important role in more departments and areas,

Table 3.1 Affected data from many areas of a sports organization: training data, performance data, medical data, and marketing data. Data metrics describe a finer granular view on included data that are worth analyzing

Data type	Data metrics
Training data	Maximal speed, maximal heart rate, stress level, ...
Performance data	Run distance, shoot efficiency, number of passes, ...
Medical data	Heart rate, oxygen, glucose, ...
Marketing data	Shirts sold, number of advertisement banners, spectators on TV, ...

and more tools and applications are being gradually added. In most cases, the systems work well within the data silos. However, when it comes to interaction and cross-departmental coordination, this results in deficiencies or unused potential. The reasons for this are technical specialization, lack of organizational coordination, and cultural differences within the sports organization in dealing with existing data and applications.

Depending on the situation, the effects of fragmented data systems can be problematic in different ways. In any case, missing links have the negative potential to lead to suboptimal decisions. However, it should be noted that silo structures do not necessarily have to be inefficient per se (de Waal et al., 2019). Sometimes data silos even work quite well, especially in their specific area. Overarching strategic decisions that focus on the entire sports organization and both the economic and sports areas suffer from fragmented data systems and pose a threat to competitiveness.

Sports organizations with highly fragmented data systems can strive to gradually merge different data silos. However, a single large data system does not necessarily have to be the goal. Rather, the aim is to reduce complexity. The focus should be on data links that are more likely to provide real added value. For future data-based decisions, one should also ask yourself if it is possible to create common standards, uniform interfaces, or a coordinated selection of analysis tools that prevent or mitigate the growth of data silos (Wang et al., 2024).

This requires strong management. Ideally, it should have the necessary technical understanding and convince employees of the need to make the necessary adjustments. Smaller sports organizations should take care not to undertake too large an integration project all at once, but rather consider a step-by-step and clearly prioritized implementation. This is the only way to achieve the goal of sustainable reduction of the fragmentation of data systems.

3.1.2 Ownership and Access Rights

Ownership and access rights (see Fig. 3.2) are key challenges facing sports organizations. Ownership refers to who owns the data (Asswad & Marx Gómez, 2021). Sports organizations sometimes work with external data providers from whom

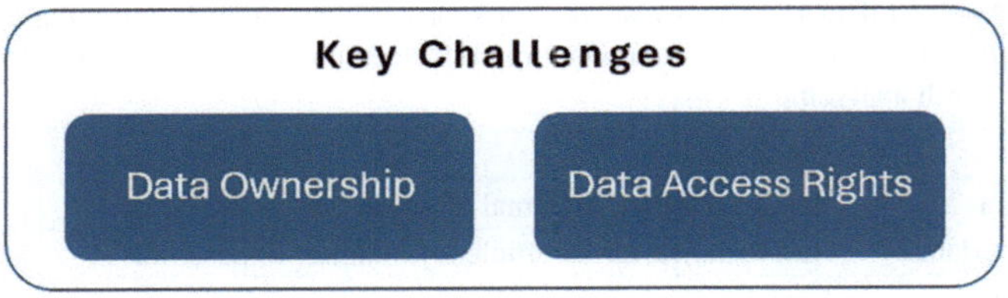

Fig. 3.2 Key challenges for sports organizations: ownership and access rights. Figure created by the authors

specific data material is purchased. The alternative to this is to collect the data independently. This is particularly useful for data on your own athletes (e.g., performance data from training). Ultimately, collecting data yourself or purchasing it is a strategic decision. Access rights refer to who is allowed to access the data. This is usually also related to data protection issues.

There are differentiation options for access rights, in particular. For example, access rights within the organization can be differentiated according to the data and areas assigned to the people concerned. This is particularly relevant for personal and medical data from athletes. As important stakeholders, athletes are also becoming increasingly sensitive when it comes to their own data (Coventry et al., 2023). Sports organizations are therefore advised to act professionally and set up appropriate solutions. A clear awareness of ownership and access rights is therefore a challenge that a sports organization should address (Bowles & McGee, 2023).

It is essential that ownership and access rights are regulated early on and, above all, transparently (Vischer & Partner, 2025). This creates trust with all stakeholders who are affected by data processing within a sports organization, be they athletes, fans, or customers. The applicable data protection laws must be considered. Data can also be sensitive for individual players, even if it does not appear at first glance. For example, an athlete may have an interest in playing despite an injury to secure a player bonus. In this case, data on the state of health can therefore have an impact on the player's financial situation. This circumstance makes the relevant performance and health data even more sensitive than it already is. A clear and transparent regulation of ownership and access rights ensures that such conflicts are avoided.

3.1.3 Data Protection and Security Requirements

Two different forms of data protection can be distinguished. The first is data protection in a narrower sense. This refers to the minimum legal requirements that must be complied with in all cases. Data security, on the other hand, refers to the actual protective measures taken, which can be technical and organizational in nature. To build trust and maintain ethical data handling, sports organizations should always consider going beyond minimum standards and taking additional data

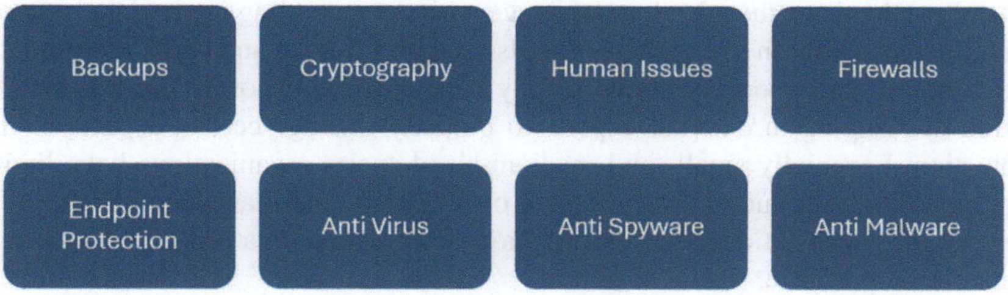

Fig. 3.3 Data protection should include various aspects. Figure created by the authors

security measures (see Fig. 3.3). This is also because it can further reduce the risks involved in data handling and protect reputation.

Medical and performance-related data, as well as personal data from individual customers or fans, must be treated with sensitivity (Jia & Fan, 2021). These allow conclusions to be drawn about individuals and therefore require greater protection. This makes strict data protection measures in this area even more important. These measures are designed to reduce the risk that data are lost or misled due to data leaks or access errors, outdated systems, or human error. These risks require specific management and should be proactively combated with appropriate countermeasures.

Once damage has been caused by overly careless handling of data or neglect of data protection, it cannot usually be easily undone. There is a risk of fines from the legislator, lasting reputational damage or a loss of trust from important stakeholders such as sponsoring partners. In team sports with transfer activities, performance data and injury data of individual athletes are of particular importance (Ferraz et al., 2023). These data are particularly sensitive, as they have a significant impact on the course of an athlete's career.

However, data-related scandals can also lead to situations in which fans and consumers are no longer as willing to share their personal data as before. As a result, a sports organization has less data and, therefore, less knowledge about its own fans. This can result in reduced economic potential. Therefore, it is important for a sports organization to always find a balance between adequate data protection and the optimization of positive effects through the intensive use of data. Ultimately, these are not two contrasting aspects, but rather complementary ones. If a good database is adequately protected, the greatest potential in sports and economics can be tapped.

Clear access regulations are a form of effective data protection. If it is clearly defined who can access which data, this is already an important element that needs to be fulfilled. Technical measures can help with this. These include aspects such as password protection (Zhao et al., 2006) or two-factor authentication (Chen & Goh, 2015). It is also advisable to define internal guidelines in the form of a code of conduct to handle data. All of this requires a high level of expertise and proper internal coordination and communication. It is also important to incorporate control mechanisms that check compliance with the prevailing internal and external guidelines. In addition to expertise, this also requires human and financial resources, which not all sports organizations simply have at their disposal. There is also the option of bringing in external experts to properly manage certain aspects of data protection. Especially small- and medium-sized sports organizations have limited legal expertise and budgets to deal with overarching data management issues. For these sports organizations, the prioritization of important data protection tasks is of particular importance.

It can be assumed that new questions regarding data protection in sports organizations will arise in the foreseeable future. Technological progress is creating new situations and protection requirements that need to be regulated by the legislator or by individual sports organizations themselves (Number Analytics, 2025). In addition, society is increasingly ethically aware of how data are handled. Sports organizations that take an early and proactive approach here by seriously addressing the newly emerging issues of data protection can anticipate more restrictive legal regulations and thus secure additional trust from their own stakeholders, as well as decisive competitive advantages.

3.1.4 Data Literacy

Data literacy (see Fig. 3.4) is a combination of individual and organizational skills in dealing with data. Sports organizations face the challenge of developing these skills or "buying in" them by hiring the appropriate specialists. Ideally, employees from various areas should be able to work with and use data independently, even without a background in data technology. This applies to both the sporting and business areas of a sports organization. People who combine specialist knowledge from a specific field (e.g., training theory, marketing, and medicine) with application-oriented skills in dealing with data are not only but also extremely sought after in sport. They make an important contribution to advance individual areas and the sports organization as a whole.

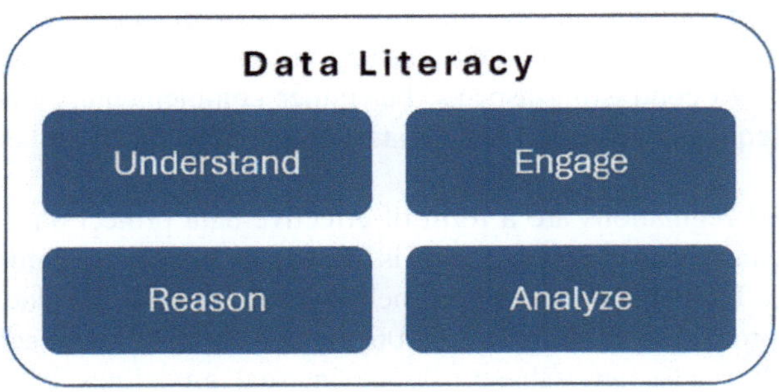

Fig. 3.4 Data literacy integrates several aspects. Figure created by the authors

However, a lack of data literacy, on the other hand, leads not only to lower success probabilities but also to potentially wrong decisions in economic and sporting matters (Balafoutas et al., 2019). Lack of data literacy means that the potential for personalization, individualization (see Sect. 2.3), and control and optimization of management decisions is not fully exploited. Depending on the level of data literacy between direct and indirect competitors in sport and among athletes (Clegg et al., 2022), this can result in a decisive competitive disadvantage. Investing in data literacy of your own employees is a long-term investment in the case of high employee retention, which can pay off not only in sporting terms but also economically. There is also the positive aspect that employees are not as dependent on data specialists but can work on many issues in their areas autonomously and efficiently.

The combination of specialist knowledge and data expertise is essential. This can be ensured both in small teams and in individuals. In sports organizations, it is often a combination of the two. Data management is not a discipline or a department in itself but is seen as an integrative element and support for the organization's own specialist work. The dynamics of cooperation also plays an important role. If a sports organization succeeds in regularly generating a sense of achievement through data-based cooperation between different employees, this promotes further cooperation and willingness to engage in data-based management and maintain an appropriate approach to data (Olaniyan et al., 2023).

However, if a sports organization relies solely on data specialists to support the various departments, smooth communication between data experts and individual departments is essential. The challenge is literally to find a common language to work on specific cases and to understand each other both linguistically and in terms of content. Ideally, it is possible to build a data-competent, learning organization (Marsick & Watkins, 2003) that improves iteratively. The conditions for this are particularly good when different specialists from individual areas work together over a long period of time. Therefore, a high degree of employee loyalty is a key element in this type of collaboration.

Data specialists or departmental specialists with strong data skills are not easy to recruit on the market. For this reason, interdisciplinary work within the sports organization and learning on the job are frequently encountered. Although it is challenging to get involved in the topic of data-based work in this way, it also represents an opportunity. It also allows a sports organization to accumulate a great deal of organization-specific knowledge, which is of significant importance for practical and case-specific applications. The sports organization must develop the skills of its own employees in the long term. This benefits both the sports organization and the individual employees. Knowledge retention occurs through long-term and systematic employee development. However, it is essential that the knowledge not only remains decentralized with the individual employees but is also documented. Some sports organizations might even set up advanced knowledge management systems (KMS) (Alavi & Leidner, 2001). This is one way to ensure that knowledge is largely retained when employees leave the company.

However, it is challenging to introduce employees to data-based work, especially if they have previously had little contact with data management. Resistance to change is expected (see Sect. 3.5). Many employees prefer to stick to old habits and tend to be skeptical of change. At this point, the management of the sports organization is required to convince employees of the benefits of the new direction and is also prepared to support employees on the way to more data-based work (Cieślak & Valor, 2024). A gradual introduction can help ensure that employees are not overwhelmed. Clear communication of the objectives of the change and the added value is also essential. If employees know why they should work in a more data-based way and why it makes sense for them, they are more willing to actively help shape major changes. After all, data competence is not only an important component for the competitiveness of the sports organization itself but can also strengthen the employability of people who work in the field in the long term.

3.1.5 Real-Time Data Processing

Real-time data processing (Rokita et al., 2025) is of particular importance in sports organizations (Vec et al., 2024). Real-time data processing refers to analysis and the use of data at the time they are generated. The aim is to make data-based decisions directly during ongoing events (Probst et al., 2018). This is particularly relevant in professional sport and in the competitive environment. Real-time data can be found in various application domains (see Table 3.2), in sports or during sporting events.

The classic example of real-time data processing in sports organizations is the analysis of performance and tactical data during a game in a team sport. This enables tactical adjustments to be made during a game for which there is data-based evidence. But real-time data processing is also relevant for sports organizations outside the game. Here, for example, the aim is to optimally manage visitor flows in the stadium and to be able to react quickly and purposefully to unexpected events. Other factors relevant to match days can also be optimized with real-time data processing. These include the management of catering services, logistics issues related to the arrival and departure of fans, and security-related issues. For many of these practical challenges, a complete solution is often not possible but rather

Table 3.2 There are various application domains that must deal with real-time data. This table provides a short list of some important ones

Application domain	Type of analyzed real-time data
Eye tracking	Reaction on gaze inputs in real time for gaze-assisted interaction
Logistics	Real-time monitoring of goods
Traffic	Analyzing vehicle numbers in real time
Medicine	Real-time monitoring of patients during surgeries
Weather	Real-time situations during hurricanes to evacuate people
Stock market	Real-time monitoring of market activity

an approximation of the optimal solution or a continuous process of optimization. However, this can result in significant improvements which, depending on the situation, can be a decisive factor for the success of sporting or economic activities of a sports organization.

Real-time data processing has both advantages and disadvantages. The advantages include faster decisions in important situations, a constant overview of the current data situation, and early recognition of impending difficulties. The disadvantages or risks include time pressure, potentially incorrect decisions due to insufficient data, and a general increased susceptibility to errors. This makes targeted preparation for situations in which real-time data processing plays a decisive role more important. It is key to properly prepare the instruments and processes and to train the employees specifically for the application situation.

There are various factors that significantly influence the success of real-time data processing. In addition to a flawless technical infrastructure and trained personnel, these include a clear organizational understanding of what is to be achieved in which situation with real-time data processing. In these situations, it must be possible to make decisions quickly and clearly. All open questions that can be clarified in advance should no longer be an issue in the situation itself. The aim is to create an optimal environment for the situation in which the key decisions are made. This is particularly important when several people are involved in the processes, e.g., when a data analyst prepares data for coaches or security officers during a match. Especially when different specialists work together, data prepared for specific target groups help to ensure optimal communication between them.

However, many sports organizations do not have enough experience or personnel to cover all situations that involve real-time data processing. Medium or small sports organizations often have difficulties in recruiting and retaining specialized personnel. This makes it even more important to consider and implement user-friendly tools in real-time data processing. In this way, employees can also be integrated into these processes who do not have a strong background in data analysis but can be integrated through application-oriented processes.

Ultimately, the need for real-time data processing varies from sports organization to sports organization. Not all sports organizations need real-time data processing to the same extent. Rather, it is vital to assess on a case-by-case basis where real-time data offer real added value to give one's own sports organization a competitive advantage. Costs and benefits must always be carefully weighed.

3.2 Data Quality

High data quality is the basis for effective decision-making in sports organizations. However, in practice, it is a major challenge to provide data that are appropriate, complete, consistent, and in a usable form (Davis et al., 2024). There are many reasons for poor data quality. These range from human error and inconsistent standards to technical limitations and unclear responsibilities. This section examines five key challenges that affect data quality in sports organizations.

Section 3.2.1 gets to the bottom of the challenge of incorrect data collection. This can be due to human inexperience, technical reasons, or organizational neglect. If errors in this area are not recognized, inaccurate data are included in the analyses and negatively influence decision-making. This leads to potentially negative impacts on athletes, wasted resources, or poor strategic decisions. A culture of responsibility, coupled with technical checks and targeted staff training and development, helps overcome challenges in this area. Section 3.2.2 focuses on incomplete data, a challenge that often remains hidden. Missing information, whether due to system errors or structural deficiencies in the data infrastructure, weakens the basis for economic and sporting decisions. Early detection, prioritization of high-impact data, and awareness of qualitative gaps are key elements for improvement. Section 3.2.3 deals with the challenge of different measurement methods. Sports organizations often use heterogeneous tools and standards, both within and between departments. Different stakeholders, such as leagues or federations, also create additional differences. Although complete standardization is hardly realistic, efforts to coordinate and harmonize measurement methods, especially within functional areas, contribute significantly to increasing the comparability of the data and thus increasing the strategic usability. The subjectivity of the data is dealt with in Sect. 3.2.4. It emphasizes how even seemingly objective data can be influenced by personal judgment, be it in scouting reports, training assessments, or player evaluations. Although subjectivity should not be completely eliminated, sports organizations must learn to collect data with certain standards, contextualize it, and conduct structured assessments. They should also focus on transparency in the interpretation of data. Finally, Sect. 3.2.5 looks at what data cleansing is all about. This deals with the technical and procedural process of correcting and validating data after they have been collected. Sports data are often highly complex. It usually contains multivariate, dynamic, and often context-dependent elements. This makes a combination of human expertise and automated tools necessary. Clear responsibilities, iterative validation, and a clean allocation of resources are the key to ensuring a well-founded and trustworthy data analysis.

In general, these sections emphasize that data quality is not a one-time effort, but an ongoing strategic task. Sports organizations that invest in addressing these challenges will be better prepared for data-driven decisions and a data culture that generates value both on and off the field.

3.2.1 Incorrect Data Collection

Incorrect data collection is a real challenge, not only in sports data management (Davis et al., 2024). There are many reasons for this. On the one hand, human errors lead to incorrect data, while technical deficits or systematic deficiencies can also lead to errors in datasets that cannot be easily corrected. An example of a human error is a lack of experience with tools or with data work in general. Systematic errors include poorly thought-out processes or lack of responsibilities.

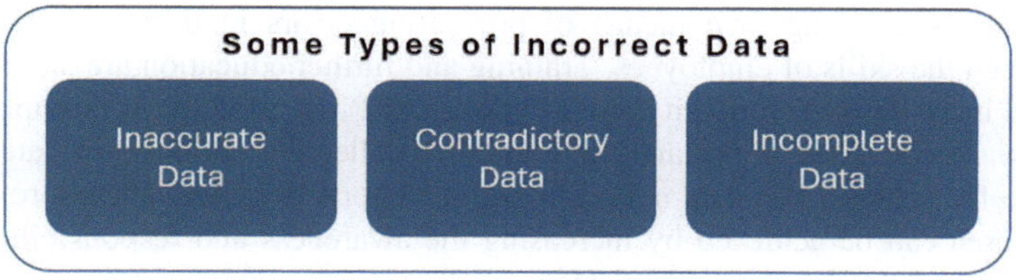

Fig. 3.5 Incorrect data can be a real challenging problem for decision-making. Figure created by the authors

The result of incorrect data collection is inaccurate, contradictory, or incomplete data (see Fig. 3.5). Unrecognized errors in data collection are particularly problematic, leading to undesirable long-term effects. Incorrect data flow into analyses and evaluations and thus influence strategic and tactical decisions. The inaccurate data are thus incorporated into reports and profiles. This creates a false consistency that provides an incorrect basis for the analysis. Depending on how pronounced the incorrect data are due to faulty data collection, this has a negative impact on the overall quality of the data work.

The consequences are multiple. For example, if an athlete's profile and performance data are incorrect, there is a high risk of many incorrect transfer decisions (Islam & Nahid, 2024). Incorrect data can also have negative consequences for individual athletes. In the medical field, for example, inefficient treatment can occur if incorrect data are used as a basis. Inadequate data due to incorrect data collection ultimately also has a negative impact on the economic sector. For example, if fans and consumers' preferences are misrepresented, this leads to a poor basis for decision-making in the economic area of a sports organization. For all these reasons, it is important that incorrect data collection is cut as much as possible.

However, countermeasures can be taken at various levels to meet the challenge. These measures can be technical, organizational, and cultural. From a technical perspective, it is possible to subject the existing data to another plausibility check (Davis et al., 2024). This means that the collected data are reviewed critically again before it is definitively entered into the database. In addition, data should always be checked for redundancies. Duplicate data also distort the results of an evaluation. Finally, it is important to integrate further possible mechanisms for early error detection in the technical area to effectively prevent as many errors as possible. At the organizational level, it is necessary to establish clear processes and responsibilities (Van der Byl & Vredenburg, 2023). Only if people are clearly responsible for the quality of the data collected can they also assume responsibility for it. Here, also, additional control measures reduce the risk of errors and inadequate data in the system. Finally, culture within a sports organization also plays a key role (see Sect. 3.5). It is important not only to promote a culture of error (Edmondson, 1999) but also to live it. It is about employees feeling safe enough to openly address potential mistakes rather than hiding them. This plays a key role in ensuring that errors can be identified and corrected early on.

An important long-term means of preventing errors in data collection is to strengthen the skills of employees. Training and further education are an important lever to increase overall quality (Salas et al., 2012). In addition, it is important to raise awareness of the importance of clean data collection not only for data quality but also for professional data management in a sports organization. Improvements in this area can be achieved by increasing the awareness and responsibility of all employees involved in data management. Employees should be motivated to take the utmost care when collecting data to achieve tangible benefits for data management. If employees become aware of the added value they generate as a result, their motivation to contribute to this area will increase further.

Future developments in the field of artificial intelligence should help identify sources of error in data collection even better and faster. However, it would be wrong to believe that all the challenges in data collection can be solved with technological applications in the foreseeable future. Technology will not replace the need for data responsibility on the part of the people involved anytime soon. The interaction between people and technology is therefore of essential importance here. Incorrect data collection is and remains a key challenge for sports organizations. Those who actively counteract this will strengthen their own data work and lay the foundation for a real competitive advantage, be it in the sporting or economic field.

3.2.2 Incomplete Data

Incomplete data are a challenge for sports organizations that is often underestimated. This is a challenge that is not readily apparent. Incomplete data can have various causes (Tenan & Adams, 2024). For example, temporary system failures can lead to missing data, but structural gaps can also be a possible cause. Structural gaps mean that data were never collected due to a lack of equipment, expertise, or resources.

The problem with incomplete data is that the gaps are not directly visible. Therefore, systematic handling of incomplete data is essential. Control mechanisms should be used to systematically check which data are available and where possible data are missing (Robertson et al., 2023). A distinction must be made between data that have never been collected and incomplete data. Incomplete or missing data can be replaced by imputation methods including several techniques such as mean, median, mode, forward- and backward-fill, interpolation, k-nearest neighbor, or even regression models (see Table 3.3).

Data with a clear qualitative background are sometimes neglected (Draper, 2009). In the sports context, for example, this includes data on mental state, sleep, or individual stress perception. Data in a historical context also often have gaps and can therefore be interpreted as incomplete datasets. Missing data is problematic because it makes it difficult to reach sound conclusions in the economic or sporting field (Tenan, 2023). The basis for decision-making is weaker in the case of incomplete data, without this being directly apparent.

Incomplete data means that the potential remains untapped. It is not easy to exploit this potential later, because incomplete data cannot be supplemented so

Table 3.3 Some imputation techniques which focus on getting rid of missing or incomplete data

Technique	Details
Mean	Summing all values, dividing by the number of values
Median	Middle number in a dataset must be ordered from smallest to largest
Mode	Value that appears most frequently in a dataset
Forward-fill	Missing value replaced with the previous non-missing value
Backward-fill	Missing value replaced with the next value observation
Interpolation	Missing values estimated between known data values
k-Nearest neighbor	Missing value found by examining the k closest data neighbors in the data
Regression model	Missing value found by computing best fitting line

easily afterward. The time of data collection is therefore very important. Ideally, the causes of incomplete data are identified early on and corrected quickly.

As human and financial resources are limited in many sports organizations, it is important to clearly prioritize the causes of incomplete data. The focus should be on completing the data that have the highest possible potential benefit. The sporting and economic areas should not be played against each other.

In the foreseeable future, new technologies and artificial intelligence should ensure that gaps in datasets can be identified and corrected at an early stage. However, systematic and complete data collection remains a key success factor in professional data management in sports organizations. Those who consciously identify gaps can increase the strategic added value, in the sporting or economic field.

3.2.3 Different Measurement Methods

Another major challenge for sports organizations is different measurement methods (Davis et al., 2024) (see Table 3.4). They also arise from the historical development of data collection methods within a sports organization. Various departments and specialists apply popular tools. Standards are used that differ from one another. The latter often has to do with the fact that there are different levels in sports management, of which sports organizations represent only one of many. For example, there is also the level of sports associations or that of leagues. These different levels also involve several types of measurement methods. In many cases, different data collection standards (see also Sects. 2.2.3 and 3.3.5) are also used, further increasing complexity. The consequences of this are the more difficult comparability, obstacles to consolidating the data, and limited benefits for strategic use (Davis et al., 2024).

When different measurement methods are available, it is not necessarily a question of completely standardized data landscapes historically grown. Rather, responsible managers should carefully weigh how much can be gained by integrating and standardizing measurement methods and where specialized methods

Table 3.4 Measurement methods with additional details about what type of data is measured and the phases (training, real sports event, and rehabilitation) in which they are typically applied

Method	Details	Phase
Direct observation	Observer qualitative feedback	Training, sports event
Physiological monitoring	Heart rate, oxygen, blood pressure	Training, rehabilitation
Training load measurement	Duration, intensity, intervals	Training
Kinematic observation	Movement speed, acceleration	Training
Biomechanical analysis	Musculoskeletal, movement data	Training, rehabilitation
Anthropometric monitoring	Body composition, BMI	Training
Performance testing	Strength, power, agility	Training
Wearable recording	GPS, heart rate	Training, sports event
Subjective measurement	Qualitative data, self-judgment	Training

and tools can continue to be used. The aim is therefore not to eliminate all data silos (see also Sect. 3.1.1) but to reduce them to a sensible level. Sometimes, the individual functional advantage within a data silo due to certain tools is so great that standardization makes little sense. An important distinction here could be between the sports and commercial areas. Therefore, the first step could be to examine the degree to which standardization can be achieved within these areas without immediately standardizing all data collection methods. In addition, it is rarely realistic to consider all external standards (e.g., leagues or associations) in an adjustment, for example, when it comes to athletes' performance data during a competition.

An important negative consequence of different measurement methods is the limited comparability. Although data may be available on similar issues, they do not complement each other because they do not meet the same standard. The context is not given, and therefore these additional data are only of limited use. They do not contribute much to the further development of the entire data system of a sports organization. This challenge of different measurement methods is therefore not just a problem limited to sports organizations themselves but affects the entire sports ecosystem with different players within a particular sport. If it is possible to establish certain uniform measurement methods within a sport through skillful coordination, this already represents great added value for all involved (Davis et al., 2024). However, this is not an easy task, as there are usually no direct actors with authority to issue directives in this area between sports organizations within a sport. However, it is more expedient to focus on coordination and incentives than on regulation.

It should already be helpful to create awareness of the distortions caused by different measurement methods. For smaller sports, this is also an opportunity to reduce the gap in data management with larger and more resourced sports by cleverly coordinating with each other and creating uniform standards on a voluntary basis. Although complete standardization is not always desirable in this case either, a minimum level of compatibility already brings decisive advantages in terms of

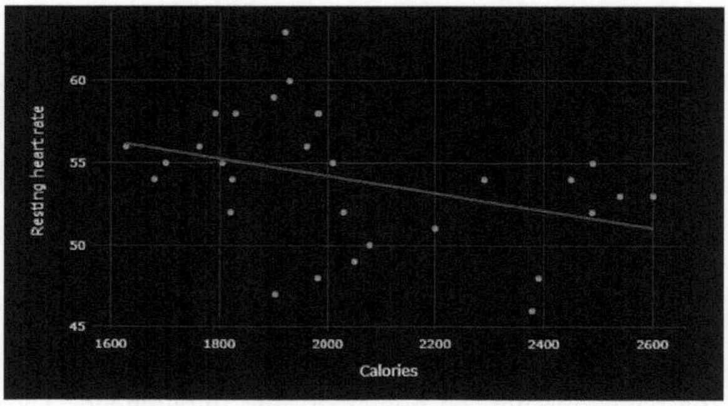

Fig. 3.6 Analyzing quantifiable values, for example, to explore the correlation behavior between the resting heart rate and the calories. Figure created by the authors by using the online version of the FitYou tool with permission of Zacheo et al. (2023)

data aggregation and comparability. This strengthens the data basis and quality for all participating sports organizations. Those who contribute to this also strengthen the entire system.

3.2.4 Subjectivity of the Data

Subjectivity is a challenge that is present in not only purely qualitative data but can also be hidden in seemingly objective data (Gaede-Illig et al., 2014). Data are not created in vacuum but are shaped in part by personal assessments. This can be the case with observations, surveys, or interpretation of data. Furthermore, not all aspects of sports data management can be measured using clearly quantifiable values (see Fig. 3.6 for the benefits of quantifiable values, for example, when analyzing them for correlation effects).

Typical examples of non-quantifiable values are certain elements of scouting (Brunnschneider & Hahn, 2022). These include aspects such as the character fit of a player to a team structure. This can be seen, for example, in the behavior before or after a game or in certain situations and is subjective to some extent. The scout must therefore determine a value that corresponds to his own assessment and cannot be completely objectified. Even when interpreting large amounts of data, specialists implicitly or explicitly make a subjective assessment based on experience and thus introduce a subjective element into the data processing procedure.

Subjective aspects can also play a role in data collection for athletes who are already within the structure of their own sports organization. For example, coaches can subjectively assess an athlete's training intensity or resilience and compare these values with other data collected in these areas. This enables a combined view through various types of data, providing a more holistic picture. Subjectivity is therefore not only a challenge but also represents a useful addition to more objective datasets when used in a targeted way.

However, data specialists involved should always be aware of whether certain data have a high degree of subjectivity or whether the data meet objective standards (Gelman & Hennig, 2017). If this awareness is not present, there is a risk that

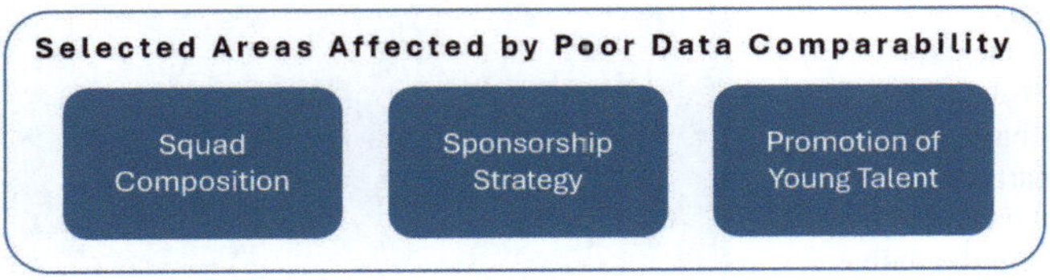

Fig. 3.7 A lack of data comparability can negatively affect areas such as squad composition, sponsorship strategy, and promotion of young talent. Figure created by the authors

the decisions will be one sided and unbalanced. The reason for this is that a high proportion of subjective assessments are not considered properly and scrutinized in this case. This leads to a lack of comparability of subjective data over time or beyond the individual sports organization. The consequences can be devastating if this leads to wrong decisions in the composition of the squad, questions about the sponsorship strategy, or the promotion of young talent (see Fig. 3.7).

There are ways and means to counteract an unfavorably high level of subjectivity in the data. For example, standardized rating scales can be used with clear definitions. The descriptions of the individual levels of the proposed scale are supported with a description, thus ensuring that the assessment is as uniform as possible, regardless of who performs it. Another option is to involve several assessors. They carry out the assessment independently of each other. This allows individual distortions to be balanced using the mean value or jointly adjusting different values. There is also the option of deliberately marking subjective assessments as such and documenting them. In selected cases, it is even possible and sensible to enrich subjective assessments with additional data that can be objectified (Montull et al., 2022). This further strengthens the informative value of mainly subjective data.

Subjective data will continue to play an important role in sports organizations in the future (Montull et al., 2022). However, artificial intelligence and learning systems are increasingly creating opportunities to recognize qualitative patterns and quantify them (Chidambaram et al., 2022). As a result, subjective assessments could become more accurate in the future thanks to algorithmic support. However, despite new technical possibilities, human experience will continue to play an important role in data management in sports organizations, especially in complex decision-making situations. Therefore, new technologies in this area should be seen as a complement to the expertise of specialists and not as a replacement.

3.2.5 Data Cleansing

Data cleansing is an ex post process to improve the quality of the data material. It involves technical data cleansing with the aim of achieving the cleanest possible and analyzable dataset. Depending on how great the need for data cleansing is, it is either a strategically central component to allow a clean basic analysis in the first place or an operational fine-tuning to increase the informative value of the data analysis.

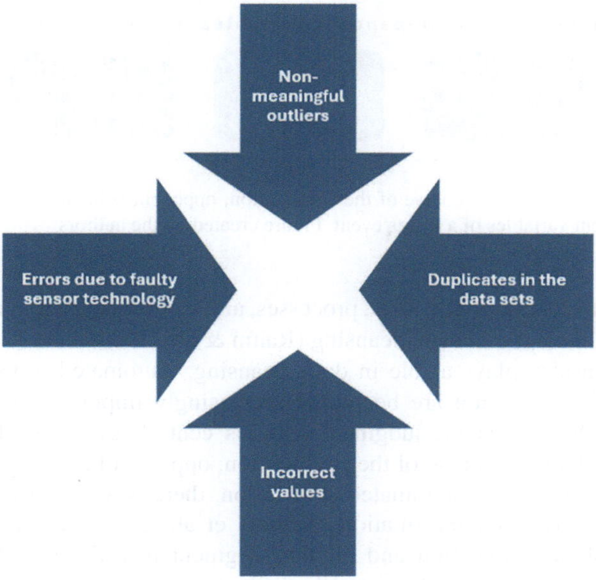

Fig. 3.8 Issues when it comes to errors and data cleansing. Figure created by the authors

Sports organizations do not know exactly when data cleansing is necessary. However, if data-based decisions do not have the desired effect, this is an indication that a closer look at data and data cleansing should be taken. These aspects indicate a lack of data quality. The need for better or more accurate data cleansing is usually not indicated by individual symptoms, but by accumulation of inconsistent or implausible events. This is precisely why it is crucial that sports organizations do not blindly trust the data but always include a plausibility check.

In data cleansing, there are several typical sources of error and cleansing goals that sports organizations pursue. These include the elimination of meaningless outliers that distort the analysis, duplicates in the datasets, obviously incorrect values (such as unrealistic GPS coordinates or incorrect time stamps), and errors due to faulty sensor technology (see Fig. 3.8). In the case of the latter, it is essential that corrections are made not only to the data but also to sensor technology to have flawless data on a sensor basis in the future. Contextualization is particularly important in the data cleansing process (Davis et al., 2024). Not all extreme values are automatically incorrect but must always be checked in context. For example, an unusual course of play can very well result in unusual values for the data.

The data cleansing process can be divided into the three main phases of identification, cleansing, and validation. The responsibility usually lies not only with the data specialists but also with the department heads such as the athletic coach or the sports director. Clear responsibilities within the sports organization are crucial

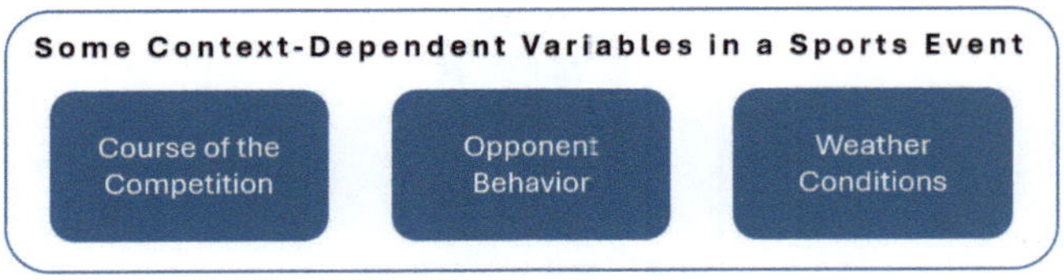

Fig. 3.9 Factors such as the course of the competition, opponent behavior, and the weather are context-dependent variables of a sports event. Figure created by the authors

for proper data cleansing. The roles, processes, and tools to be used should be clearly assigned to allow optimal data cleansing (Rahm & Do, 2000).

Automation also plays a role in data cleansing. Automated processes such as AI-based outlier detection are becoming increasingly important (Panwar, 2024). Nevertheless, human expert judgment remains central, as sports data are often context-dependent (cf. course of the competition, opponent behavior, weather, etc.) (see Fig. 3.9). In a purely automated application, there is a risk of overadjustment and the loss of relevant information (Neutatz et al., 2022). Therefore, it makes sense to combine automation and human judgment in order to achieve optimal solutions in data cleansing. Automated prefiltering should always be checked by human validation.

In the sports context, there are some special features to consider when it comes to data cleansing. For example, data collection conditions in sport are sometimes highly variable, especially in game sports with an opponent on the pitch. In addition, sports data are often dynamic, nonstandardized, and multivariate (Davis et al., 2024). The comparability of historical data is made more difficult by data cleansing processes that are pursued with varying degrees of intensity. This is also because individual data differ due to changes in game mode, calendar structure, or other factors. For example, it is only possible to directly compare load data over several seasons to a limited extent because, for example, the season length or the match frequency are not identical. In this case, normalization is necessary to ensure at least approximate comparability.

However, in the daily practice of sports organizations, the challenge is not only to properly perform data cleansing but also to simply provide the necessary resources and expertise (Postma, 2023). Sometimes external support is also required. Lack of resources can also lead to processes being slowed down or requiring greater prioritization. Finally, data cleansing processes are made more difficult by fragmented data landscapes (see Sect. 3.1.1). Therefore, the prevention of data fragmentation should also be given the attention it deserves.

Data cleansing is an important prerequisite for meaningful data analysis. Therefore, it is a central element for sound decisions in the data management of a sports organization. Without consistent data cleansing, sports organizations run the risk of making wrong strategic decisions or missing potential.

3.3 Data Integration

There is a great body of research and literature on the topic of data integration (Doan et al., 2012), which is less studied in the field of sports and sports management. However, we will consider the most important challenges, including data sources and their heterogeneity (Sect. 3.3.1). Semantics plays a crucial role in obtaining data alignments (Sect. 3.3.2). Large amounts of data are becoming increasingly problematic for sports organizations (Sect. 3.3.3). Data must even be synchronized to get them to a comparative level, which gives an additional burden for data integration (Sect. 3.3.4). Finally, even a lack of standards is a real challenge to get all these steps of data integration done in a reliable, efficient, and effective manner (Sect. 3.3.5).

3.3.1 Heterogeneous Data Sources

Sports data exist in a variety of forms, consisting of several data types (see Sects. 2.1.2 and 4.4.2), being stored in several data formats, and accessible from various data sources, including file systems, databases, or data streams from a remote server or from a local machine (see Fig. 3.10 for some of the most prominent data types) (Anzer et al., 2025). The data itself can be static, dynamic, structured, unstructured, cleaned, or even full of errors (see Sect. 3.2.5) and missing values (see Sect. 3.2.2). There is no guarantee that the data are already useful and well prepared for a data analysis or visualization. Consequently, heterogeneous data are a real challenge for data scientists with the goal of finding rules, patterns, correlations, or anomalies and outliers in them, i.e., insights and knowledge.

With an increasing number of data generation technologies, more powerful hardware, and a larger variety of data-related disciplines, we can see a never-ending trend in the production of digital data. Even social networks can be part of heterogeneous data sources in sports organizations, for example, including fan feedback, discussions, or critical thoughts on a sports team and its management crew. Analyzing all available data can be a great benefit in improving management

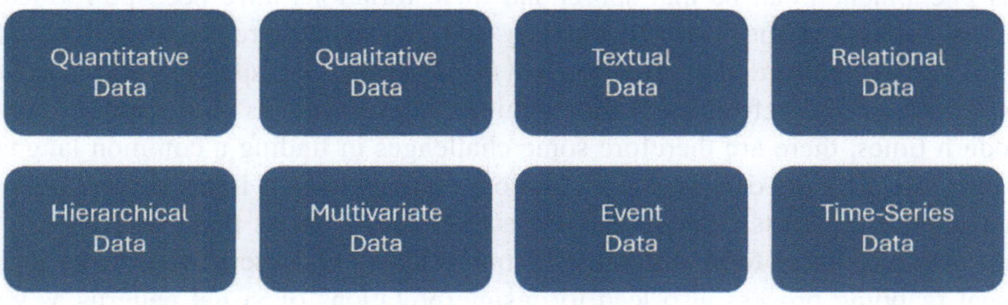

Fig. 3.10 Heterogeneous data exist in a variety of data types, data formats, data sources, and data structures. Figure created by the authors

strategies, but on the negative side, a data analyst is typically faced with challenging issues that require more than one domain expert, involving many research fields in some kind of interdisciplinary and multidisciplinary style (Piggott et al., 2020) (see Sect. 3.4.2). This interdisciplinary aspect brings into play several opinions, sometimes conflicting, and makes decision-making very difficult in some situations.

Data integration (Sect. 3.3) is also a big problem when dealing with heterogeneous data sources, as the way in which we integrate the data is often not well defined and unclear, leading to a loss of data quality (Daraio et al., 2022). Moreover, to successfully work with heterogeneous data and all the data analysis techniques involved, data analysts must apply well-performing algorithmic approaches which are sometimes not available due to computationally NP-hard or intractable problems (Garey & Johnson, 1979). Heuristic approaches are required, in particular when real-time analyses need to be applied, for example, during a sports event that includes various types of data and data sources to get reliable analytical results. Even if analysis techniques perform well now, they can suffer from scalability issues in the future, in the case where heterogeneous datasets grow, leading to performance problems during a data analysis stage.

3.3.2 Semantic Data Alignment

The various data sources and data formats create challenges for data integration, data linkage, and data merging (Putrama & Martinek, 2024). These challenges cannot be solved with a single algorithm. Often a semiautomatic solution is required, including human experts in the form of data analysts and domain experts to find the optimal solution. To be successful, a common language is needed that everyone involved can understand, even the algorithms (Koutras, 2019). Otherwise, there will be inconsistencies in the data, and finally the data could be prone to errors and patterns or insights are distorted. With semantic data alignment it should be guaranteed that such miscommunications are avoided, and the data are reliably and consistently integrated for further use.

For sports organizations, this can be problematic since sport is an international discipline, and consequently there exist different terminologies. The reason for this phenomenon can be that sports and their variations have been performed in various regions of the world divergently and evolved differently over time (Zhai et al., 2020). Before the invention of the Internet, the sports world was less connected, and therefore, each subcommunity developed its own terminology. In modern times, there are therefore some challenges in finding a common language to integrate different data sources. This common language is important not only for data science concepts but also for interactive visualizations that must display the data in some visual form that must be presented to end users. The errors in this visual mapping process also lead to misinterpretations of visual patterns as well. It is not just a mapping but also a semantic mapping that requires the different terminologies (which mean the same or similar things) to be brought into a common and understandable language for everyone (Suzani, 2024).

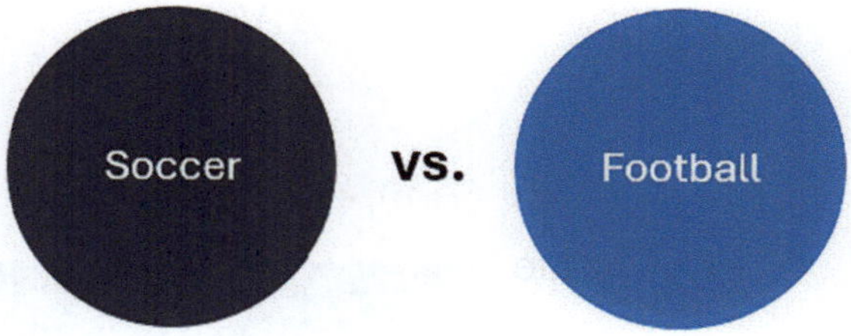

Fig. 3.11 Soccer vs. football: Both terms mean the same game, but in different parts of the world. Figure created by the authors

One example includes the term that describes a prominent game that can be slightly different in some of the world's regions. The most popular example of such a phenomenon is the term for soccer vs. football (see Fig. 3.11) which means the same game. However, soccer is used more in North America and Australia, whereas football is used in most other parts of the world. Another example in the sports domain could be a certain set of rules, for example, in soccer, where some countries have special and extra rules due to natural circumstances. A head organization like FIFA or UEFA must decide which rules apply in a more general, perhaps international setting. In addition, for the mass media it is important that sports terms are used consistently, for example, when broadcasting an international event such as the FIFA World Cup or the Olympic Games. The general language may be English, but each radio station or TV station has a language-specific native speaker who uses his own words to explain events during a sports competition.

3.3.3 Large Amounts of Data

Large amounts of data pose a variety of challenges for sports organizations (Postma, 2023). Professional sports are generating ever-increasing amounts of data. The reasons for this are digitalization, the diversity of sensor technology (e.g., GPS, heart rate, tracking systems), and the increasing expectations of data-based decisions. One of the main challenges is maintaining an overview, separating relevant from irrelevant data, and recognizing meaningful correlations. Technical limitations such as storage capacities or data processing times also play a role here. For example, even a single player in a soccer match generates many data points in a short period of time. These include position data, running intensity, heart rate, ball contact, and many more.

When it comes to large amounts of data in the sports context, we sometimes also talk about the 5 Vs of big data (Postma, 2023): volume, velocity, variety, veracity, and value (see Fig. 3.12). Volume is generally understood to mean that large amounts of data are constantly being generated in sport. Velocity stands for the frequent need for real-time processing, which is becoming increasingly important in game sports, for example, for making tactical adjustments during a match. Variety stands for the different data sources. In sports, this includes movement data, subjective assessments, medical data, video footage, and more. Veracity stands for the challenge that data collected in sports are not always clean. Sensor errors,

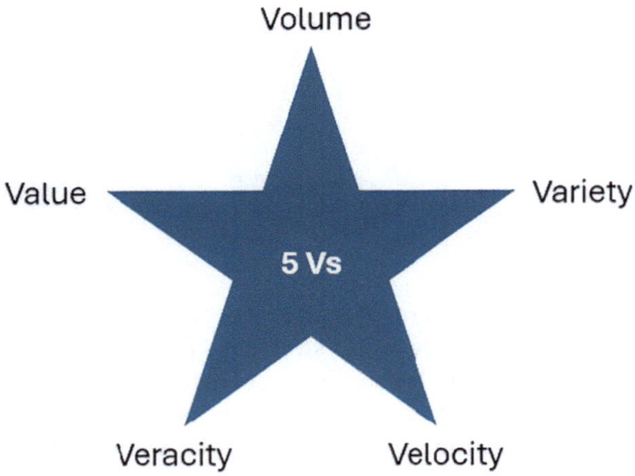

Fig. 3.12 Big data focus on the 5 Vs including volume, velocity, variety, veracity, and value. Figure created by the authors

transmission problems, or context errors can occur. All these errors make the reliability of sports data more difficult. After all, not all data have the same value. The handling of data in sports organizations requires strategic prioritization to focus on meaningful data.

There are various risks associated with an inadequate scope with large volumes of data (Dello Iacono et al., 2025). For example, there is a risk of not evaluating important data or interpreting it incorrectly. There is also a risk of wasting resources on data that offer little analytical added value. Furthermore, misjudgments can occur, for example, in player ratings, match analyses, or medical evaluations. Inefficient data work can easily lead to frustration, loss of time, and wrong strategic decisions. Inefficient handling of large amounts of data is also expensive.

To handle the 5 Vs of big data well in sports organizations, certain requirements are placed on data managers. First, data managers should know for what they need the data and for what they do not. In addition, it is important to maintain an overview of existing data sources and their quality. Furthermore, relevant data should be identified and irrelevant data ignored for the time being. It is also crucial that the data are correctly contextualized and that any correlations are recognized. In addition, one should be aware of the cases in which real-time analyses are necessary (e.g., for live coaching) and where a downstream analysis is sufficient. Finally, awareness should also be raised about where it makes sense to understand and interpret data over the course of time (e.g., season or over an entire career).

Big data in sports organizations is not the ultimate objective. More data are collected for specific reasons. This flood of data has opportunities and also entails risks if used without due consideration. Not only is the amount of data crucial, but also the methodical and strategic ability to handle these data. Sports organizations that remain adaptive, set clear priorities, and develop their own data

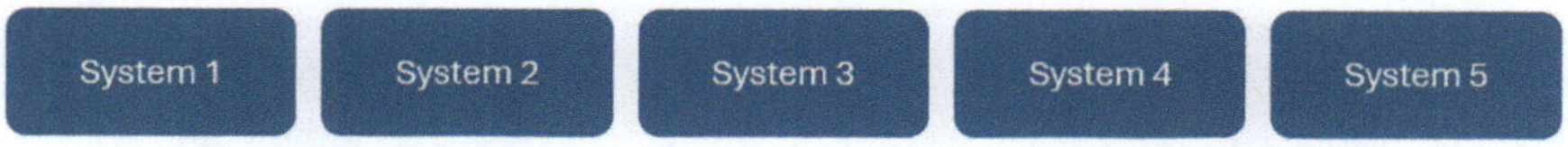

Fig. 3.13 There can be several systems that have to be updated regularly and at the same time they must be synchronized to avoid errors. Figure created by the authors

skills systematically can generate real, organization-specific added value from the wealth of data.

3.3.4 Data Synchronization

There are typically multiple data sources such as heterogeneous data, which must be kept up to date for certain periods of time. Update rates can be based on different time granularities ranging from days, hours, minutes, seconds to even milliseconds. Having the same information contained in each of the data sources involved is a challenging task; however, it can be very important if the data must be accessed in real time to make the necessary prediction or a quick decision. For sports events, this can happen during the running event in which several data sources have to be analyzed in real time to come up with the right selection of player substitutions in a soccer match, for example. When data are refreshed, there should be consistency in all data sources, systems, and devices involved (Davis et al., 2024). This reflects a high level of data integrity. A challenging problem is also the time shift with which different broadcasting stations in the world must live. In cases in which data are not synchronized, the time shift, for example, a different time zone, can create an additional burden for the synchronization process.

However, there is a certain delay between the updates of different systems (see Fig. 3.13). This means that if one data source is updated, it will take some time until the updates are also available in all other relevant systems and data sources. This is called data synchronization latency. For real-time analyses this can be a problem because algorithms that work on real-time data need the current version of the data and not the data a few milliseconds before. If synchronization does not work properly or is fast enough, such algorithms can take the wrong values and might produce inaccurate or even erroneous results (Biermann et al., 2023). This can again have a negative impact on decision-making when this must occur quickly, for example, during a sporting event.

3.3.5 Lack of Standards

Lack of standards makes data integration difficult. There is a lack of uniform standards for data exchange in sport. This makes interoperability between different systems and integration of data from different sources more challenging. The establishment of open standards could facilitate data integration. Standardization

Fig. 3.14 Input data must be standardized to avoid inconsistency, inaccuracy, and inefficiency. Figure created by the authors

is very important when data scientists need to deal with data. It can support the way data are stored, parsed, and processed. If there is no standard, there is also no common data language that describes how data are stored and, finally, analyzed for patterns and anomalies. Consequently, if data standards are supported, there is a higher probability of data consistency, accuracy, and efficiency in the way data are read and interpreted (Cong et al., 2007). This can again drastically reduce the computation time and costs due to the lower chance of getting errors and misinterpretations.

A standard in the field of sports management should be established when it comes to storing data from various data sources, i.e., heterogeneous data (see Sect. 3.3.1). For example, match events that happen over time and additional player data must follow a certain rule to make it consistent and analyzable (Burch & Dannehl, 2025). This requires a mechanism that converts each incoming data segment into the corresponding supported and understandable uniform data format (see Fig. 3.14). Machine learning algorithms are typically based on a standardized data format, for example, a normalization of data values to define feature ranges to allow smooth and reliable running of the machine learning algorithms. Data during a sports event can be measured on different scales or even different measurement units are used, such as kilometers and miles, which must be transformed first before using them in an algorithm. An efficient way to standardize the data is based on the so-called Z-score normalization (Fei et al., 2021) that transforms the data to have a mean of 0 and a standard deviation of 1 which means that all data points are based on the same scale.

3.4 Data Analytics Skills

The strategic use of data is increasingly becoming a key success factor in professional sports organizations. However, many sports organizations are confronted with major challenges that go beyond the purely technical dimension of data management. These challenges are related to human components and organizational structures. They require cultural change and current technological knowledge.

Section 3.4.1 addresses the widespread lack of data literacy. In many sports organizations, this factor is a key barrier to the launch of data-based work. Without a basic understanding of how to read, interpret, and use data for specific questions, sports organizations cannot use their data in a meaningful and effective way, regardless of what tools are available (Makkubhai & Veeragond, 2024). The lack of specialized data scientists in Sect. 3.4.2 is closely related to this. Sports organizations often find it difficult to attract professionals who combine data competence and technical expertise. These profiles are rare on the market and in high demand. They make the war for talent particularly intense. Even if sufficient data experts are present in a sports organization, the increasing complexity of data and analysis methods poses a challenge, as further explained in Sect. 3.4.3. A high level of analytical and contextual expertise is required to understand correlations, interpret models correctly, and prioritize relevant factors. Without this expertise, data are quickly misinterpreted. Section 3.4.4 addresses the importance of communicating and interpreting the results of data analysis. Analytical insights are only fully effective if they are clearly translated and communicated in a way appropriate for the target group. They should also lead to specific decisions. Sports organizations must therefore close the gap between pure data experts and functional teams, be it in coaching, marketing, or management. Finally, Sect. 3.4.5 is about proactively addressing cultural change. Moving toward a data-based way of working requires a different way of thinking. Habits and processes should be questioned and redesigned where necessary. This requires leadership, trust, and willingness to learn from mistakes. This change cannot be imposed but must also be shaped by the employees themselves, at all levels of the sports organization.

In general, these five sections are about one important insight: data-based transformation is not just a question of systems and applications but is first and foremost a question of culture.

3.4.1 Lack of Data Literacy

Sports organizations operate in a dynamic and complex environment. Data are becoming increasingly important in the management of this dynamism and complexity, both in sports and in business. The existence of data literacy in the sense of competent and targeted data handling in the sports organization is therefore a key success factor to exploit potential. However, many sports organizations face the challenge of having limited human and financial resources to drive this development forward.

The symptoms of lack of data literacy in a sports organization can be multiple: general uncertainty in dealing with data, a lack of understanding of how to collect, read, or use data correctly, using data without a deeper understanding of the underlying concepts or taking data out of context (see Table 3.5). Simple misinterpretations of data or ambiguities in data language can also be additional elements indicating a lack of data literacy.

Table 3.5 There are several symptoms of lack of data literacy in a sports organization

Lack of literacy	Consequence
Uncertainty	Dealing with data not well defined
Understanding	Wrong interpretation during collecting/reading/using data
Context	Error-prone results due to out-of-context interpretation

Lack of data literacy has an impact on the sports organization and its decisions. The potential remains untapped, and the risk of wrong decisions or inefficient processes increases. Data-based work turns into a superficial routine. Although figures are used, they are not really understood. The reason for this is often a lack of acceptance of data-based work or a lack of implementation skills among employees.

There are sometimes structural barriers and blind spots in sports organizations that make it difficult for data literacy to emerge. This includes a lack of targeted support at the strategic level. If it is not clear who is responsible for the promotion of data literacy development, improvements in this area will become more difficult. The lack of learning culture in dealing with data also makes the task of data-based work more difficult. Furthermore, it is not enough to simply acquire technical solutions without training employees in their use and understanding.

Managers play an important role in the development of greater data literacy. They are a critical factor. If managers themselves have little data literacy, they cannot promote or exemplify data literacy (Koloski et al., 2025). This creates a credibility problem. Managers should therefore develop a minimum level of understanding for data and its handling and send clear signals. Data literacy in a sports organization is generally not just a specialist task but also a management task (Capgemini Research Institute, 2023).

When developing data literacy in sports organizations, there are several special characteristics to consider. For example, it is difficult for sports organizations to recruit well-trained data specialists because they are in competition with better-paying industries. Therefore, the relevant expertise often must be built up internally. However, a combination of sports expertise and strong data skills is rare, although increasingly in demand (Glebova et al., 2024). Therefore, the internal development of data literacy is particularly important.

3.4.2 Lack of Specialized Data Scientists

Data play an increasingly important role in sport. Meanwhile, sports organizations are often confronted with a lack of data literacy internally (see Sect. 3.4.1). Therefore, they sometimes need to rely on specialized data scientists. These can act as bridge builders between the data and specialist worlds. They have the relevant skills to support targeted solutions in sport, be it at a sporting or economic level: the ability to classify data in the right context, perform well-founded analyses, communicate with the right target group (e.g., coaching staff versus management), and visualize complex relationships.

Fig. 3.15 Different perspectives are required to meet high professional requirements including analytical, sporting, and economic ones. Figure created by the authors

Proven data experts with a sporting background are rare. They must meet high professional requirements, that is, a combination of analytical, sporting, and economic perspectives (see Fig. 3.15). It is not easy to find such profiles on the job market. Added to this are the limited human and financial resources with which many sports organizations are confronted. In addition, specialization in sport and the fragmented nature of tasks make it difficult to create attractive positions that cover all relevant areas of a sports organization.

The battle for talented employees with data skills is fierce. This is also because the competition for this talent extends beyond sport. Sectors, such as the tech industry, finance, or retail, can generally offer data managers even more attractive working environments. In sport, on the other hand, specialists are often faced with below-market salaries and limited career prospects (Yellowbrick, 2023). Added to this are irregular working hours, e.g., for real-time data analysis during matches or tournaments. These conditions make it difficult to recruit and retain talent.

Lack of expertise does not remain without consequences but has concrete effects. Important analyses are not performed at all or are methodologically weak. As a result, many decisions continue to be based on pure experience and gut feeling rather than on reliable data. If there is too little expertise available, sometimes internal staff are trained. Although this is not the wrong approach, it is usually inefficient and sometimes even overburdening. An alternative to this is the increasing use of external service providers or tools. There is often the problem of limited contextual knowledge. However, this is important for the correct interpretation of the data and for the strategic development of data management.

Small- and medium-sized sports organizations are particularly affected by a lack of expertise. However, there are ways and opportunities for them to meet the challenges of data management. For example, explore collaborations with other sports organizations to share experts for data analysis (Postma, 2023). They should also place a particularly strong emphasis on the right prioritization. The aim is to focus on a small number of key issues with high impact. One can also consider temporarily integrating additional external expertise, for example, for a start-up phase, special projects, or employee training. The aim in this case is to find a good balance between progress and the burden on resources.

Sports managers can create structural conditions to ensure the effective use of data. This also includes low-threshold data access through simplified interfaces and

Fig. 3.16 Sports videos create a wealth of data that must be analyzed to find insights and patterns in the data. Video recorded by one of the authors

clear responsibilities. Suitable tools and technologies should also be easily available. Another key factor is the provision of resources in the form of budget, time, and personnel. In addition, interdisciplinary collaboration must be promoted, and data scientists must be integrated into decision-making processes rather than being only assigned a technical support role (Ward et al., 2019).

3.4.3 Complexity of Data and Analysis Methods

Data and analysis methods in sports organizations have a variety of data types (see Sect. 4.4.2) and not just due to the different fields of application (e.g., economic data vs. sports-related data). Data specialists in sports organizations work with structured data such as tables, scores, and KPIs, as well as unstructured data such as videos (see Fig. 3.16 for an example of some frames of a video data sequence from a handball match), audio, and text, and real-time data such as live tracking, sensor technology, and spectator flows. The challenge is to integrate these different types of data into meaningful analysis processes.

Data management in sports organizations is complex and requires a high level of expertise (Postma, 2023). The requirement is to measure exactly what you want to measure (Davis et al., 2024). It is essential to avoid using spurious correlations instead of real ones as a basis for decision-making. Complex methods therefore require a high level of data competence at the individual and organizational levels. Without sufficient expertise, it is not possible to use complex analysis methods in a well-founded manner.

There are various barriers to understanding and interpretation risks that must be considered. These vary depending on the sports organization and are particularly dependent on expertise and resources. Ultimately, the correct interpretation of the data also determines the success or failure. If data management lacks the necessary contextualization, this can quickly lead to poor strategic decisions, the adoption of inefficient measures, and a decrease in the credibility of data-based approaches.

There are various bottlenecks at both the technical and the time levels. In the absence of active management, the complexity of data and analysis methods can easily mean that the necessary tools are not available or that existing applications cannot be used effectively due to a lack of expertise. Time scarcity can also easily prove to be a real stumbling block in day-to-day operations. In the end, even good tools are useless if they are not understood or prioritized properly.

There is also a danger in mapping the overcomplexity (Davis et al., 2024). Complex models often appear to be more precise than they are. As a result, there is a risk of overinterpretation and fictitious precision. Complexity per se is not negative but is only valuable if understood. However, a lack of control over the model can lead to incorrect decisions. Therefore, it is crucial to find the right balance between depth and comprehensibility and to communicate even complex results clearly (Liu et al., 2023). The success factors here include audience-oriented storytelling and selective visualization (see Sect. 4.4.5), focusing on key messages instead of overwhelming detail. Only if the data can be communicated clearly and effectively will it have the desired effect on decision-makers.

Finally, it is also important to apply pragmatic strategies when dealing with complexity. Here, a well-thought-out step-by-step approach is the key. In addition, tasks should be clearly prioritized, even or especially when they are highly complex. It is important to have the courage to make data-based decisions and optimize them on an ongoing basis, even in the face of high complexity. Where internal expertise reaches its limits, external specialists can be called in, as completely dispensing with complex analyses is rarely an effective strategy. Rather, a conscious and reflective approach to the high level of complexity is required.

3.4.4 Communication and Interpretation of the Results

Today in sports organizations, it is still common for many specialists to be employed who do not have a vast knowledge of the data. Therefore, it is even more important that the results of the analysis are put in the right context by the data specialists. This is the only way to derive meaningful recommendations for action. Communication and interpretation of the results of data analysis are crucial for meaningful data-based decisions in sports organizations.

A central aspect of communication at the interface between specialists and the respective target group is the orientation toward the recipient of the information of the data analysis. The lack of adequacy of the target group makes it difficult to understand and derive suitable recommendations for action. Data should be prepared cleanly and according to the target group (Davis et al., 2024). This creates a basis for decisions of the department heads, who can then draw their own conclusions.

If data are not adequately prepared and communicated, there is a risk of misinterpretation. Incorrect interpretations of the analyses lead to poor strategic decisions (Watanabe & Rewliak, 2022), such as incorrect marketing measures in the economic sector or misjudgments in player transfers in the sporting sector. Trust in data-based decisions also suffers if there are recognizable errors.

Good visualizations (see Sect. 4.4.5) make it easier to understand even complex relationships (Liu et al., 2023) (see Fig. 3.17 for a visual representation of the resting heart rate over time during a sports activity). Data specialists should always consider the specific information needs of the respective target groups. There are not only differences according to the function but also according to the personal context. If elements such as storytelling and linguistic translation are used sensibly, these are important keys to making an impact on the target group. Only when the essence of

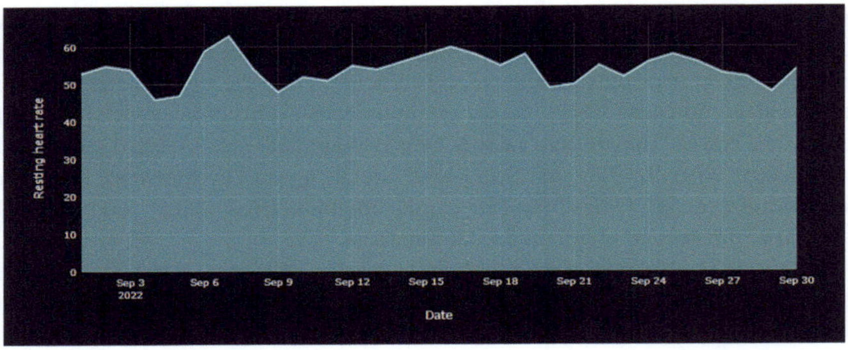

Fig. 3.17 Simple visualizations can be useful to understand dynamic patterns and correlations, for example, the resting heart rate metric over time. (Image created by the authors with permission from Zacheo et al. (2023))

the data is clearly defined and communicated is there an optimal basis for important decisions and continuous improvement (Mansurali & Mahmoud, 2024).

If possible, it makes sense to combine data expertise and specialist knowledge in the same person. However, this is the ideal case and cannot always be implemented. Therefore, there is often a need for proper coordination between data analysts and departmental experts (Davis et al., 2024). This collaboration requires clear processes, responsibilities, and interface regulations. The more know-how is combined in one person, the less communication effort is required.

Investing in good communication is worthwhile. With successful communication, the existing data potential is used optimally and effectively. There is less friction and better understanding at all levels. Data become a genuine basis for decision-making rather than randomly compiled dashboards. In general, this can strengthen the entire data-based culture within the sports organization.

Sports organizations can adopt several pragmatic approaches to improve communication. These include, for example, recording the needs of the respective target groups through small surveys. What do they need? In what form would they like to receive the results? Data specialists should be guided by real decision-making processes and information channels. Establishing a feedback cycle between data analysts and recipients with appropriate communication as a link can also be a key success factor (Trilling, 2024). Finally, initial pilot tests can also be attempted with small teams that have specific data requirements. If the experience is positive, these processes can be transferred to other specialist areas.

3.4.5 Cultural Change

Working with data is more than just working with technology. Building a truly data-driven sports organization requires a cultural shift. As data become increasingly important in sport, cultural change toward a data-driven sports organization is an important competitive factor (Szukits & Móricz, 2024). Only those who correctly use the data can identify specific levers for improvement. Therefore, many professional sports organizations are recommended to make data orientation a natural way of working. However, the path to a data-driven sports organization is challenging. Especially when many employees have little or no access to the data, they are often skeptical or simply uncertain (Wenzel & Quaquebeke, 2017). Attitudes and routines based on experience rather than analysis dominate. With this starting position, it is important to break new ground, endure uncertainty, and gradually move toward a data-driven sports organization. Cultural change requires abandoning old ways of thinking and courage to adopt new approaches.

Managers have an important role to play here. They are both trailblazers and role models. They must not only promote data-based thinking but also set a credible and authentic example (Niggl et al., 2025). However, data expertise alone is not enough; it also requires a great deal of persuasiveness and visionary thinking. It is crucial that employees see the meaning and benefits behind cultural change and recognize the work of the data as valuable for themselves (Kesari, 2025). Data often appear abstract and confusing. As a result, there is a risk of data overload and loss of orientation, especially for employees who are not yet used to working with data. The previous ways of working come under pressure. This can lead to uncertainty and excessive demands. Trust and structure are therefore needed to deal with this additional complexity and challenge. The emotional stress on employees should not be underestimated.

Some elements particularly characterize an open-data culture. These include openness to experimentation and learning, room for mistakes and interactive improvements, a dialog between technical expertise and data logic, and a culture in which critical questions can also be asked. Sports organizations can take some pragmatic steps toward change to tackle cultural change. These include, for example, the development of an organization-specific roadmap for gradual cultural change, in which employees are consciously involved. A step-by-step turnover with feedback loops and adjustments is also important. It can also be helpful to make small advances and successes visible and focus on role models and best practices. Patience, time, and authenticity are important factors that contribute significantly to the success of the change (see Fig. 3.18).

3.5 Data-Driven Culture

In this section, we examine a data-driven culture and first focus on resistance to change (Sect. 3.5.1). We also see the lack of trust in the data as an additional challenge (Sect. 3.5.2). Learning processes and targeted training are important to initialize culture change (Sect. 3.5.3). In addition, incentives are crucial to find solutions in this challenging area (Sect. 3.5.4). Leadership can be a great step toward the right direction, but it requires people who take responsibility (Sect. 3.5.5).

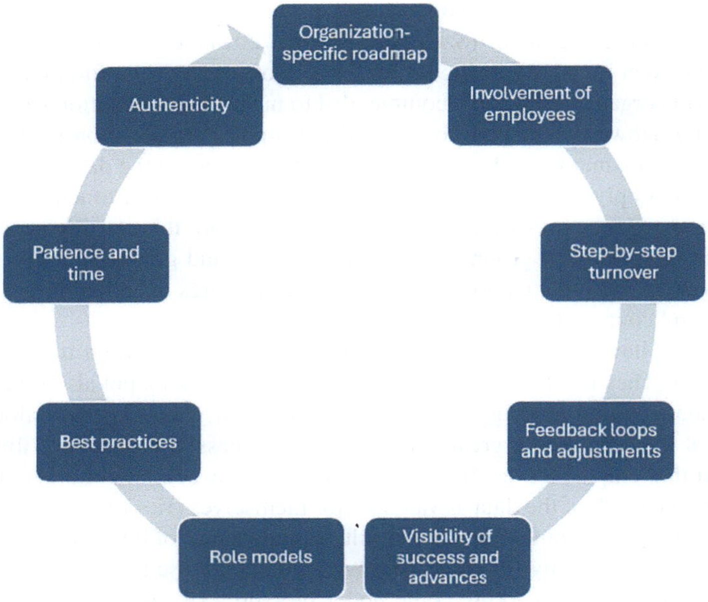

Fig. 3.18 Tackling cultural change is a challenging problem, but some pragmatic steps can be useful. Image created by the authors

Table 3.6 Various forms of resistance can lead to challenging problems in sports organizations

Resistance form	Consequence
Passive rejection	Inner withdrawal, lack of participation, increasing standstill
Active resistance	Agitation, deliberate sabotage, open protest
Subtle resistance	Destructive conversations, awkward behavior

3.5.1 Resistance to Change

If sports organizations want to develop further on the basis of data, certain resistance is expected (Qi et al., 2024). The focus is not only on technological changes but also on far-reaching cultural changes. These affect employees directly. Employees will have to question the existing ways of thinking and working and adapt to new processes. This causes uncertainty and anxiety. Therefore, it is likely that there will be resistance to the change in individual cases or even on a broad basis. This resistance can be explicit or subtle and destructive (Cieślak & Valor, 2024).

There are various forms of resistance (see Table 3.6). Passive rejection leads to inner withdrawal on the part of those involved. This is reflected in a lack of participation and an increasing standstill in the subsequent development processes. However, there is also the form of active resistance. This manifests itself in agitation, deliberate sabotage, or open protest. And finally, there is an intermediate form of subtle resistance. This manifests itself in destructive conversations in the background or in underlying behavior. All forms of resistance should be taken seriously. Open criticism can also be helpful if it is actively considered in the transformation process.

The causes of resistance are numerous. For example, a lack of clarity about new roles, fear of losing control, or excessive demands can lead to resistance coming to light. There is also often concern about being replaced by digital elements and no longer being needed as an employee in the future (Firk et al., 2024). In sports, there is also constant pressure to succeed in the short term, which increases risk sensitivity. This makes many types of change seem even more threatening. In addition, there is usually already a relatively high workload due to demanding working conditions in the sports industry with a tendency toward lower pay levels, a high level of dynamism, and high pressure to perform.

Hidden resistance poses a particular challenge. This is more difficult to recognize than to express explicit criticism. Elements such as a certain proximity to employees, trust, and an open communication culture are crucial in identifying hidden resistance approaches at an early stage. An open feedback culture should be established before the data-driven change, not just during it. There are many indications of hidden resistance: lack of feedback, signs of demotivation, high fluctuation, and delaying tactics.

If resistance is not addressed, transformation projects in the data sector can fail or be massively delayed. Negative group dynamics quickly creates a critical mass that rebels against data-driven change. In extreme cases, it may even become necessary to dismiss employees who do not support the change. However, this would be an extreme measure to allow progress and is not without risks. If the change fails, there is a risk of strategic regression, and the organization will lose contact with its data-based competitors.

The role of leadership in cultural change is very important. Active listening and professional proximity to employees can help identify resistance early (Cieślak & Valor, 2024). It is also important to offer psychological security to employees (Mutonyi et al., 2025). They should feel comfortable enough to embrace and support the changes. The change should make sense not only for the sports organization but also for everyone involved and from their point of view. In other words, there must be both a personal and an organizational benefit. In this situation, management should not only set guidelines but also invite people to help shape them.

Some phases of change are particularly critical. Abrupt changes in working methods or responsibilities often lead to high levels of resistance. In addition, setbacks in the initial phase are particularly discouraging. In contrast, early successes can reinforce positive change (Stouten et al., 2018). Therefore, it is important to understand the transformation process as an incremental change and to proceed step by step.

Proactively shaping the change toward a data-based sports organization is essential. The advantages and opportunities of data-based action and thinking should be actively demonstrated to employees. Furthermore, employees should be directly involved. They should have the opportunity to help shape the organization. In addition, managers should ensure that individual development paths are made

Table 3.7 Reasons for lack of trust can be manifold and have serious consequences for sports organizations. Own table based on (Cieślak & Valor, 2024)

Lack of trust reason	Consequences for sports organizations
No familiarity	Unclear or wrong decisions due to missing experience
Uncertainty	Missing understanding of topics
Fear	Unable to cope with digital transformation
Bad experience	Avoiding the same experiences repeatedly
Unconvincing results	Skeptical opinions about future projects
No transparency	Mistrusting the interpretation of data and the results

possible. Criticism should be taken seriously. Resistance can also be an important source of information for taking a closer look at certain situations or processes (Heiland & Schaupp, 2021). Change requires not only time, energy, and patience but also courage and decisive leadership. A worthwhile goal is not only to initiate a transformation toward a data-based sports organization but also to shape the path toward this goal productively and as a learning organization.

3.5.2 Lacking Trust in Data

Data mistrust is often particularly widespread in areas where data-based work has played little or no role to date. In many cases, there is a lack of trust not only in data quality but also in the entire data-related process. Employees in sports organizations with a strongly experience-based approach (e.g., old-school coaches) often find it difficult to switch to data-driven work. However, a goal could be to convince these stakeholders to adopt a more data-driven approach by communicating the benefits of data applications. If the applications are concrete and comprehensible, the first steps can be taken in this direction.

There are various reasons for lack of trust (see Table 3.7) (Cieślak & Valor, 2024). These include a lack of familiarity with the data or uncertainties in understanding the topic of the data. There are also fears among the employees that they will not be able to cope with the digital transformation. Individual employees may already have bad experience with data projects, or that unconvincing results in the past have led to skepticism. Lack of transparency on the origin, processing, or interpretation of data can also lead to mistrust.

This is why communication is so important. Data-based decisions must be explained and made comprehensible. Interfaces and visualizations can help facilitate access and understanding of the data (Li, 2020). If it is possible to turn employees into participants and cocreators of the data-based approach in a sports organization, this will also promote acceptance of data-driven transformation.

In addition, a clear plan that is implemented step by step helps to create trust. Small, visible successes increase motivation and strengthen credibility. If employees can be actively involved in shaping the change process, they will develop a greater sense of identification with the new way of working. This can create a positive dynamic that also attracts skeptics and increases pressure on blockers.

In some situations of data-driven transformation, sports organizations also work with external providers. These can also help build more trust between employees. It is important that good communication is also established. This not only strengthens understanding among internal employees but also acceptance of change. Nontransparent systems or black box solutions increase uncertainty. Finally, the roles of internal employees and external service providers should be clarified (Gunklach et al., 2025). Trust in one another can only grow through well-organized collaboration.

When it comes to lack of trust in the data, there are some typical misconceptions and misunderstandings. Sometimes, it is wrongly assumed that data and experience are the decisive factors for success, whether in business or sports. However, today it is not data or experience that is needed, but a skillful combination of both in coordinated interaction (Kling et al., 2025). There is also a widespread fear that data-based work will replace human factors. As a rule, this is not the case, but a supplement rather than a replacement for human factors. It is not the case that the data automatically lead to better decisions, but that context and interpretation are decisive elements.

Therefore, it is also important that the preparation and visualization of the data are easily accessible, intuitively understandable, and context sensitive. Good interfaces facilitate access, especially for employees with little affinity for data. Best practice examples of an internal or external nature can also provide important role models to follow. This can strengthen the belief in a functioning, data-trusted sports organization that makes data-based decisions with a sense of proportion.

3.5.3 Training for Cultural Change

Cultural change toward a data-based sports organization requires targeted training and learning processes (Cruickshank et al., 2015). This change must be moderated and shaped and does not just happen. Change affects both abstract ways of thinking and concrete ways of acting. Therefore, it involves both cultural and technological issues. Employees need to be taken along on the transformation journey. Change requires support and sufficient time. This is the only way to establish a new, data-oriented culture within a sports organization without devaluing existing skills across the board or losing the support of employees for transformation.

Setting up suitable training programs is challenging. Ideally, training should be individually tailored to different roles and needs. There are hardly any one-size-fits-all solutions here. Different previous experiences and attitudes require differentiated training. Management can also support the process by showing genuine interest in employees and proactively shaping their development paths. Culturally influenced training formats such as joint workshops or reflection events can also have a unifying effect among employees.

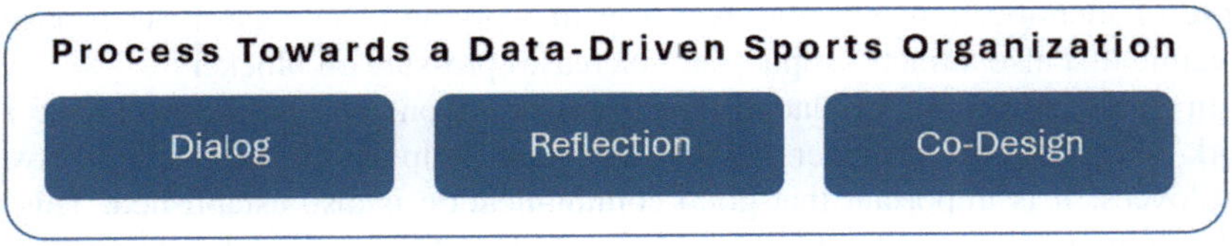

Fig. 3.19 Dialog, reflection, and codesign are required for a process that includes conscious development toward a data-driven sports organization. Figure created by the authors

There is a wide spectrum of possible training formats. These range from abstract and reflective (e.g., working on your own values) to application-oriented (e.g., tools and dashboards). A combination of internal and external formats is also possible. This depends on the needs of the individual sports organization and the available resources. Theoretically, certain standardized modules are also possible but are usually not sufficient. In-depth individual training is often necessary. However, regular guided exchange formats are particularly important for anchoring and further developing data-driven transformation.

Training programs for transformation in data-driven sports organizations focus not only on traditional knowledge transfer but also on changing organizational culture (Glebova et al., 2025). The starting point is an understanding of the existing culture. The goal, in turn, is the conscious development toward a data-driven sports organization. This process requires dialog, reflection, and participatory codesign (see Fig. 3.19).

Managers play an important role in the transformation process. They must not only facilitate change but also participate and learn. Managers should set an example of change. Their presence in training sessions strengthens their relevance and credibility. At the same time, this also gives managers a better feel for the challenges and progress of their teams. In this way, the development of the joint vision leads to a better identification of employees with the change.

An error-friendly environment is essential for cultural change (Lin et al., 2023). Psychological safety motivates employees to engage in new content and assume responsibility (Jin & Peng, 2024). If employees feel comfortable within the sports organization, it is easier to ensure the development of a learning organization with long-term adaptability.

However, training for change does not only take place in seminar rooms and formal training courses, but also the integration of continuous learning into everyday work life is also key (Beier et al., 2025). For example, forms of peer learning, learning on the job, and an informal exchange of experience can contribute to change just as much as formal training courses. Training should therefore not be seen as an isolated project but as a continuous process.

When organizing cultural change training, it is important to avoid typical mistakes and anticipate challenges. For example, over-standardization of training programs can quickly become untrustworthy and is often not sufficiently connectable. Furthermore, training should not be perceived as compulsory exercise or a

Fig. 3.20 Incentives can come in different forms and can help encourage active employee engagement, extrinsically and intrinsically. Figure created by the authors

fig leaf measure. Real transformation can only be achieved with genuine interest, a long-term perspective, and openness to feedback (Khaw et al., 2022).

3.5.4 Need for Incentives

Data-driven cultural change in sports organizations requires active participation of employees (Cruickshank et al., 2015). Incentives can help to encourage this participation, both extrinsically and intrinsically (see Fig. 3.20). This is not just about financial rewards but also about development opportunities, recognition, and codesign.

Incentives should motivate and encourage new behavior (Gneezy et al., 2020). What is important here is a coherent overall moderation of cultural change. Incentives alone are not enough. A shared understanding of the desired changes is the basis for creating incentives. Incentives are ultimately part of the way there. Part of the motivation can also come from the feeling of contributing to an evolving, future-oriented organization.

When it comes to incentives, it is important to focus on clear and transparent communication (Kim & Uysal, 2025). It must be clear who receives which incentives and why. Incentive systems should also remain understandable. Overly complex sets of rules not only overwhelm employees but also the sports organization itself, which often does not have the resources to develop sophisticated incentive systems. Incentives should also precisely reward the behavior that contributes to the desired change.

Of course, it is also possible to eliminate all incentives for change. However, a lack of incentives or even the wrong incentives also entail certain risks. For example, the transition to a data-based sports organization can be delayed or too few employees participate in the change. The absence of incentives can also lead to an insufficient focus on the objectives. If the wrong incentives are set, this encourages short-term thinking and opportunism.

In incentive systems, it is often helpful to combine individual and collective rewards (Klindžiç & Galetić, 2020). Individuals should be specifically encouraged by receiving individual feedback and bonuses. However, there should also be a place for collective incentives. Joint target agreements for entire teams or departments promote the collective pursuit of goals. The last level includes incentives for the entire sports organization. Thanks to a shared vision and a sense of achievement, cultural change is driven quickly and purposefully.

Feedback plays a particularly important role at the individual level. It enables an individual assessment of where they are at and promotes self-regulation. It also shows employees whether they are on the right track and enables them to make corrections at an early stage. Feedback increases the effectiveness of incentives and promotes their acceptance.

Incentives should support sustainable transformation and should not primarily reward short-term performance (Johnstone & Beusch, 2025). Transformational leadership can help set common goals that are attractive and achievable for everyone. However, it is crucial that incentives always contribute to the longer term development steps and value orientation of the sports organization.

3.5.5 Importance of Leadership

Cultural change requires people to take responsibility and bring others with them (Miller et al., 2025). This includes both formal managers and informal or technical leaders, such as data experts. In this context, leadership means shaping change, providing orientation, and empowering employees to find their role. Credible and adaptable leadership is needed in data-driven transformation processes (Müller et al., 2025).

The demands for leadership in cultural change in sports organizations are diverse. For example, it is necessary to formulate a clear and attractive vision and keep it alive. Employees' fears and resistance should be addressed (Abhari, 2025). Their concerns should be taken seriously. Change cannot be imposed but can be communicated through inspiration. It is also important to maintain agility and adjust the goals as necessary without losing focus. The advantage of data-driven change is that leadership can be supported by measurability. Progress becomes visible and has a motivating effect. However, at the same time, the responsibility to constantly reflect on the cultural context of data use increases.

Management is regularly confronted with resistance. Resistance is a signal. It is not primarily a disruptive factor, but a reason to take a closer look (Rehman et al., 2021). Too much resistance jeopardizes the transformation project. Reflective leadership is required here. Successful leaders have a strong instinct and recognize when course corrections are necessary. Furthermore, the leadership must be credible (Williams et al., 2023). Announcements alone are not enough. It is also necessary to act on them. The keyword is walk the talk. Only those who are open to change themselves can take others with them. Authenticity increases acceptance and identification.

Ideally, managers and coaches themselves should have very strong data skills (Olaniyan et al., 2023). However, this is not essential. What is key is understanding the importance of data-based processes. Managers can certainly rely on specialists but must recognize strategic relevance. Ultimately, the change is more successful if it is widely supported and not exclusively controlled from the top down. A vision that convinces the employees creates identification and intrinsic motivation. The goal of this is a dynamic sports organization with a common direction, not just management control.

References

Abhari, K. (2025). Employee participation in digital transformation: From digitalization sentiment to transformation predisposition. *Information & Management, 62*(8), 104212.

Alavi, M., & Leidner, D. E. (2001). Knowledge management and knowledge management systems: Conceptual foundations and research issues. *MIS Quarterly, 25*(1), 107–136.

Anzer, G., Arnsmeyer, K., Bauer, P., Bekkers, J., Brefeld, U., Davis, J., Evans, N., Kempe, M., Robertson, S. J., Smith, J. W., & Haaren, J. V. (2025). A standardized format for match-data in football (soccer). arXiv preprint. Version 1.0.0, July 8, 2025.

Asswad, J., & Marx Gómez, J. (2021). Data ownership: A survey. *Information, 12*(11), 465.

Balafoutas, L., Chowdhury, S. M., & Plessner, H. (2019). Applications of sports data to study decision making. *Journal of Economic Psychology, 75*(Part B), 102153.

Beier, M. E., Saxena, M., Kraiger, K., Costanza, D. P., Rudolph, C. W., Cadiz, D. M., Petery, G. A., & Fisher, G. G. (2025). Workplace learning and the future of work. *Industrial and Organizational Psychology, 18*(1), 84–109.

Biermann, H., Komitova, R., Raabe, D., Müller-Budack, E., Ewerth, R., & Memmert, D. (2023). Synchronization of passes in event and spatiotemporal soccer data. *Scientific Reports, 13*, 19658.

Bowles, H., & McGee, D. (2023). Data ownership, athlete rights and the global sports gambling industry. In D. McGee & C. Bunn (Eds.), *Gambling and sports in a global age*, volume 18 of Research in the sociology of sport (pp. 41–56). Emerald Publishing Limited.

Brunnschneider, M., & Hahn, M. (2022). Scouting. In D. Memmert (ed.), *Spielanalyse im Sportspiel* (pp. 183–192). Springer Spektrum.

Burch, M., & Dannehl, S. (2025). Analyzing player types in football. In *Proceedings of the International Convention on Information and Communication Technology, Electronics and Microelectronics, MIPRO*.

Capgemini Research Institute. (2023). Datengetriebene Organisationen: Mit Daten den Veränderungserfolg beflügeln.

Chen, A. Q., & Goh, W. (2015). Two factor authentication made easy. In P. Cimiano, F. Frasincar, G. Houben & D. Schwabe, (Eds.), *Proceedings of the 15th International Conference on Engineering the Web in the Big Data Era - 15th International Conference, ICWE*, volume 9114 of Lecture notes in computer science (pp. 449–458). Springer.

Chidambaram, S., Maheswaran, Y., Patel, K., Sounderajah, V., Hashimoto, D. A., Seastedt, K. P., McGregor, A. H., Markar, S. R., & Darzi, A. (2022). Using artificial intelligence-enhanced sensing and wearable technology in sports medicine and performance optimisation. *Sensors, 22*(18), 6920.

Cieślak, V., & Valor, C. (2024). Moving beyond conventional resistance and resistors: An integrative review of employee resistance to digital transformation. *Cogent Business & Management, 12*(1), 2442550.

Clegg, T. L., Cleveland, K., Weight, E., Greene, D., & Elmqvist, N. (2022). Data everyday as community-driven science: Athletes' critical data literacy practices in collegiate sports contexts. *Journal of Research in Science Teaching, 59*(10), 1662–1687.

Cong, G., Fan, W., Geerts, F., Jia, X., & Ma, S. (2007). Improving data quality: Consistency and accuracy. *Proceedings of the VLDB Endowment, 1*(1), 315–326.

Coventry, T., Timler, A., Mosler, A. B., Russell, K., Travers, M., Mitchell, L., & Murphy, M. C. (2023). "I lied a little bit." A qualitative study exploring the perspectives of elite Australian athletes on self-reported data. *Physical Therapy in Sport, 60*, 91–97.

Cruickshank, A., Collins, D. J., & Minten, S. (2015). Driving and sustaining culture change in professional sport performance teams: A grounded theory. *Psychology of Sport and Exercise, 20*, 40–50.

Daraio, C., Leo, S. D., & Scannapieco, M. (2022). Accounting for quality in data integration systems: A completeness-aware integration approach. *Scientometrics, 127*(3), 1465–1490.

Davis, J., Bransen, L., Devos, L., Jaspers, A., Meert, W., Robberechts, P., Van Haaren, J., & Van Roy, M. (2024). Methodology and evaluation in sports analytics: Challenges, approaches, and lessons learned. *Machine Learning, 113*, 6977–7010.

de Waal, A., Weaver, M., Day, T., & van der Heijden, B. (2019). Silo-busting: Overcoming the greatest threat to organizational performance. *Sustainability, 11*(23), 6860.

Dello Iacono, A., Datson, N., Clubb, J., Lacome, M., Sullivan, A., & Shushan, T. (2025). Data analytics practices and reporting strategies in senior football: Insights into athlete health and performance from over 200 practitioners worldwide. *Science and Medicine in Football*, 1–16.

Doan, A., Halevy, A., & Ives, Z. (2012). *Principles of data integration.* Morgan Kaufmann Publishers.

Draper, C. E. (2009). Role of qualitative research in exercise science and sports medicine. *South African Journal of Sports Medicine*, 21(1), 27–28.

Edmondson, A. C. (1999). Psychological safety and learning behavior in work teams. *Administrative Science Quarterly, 44*(2), 350–383.

Fei, N., Gao, Y., Lu, Z., & Xiang, T. (2021). Z-score normalization, hubness, and few-shot learning. In *Proceedings of the IEEE/CVF International Conference on Computer Vision, ICCV* (pp. 142–151). IEEE.

Ferraz, A., Duarte-Mendes, P., Sarmento, H., Valente-Dos-Santos, J., & Travassos, B. (2023). Tracking devices and physical performance analysis in team sports: A comprehensive framework for research—trends and future directions. *Frontiers in Sports and Active Living, 5*, 1284086.

Firk, S., Gehrke, Y., & Wolff, M. (2024). Digital anxiety in the finance function: Consequences and mitigating factors. *Journal of Management Accounting Research, 36*(1), 95–118.

Gaede-Illig, C., Zachariae, S., Menzel, C., & Alfermann, D. (2014). Körperliche Aktivität erfassen – ein Vergleich vom IPAQ-SF und dem SenseWear Pro Armband. *German Journal of Sports Medicine/Deutsche Zeitschrift für Sportmedizin, 65*(6). Accessed August 5, 2025.

Garey, M. R., & Johnson, D. S. (1979). *Computers and Intractability: A Guide to the Theory of NP-Completeness*. W. H. Freeman.

Gelman, A., & Hennig, C. (2017). Beyond subjective and objective in statistics. *Journal of the Royal Statistical Society: Series A (Statistics in Society), 180*(4), 967–1033.

Glebova, E., Madsen, D. O., Mihal'ová, P., Géczi, G., Mittelman, A., & Jorgič, B. (2024). Artificial intelligence development and dissemination impact on the sports industry labor market. *Frontiers in Sports and Active Living, 6*, 1363892.

Glebova, E., Su, Y., Desbordes, M., & Schut, P.-O. (2025). Emerging digital technologies as a game changer in the sport industry. *Frontiers in Sports and Active Living, 7*, 1605138.

Gneezy, U., Kajackaite, A., & Meier, S. (2020). Incentive-based interventions. In M. S. Hagger, L. D. Cameron, K. Hamilton, N. Hankonen & T. Lintunen (Eds.), *The handbook of behavior change* (pp. 523–536). Cambridge University Press.

Gunklach, J., Nadj, M., Michalczyk, S., Jacob, K., Gröger, C., & Mädche, A. (2025). Beyond the unicorn? Job roles in data science. *Business & Information Systems Engineering*, 1–25.

Heiland, H., & Schaupp, S. (Eds.). (2021). *Widerstand im Arbeitsprozess: Eine arbeitssoziologische Einführung*, volume 11 of Arbeit und Organisation. Nomos.

Islam, K. T., & Nahid, M. H. (2024). Applications & implications of data-driven analytics in the football player valuation. In *SHS Web of Conferences* (Vol. 204, pp. 04006).

Jacobsen, A. (2023). Managing institutional complexity in a football organization. *Managing Sport and Leisure*, 1–20.

Jia, L., & Fan, W. (2021). Medical sports data privacy protection method based on legal risk control. *Journal of Healthcare Engineering, 2021*, 6630429.

Jin, H., & Peng, Y. (2024). The impact of team psychological safety on employee innovative performance: A study with communication behavior as a mediator variable. *PLoS ONE, 19*(10), e0306629.

Johnstone, L., & Beusch, P. (2025). Motivating sustainable behaviour in the workplace through control. *Journal of Management Control*, 1–36.

Kesari, G. (2025). *Building a data-driven culture: Four key elements*. MIT Sloan Management Review.

Khaw, K. W., Alnoor, A., Al-Abrrow, H., Tiberius, V., Ganesan, Y., & Atshan, N. A. (2022). Reactions towards organizational change: A systematic literature review. *Current Psychology, 13*, 1–24. Advance online publication.

Kim, Y., & Uysal, N. (2025). Transparent communication and employee outcomes: The mediating role of workplace sense of community in enhancing voice, loyalty, and positive work behaviors. *International Journal of Business Communication*. Advance online publication.

Klindžić, M., & Galetić, L. (2020). Combining individual and collective employee incentives to enhance organizational performance. *Društvena istraživanja/Journal for General Social Issues, 29*(1), 71–90. Empirical study on the effects of combined incentives.

Kling, N., Haugk, S., & Gebauer, H. (2025). Towards a data-driven organisation: Making data a strategic knowledge asset in SMEs. *Journal of the Knowledge Economy*, 1–19.

Koloski, D., Porter, C., Almand-Hunter, B., Gatchell, S., & Logan, V. (2025). Data literacy in industry: High time to focus on operationalization through middle managers. *Harvard Data Science Review, 7*(1).

Koutras, C. (2019). Data as a language: A novel approach to data integration. In *PhD@ VLDB*. Accessed August 6, 2025.

Li, Q. (2020). Overview of data visualization. In *Embodying data: Chinese aesthetics, interactive visualization and gaming technologies* (pp. 17–47). Springer.

Lin, M., Xie, M., & Li, Z. (2023). Organizational error tolerance and change-oriented organizational citizenship behavior: Mediating role of psychological empowerment and moderating role of public service motivation. *Psychology Research and Behavior Management, 16*, 4133–4153.

Liu, A., Mahapatra, R. P., & Mayuri, A. V. R. (2023). Hybrid design for sports data visualization using AI and big data analytics. *Complex & Intelligent Systems, 9*, 2969–2980.

Makkubhai, I. M., & Veeragond, V. B. (2024). Leveraging library information sciences to advance research and data literacy in sports sciences. *International Journal of Sports, Exercise and Physical Education, 6*(2), 114–121.

Mansurali, A., & Mahmoud, A. B. (2024). Data-driven sports and decision intelligence. In A. Mansurali, P. M. Jeyanthi, D. Hack-Polay & A. B. Mahmoud, (Eds.), *Sports analytics: Data-driven sports and decision intelligence* (pp. 1–17). Springer.

Marsick, V. J., & Watkins, K. E. (2003). Demonstrating the value of an organization's learning culture: The dimensions of the learning organization questionnaire. *Advances in Developing Human Resources, 5*(2), 132–151.

Miller, R., Waterman, C., Jackson, C., Mahesh, S., Tingle, A., Mayrhofer, A., and Toma, M. (2025). Leading by example? Culture, change, and strength-based social work. *British Journal of Social Work, 55*(6), 2755–2774. Advance online publication.

Müller, S. D., Zaggl, M., Svangaard, R., & Jakobsen, A. M. (2025). Digital transformation toward data-driven decision-making: Theorizing action strategies in response to transformation challenges. *Communications of the Association for Information Systems, 56*, 961–999.

Montull, L., Slapšinskaitė-Dackevičienė, A., Kiely, J., Hristovski, R., & Balagué, N. (2022). Integrative proposals of sports monitoring: Subjective outperforms objective monitoring. *Sports Medicine - Open, 8*(1), 41. Accessed August 5, 2025.

Mutonyi, B. R., Fredheim, R., & Slåtten, T. (2025). The role of psychological safety and psychological capital in linking leadership curiosity to employee creative performance. *Cogent Social Sciences, 11*(1), 2458060.

Neutatz, F., Chen, B., Alkhatib, Y., Ye, J., & Abedjan, Z. (2022). Data cleaning and AutoML: Would an optimizer choose to clean? *Datenbank-Spektrum, 22*(2), 121–130.

Niggl, S., Krause, V., Nedelchev, A., & Smerat, S. (2025). The impact of leadership on establishing a data-driven organization: A qualitative study. In V. Salminen (Ed.), *Human factors, business management and society*, volume 176 of AHFE open access, USA. AHFE International.

Number Analytics. (2025). Data protection in sports: A policy perspective. Retrieved August 26, 2025, from https://www.numberanalytics.com/blog/data-protection-sports-policy-perspective

Olaniyan, O., Dehe, B., Bamford, D., & Ward, S. (2023). Enhancing on-pitch learning capabilities with data analytics and technologies in elite sports. *European Sport Management Quarterly, 24(6)*, 1195–1214.

Panwar, V. (2024). AI-powered data cleansing: Innovative approaches for ensuring database integrity and accuracy. *International Journal of Computer Trends and Technology (IJCTT), 72*(4), 116–122.

Piggott, B., Müller, S., Chivers, P., Cripps, A., & Hoyne, G. (2020). Interdisciplinary sport research can better predict competition performance, identify individual differences, and quantify task representation. *Frontiers in Sports and Active Living, 2*, 14.

Postma, M. (2023). *Best practices for big data management in the sports industry* (pp. 1–8). TScIT 39, University of Twente. Accessed July 10, 2025.

Probst, L., Rauschenbach, F., Schuldt, H., Seidenschwarz, P., & Rumo, M. (2018). Integrated real-time data stream analysis and sketch-based video retrieval in team sports. In N. Abe, H. Liu, C. Pu, X. Hu, N. K. Ahmed, M. Qiao, Y. Song, D. Kossmann, B. Liu, K. Lee, J. Tang, J. He & J. S. Saltz (Eds.), *Proceedings of the IEEE International Conference on Big Data, IEEE BigData* (pp. 548–555). IEEE.

Putrama, I. M., & Martinek, P. (2024). Heterogeneous data integration: Challenges and opportunities. *Data in Brief, 56*, 110853.

Qi, Y., Sajadi, S. M., Baghaei, S., Rezaei, R., & Li, W. (2024). Digital technologies in sports: Opportunities, challenges, and strategies for safeguarding athlete wellbeing and competitive integrity in the digital era. *Technology in Society, 69*, 101012.

Rahm, E., & Do, H. H. (2000). Data cleaning: Problems and current approaches. *IEEE Data Engineering Bulletin, 23*(4), 3–13.

Rehman, N., Mahmood, A., Ibtasam, M., Murtaza, S. A., Iqbal, N., & Molnár, E. (2021). The psychology of resistance to change: The antidotal effect of organizational justice, support and leader-member exchange. *Frontiers in Psychology, 12*, 678952.

Robertson, S., Zendler, J., De Mey, K., Haycraft, J., Ash, G. I., Brockett, C., Seshadri, D., Woods, C., Kober, L., Aughey, R., & Rogowski, J. (2023). Development of a sports technology quality framework. *Journal of Sports Sciences, 41*(22), 1983–1993.

Rokita, M., Modrzejewski, M., & Rokita, P. (2025). PyBrook—a Python framework for processing and visualising real-time data. *SoftwareX, 30*, 102116.

Salas, E., Tannenbaum, S. I., Kraiger, K., & Smith-Jentsch, K. A. (2012). The science of training and development in organizations: What matters in practice. *Psychological Science in the Public Interest, 13*(2), 74–101.

Stouten, J., Rousseau, D. M., & Cremer, D. D. (2018). Successful organizational change: Integrating the management practice and scholarly literatures. *Academy of Management Annals, 12*(2), 752–788.

Suzani, S. M. (2024). Duality of meaning in sports specific terminology: Toward better competence in "playing the game". *Journal of Teaching English for Specific and Academic Purposes, 12*(3), 593–607.

Szukits, A., & Móricz, P. (2024). Towards data-driven decision making: The role of analytical culture and centralization efforts. *Review of Managerial Science, 18*(10), 2849–2887.

Tenan, M. S. (2023). Missing data in sport science: A didactic example using wearables in American Football. *Sports Medicine, 53*(6), 1109–1116.

Tenan, M. S., & Adams, W. (2024). Real-world evidence in sport. *Sports Science Exchange, 37*(252), 1–7. Accessed August 5, 2025.

Trilling, D. (2024). Communicative feedback loops in the digital society. *Weizenbaum Journal of the Digital Society, 4*(2).

Van der Byl, C. A., & Vredenburg, H. (2023). The interrelatedness of error prevention and error management. *Frontiers in Psychology, 14*, 1032472.

Vec, V., Tomazic, S., Kos, A., & Umek, A. (2024). Trends in real-time artificial intelligence methods in sports: A systematic review. *Journal of Big Data, 11*(1), 148.

Vischer & Partner (2025). Fair play mit KI: Wie Sportorganisationen Athletendaten nutzen dürfen. Retrieved August 25, 2025, from https://www.vischer.com/know-how/blog/teil-11-fair-play-mit-ki-wie-sportorganisationen-athletendaten-nutzen-duerfen/

Wang, X., Zhang, L., & Chen, Y. (2024). Diversifying configurational paths for athlete data protection: A systematic analysis. *Scientific Reports, 14*, 83792.

Ward, P., Windt, J., & Kempton, T. (2019). Business intelligence: How sport scientists can support organization decision making in professional sport. *International Journal of Sports Physiology and Performance, 14*(4), 544–546.

Watanabe, N. M., & Rewliak, J. (2022). Where analytics gets it wrong. *Journal of Applied Sport Management, 14*(4), 2.

Wenzel, R., & Quaquebeke, N. V. (2017). The double-edged sword of big data in organizational and management research: A review of opportunities and risks. *Organizational Research Methods, 21*(3), 548–591.

Williams, R. I. J., Raffo, D. M., Clark, W. R., & Clark, L. A. (2023). A systematic review of leader credibility: Its murky framework needs clarity. *Management Review Quarterly, 73*(4), 1751–1794.

Yellowbrick. (2023). Sports researcher salary: A comprehensive analysis. Retrieved August 25, 2025, from https://www.yellowbrick.co/blog/sports/sports-researcher-salary-a-comprehensive-analysis

Yue, B., Li, C., Hu, H., Shao, R., & Zhang, X. (2025). Harnessing big data in sports content: Current applications and future directions. In *Proceedings of the 3rd International Conference on Big Data Economy and Digital Management (BDEDM 2025)* (pp. 20–28).

Zacheo, G., Buzimkic, A., Roi, A. L., van Schie, A., Staudt, Y., & Burch, M. (2023). FitYou: A personalized dashboard for health data. In R. Malina, K. Zhang, W. Zeng & G. Wallner (Eds.), *Proceedings of the 16th International Symposium on Visual Information Communication and Interaction, VINCI* (pp. 4:1–4:5). ACM.

Zhai, Z., Guo, Y., Li, Y., Zhang, S., & Liu, H. (2020). The regional differences in game-play styles considering playing position in the FIBA female continental basketball competitions. *International Journal of Environmental Research and Public Health, 17*(16), 5827.

Zhao, Z., Dong, Z., & Wang, Y. (2006). Security analysis of a password-based authentication protocol proposed to IEEE 1363. *Theoretical Computer Science, 352*(1–3), 280–287.

Sports Data Management Framework

4

In professional sports, data are considered a decisive lever for sustainable success (Pradhan et al., 2025). The ability not only to collect data but also to use it systematically and strategically is increasingly becoming a competitive factor for sports organizations. As a first component of the Sports Data Management Framework, we introduce the Sports Data Strategy Framework. It offers a structured orientation and supports organizations in understanding data management not as an individual technological issue, but as an integrated management task. The purpose of the framework is to provide organizations with professional structures with a solid foundation to reflect on the relevant issues surrounding the use of data according to their sporting and economic objectives. It provides clarity on how data-related decisions can be prepared and managed so that operational measures in training, medicine, fan loyalty, or sponsorship can be effectively implemented.

The framework (see Fig. 4.1) distinguishes between three core strategic dimensions: first, the management area, which differentiates between sports and business, second, the organizational level at which data management takes effect: athlete, sports organization, or sports system, and third, the time horizon is considered, ranging from short-term event management to seasonal planning and long-term cycles, such as those relevant in the Olympic context. These three perspectives make it possible to holistically analyze and further develop the data management of a sports organization. The framework is aimed at professional clubs and sports organizations in which initial data management structures are already in place or are about to be established. The goal is to promote a strategic mindset that enables the potential of data-based management to be systematically tapped and anchored throughout the organization.

As a second component of this framework, we introduce the part of sports data analytics that is also visually depicted in Fig. 4.1. This includes several steps such as data recording, for example, by modern sensor (Kim & Kim, 2017) or camera technologies (Bengoa & Méndez-Zorrilla, 2021), which can also be integrated into sportswear (Koyama et al., 2015). The data recording stage is responsible

D. Schwizer, M. Burch, *Data Excellence in Sports*, Management for Professionals,
https://doi.org/10.1007/978-3-032-10993-4_4

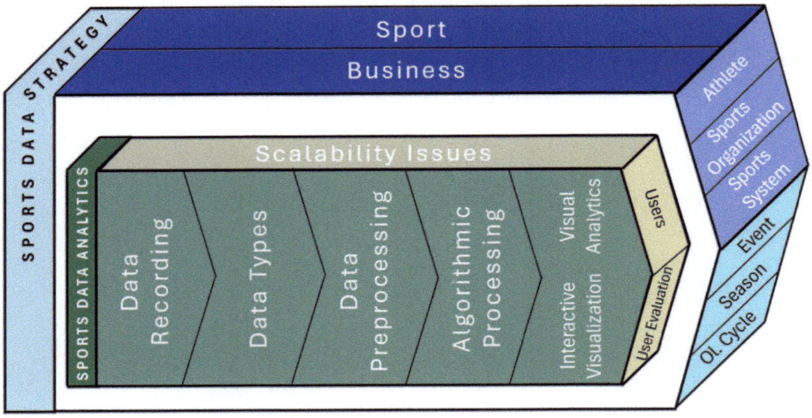

Fig. 4.1 The Sports Data Management Framework combines the strategic perspective of sports data management with the analytical perspective within a sports organization. Figure created by the authors

for generating static and dynamic data sources of various data types. Dynamic data might even be real-time data, for example, measured and recorded during a sports event. Typically, such data sources cannot be used in their raw form but must be preprocessed, cleaned, filtered, and transformed in a first stage to make them usable by data analytics and visualization systems (Keim et al., 2012). The resulting data are then algorithmically processed, further transformed, and structured into certain group and cluster patterns, but anomalies and outliers can also be discovered at this algorithmic stage (Bouman et al., 2024). In addition, more advanced algorithmic processes are imaginable such as data mining, machine learning, time series analyses, or dimensionality reduction and projection methods. Finally, the output of the processing steps is another kind of data that cannot be explored by users in a rapid manner. Hence, there should be some kind of visual representation that allows for rapid visual pattern recognition (Ware, 2004, 2008) and quick navigation in the data using advanced interaction concepts (Yi et al., 2007). Typically, these are based on the display technologies used (Belkacem et al., 2024). For example, the integrated interactions in a small-scale smart phone system are different from those integrated in a large high-resolution display (LHRD). Even immersive environments making use of virtual, augmented, or mixed reality are modern visual support systems for finding insights and knowledge in such typically large, heterogeneous, and time-varying data sources. In addition, users-in-the-loop (Rüger, 2005) with their tasks at hand play crucial roles in guiding the data exploration process, be it as a postprocess or in a more real-time data analytics setting. Users are important in nearly all application domains and in sports in which we can find several interest groups including the athletes themselves, trainers, club managers, or even the press and mass media.

The chapter is organized in a way that introduces general strategies to address these challenges (Sects. 4.1, 4.2, and 4.3). Based on these data challenges, we describe the part of sports data analytics and the most important components to find solutions (Sect. 4.4). Users-in-the-loop (Sect. 4.5) are important actors in applying the tools developed and improving them step by step. These improvements are based on user evaluation concepts that require the design and execution of user studies (Sect. 4.6). Finally, a developed tool or system for sports data analytics must be efficient and effective in solving the tasks at hand. These ideas are reflected when considering some thoughts on performance and scalability issues (Sect. 4.7).

4.1 Management Area

Sports organizations have two main management areas that function according to different mechanisms: the sporting aspects (Sect. 4.1.1) and the business aspects (Sect. 4.1.2). These two components of a sports organization are described in this section.

4.1.1 Sport

Management of the sports area of a sports organization includes all activities and processes related to training, regeneration, and medical aspects (Dijkstra et al., 2014). The aim of this area is to create optimal conditions for key employees of a sports organization, that is, athletes themselves. To monitor the performance of athletes and improve them in a targeted and continuous manner, sports organizations collect and analyze a wide range of data for various purposes (see Fig. 4.2).

Training data provide important information for load control and progress monitoring (Houtmeyers et al., 2021). They focus on aspects such as the scope and intensity of training and the type of exercise. The load monitoring (Brink et al., 2021) is based on various elements, such as monitoring the heart rate, recording lactate values, or the rate of perceived exertion (RPE). The latter is a subjective scale that measures the exertion of a person during a particular activity. This allows controlling the intensity of training and assessing individual differences. In general,

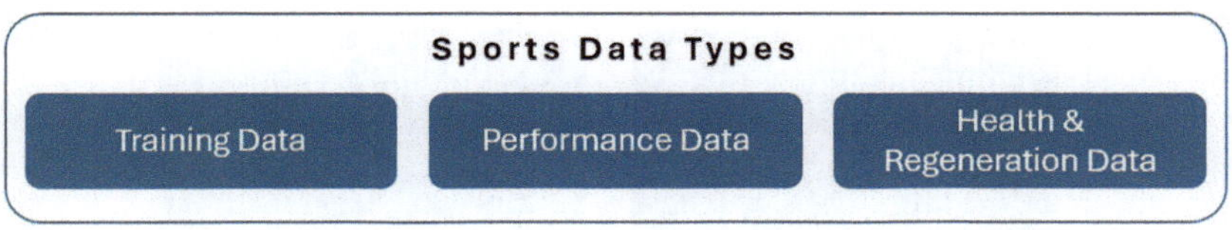

Fig. 4.2 Sports data types consist of training data, performance data, and health and regeneration data. Figure created by the authors

training data help measure progress and individualize training sessions to ensure optimal progress and maximum performance.

Performance data are collected in the competition situation and are often evaluated in real-time analyses to use the results for tactical decisions (Obi et al., 2024). Recording running times, speeds, technical execution, ball possession, and other statistics and comparable values help to analyze performance in the competition situation and optimize it for future matches.

Health data and regeneration data also play a central role in performance-oriented sports (Lee et al., 2017). In the event of injury or after high levels of stress during training and competition, these data help athletes recover to full performance as quickly as possible. These data include information on injuries, illnesses, sleep quality, nutrition, hydration, mental well-being, and individual data on completed physiological tests and rehabilitation measures. These data are particularly worthy of protection as they lie at the interface between pure athletic data and medical data (Guo et al., 2024).

Effective data management in the sports sector is essential to gain the right insights from the multitude of possible data and analyses and to make well-founded decisions for the future. The main recipients of these data are usually trainers, coaches, physiotherapists, and medical personnel. Training data and performance data provide important clues about how training, regeneration, or medical measures can be further improved to make athletes even more efficient. The data make it possible to monitor progress and make any necessary adjustments to training and regeneration.

4.1.2 Business

The business area of a sports organization includes all activities and processes that aim to provide financial stability and sustainable growth (see Fig. 4.3). The focus is not primarily on achieving maximum performance with existing resources but on pursuing a continuous path to economic success that will position the sports organization in the long term to create an even better basis for both sporting

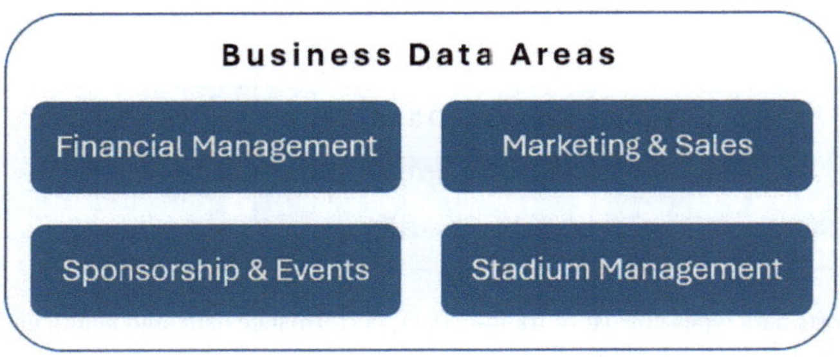

Fig. 4.3 Business data cover areas such as financial management, marketing and sales, sponsorship and events, and stadium management. Figure created by the authors

success and economic prosperity. It is about generating revenue, using existing resources sparingly and effectively, and making intelligent strategic decisions for the future. Typical key players in this area are general management, finance department, marketing and sales, as well as sponsorship and event or stadium management.

Financial management is responsible for recording, analysis, and controlling all financial matters of a sports organization (Gümüşdağ, 2024). Data are a central basis for this activity. They show income and expenditure according to specified accounting standards. This not only ensures correct accounting but also serves as a basis for strategic management decisions. The income of sports organizations is diverse in nature and ranges from ticket sales, sponsorship and merchandising income, revenue from TV rights to victory bonuses for sporting success or even transfer surpluses (Gümüşdağ, 2024). The expenses cover all the costs of a sports organization. These range from salaries for players, coaches, support staff, and management to operating costs for stadium rental, travel, and energy, as well as marketing expenses, transfers expenses, and the organization of sporting events (Lalić & Lučić, 2023). The links to the sports area of the organization are particularly evident in the salaries of employees in the sports area and the transfer expenses. In financial reporting with balance sheet, income statement, and cash flow statement, sports organizations show how healthy they are financially. This financial reporting also serves as an important basis for strategic decisions and communication with external stakeholders.

The marketing and sales department bundles activities and measures that strengthen the brand of the sports organization, attract and retain fans and market products such as merchandising items, and services such as stadium experiences. The collection and analysis of different types of data play a role here. Sports organizations collect data about their fans and customers (Yiapanas, 2025). This includes, for example, demographic data and information on purchasing behavior for tickets and merchandising articles and stadium visits, including consumption behavior. This allows products and services to be personalized and the fan experience to be improved. The data thus enable more targeted marketing communication (Zhou & Huang, 2018). The marketing and sales department also records sales figures for tickets, merchandise articles, and other offers from the sports organization. This allows trends and developments in customer preferences to be identified (Wang, 2024). Furthermore, this leads to targeted product development and a pricing strategy to optimally exploit the willingness to pay to the organization's own fans and thus customers and get them excited about the products. Finally, marketing also takes care of the digital marketing activities of a sports organization. Data on social media and website visits are essential here. Today, fans expect not only an attractive stadium experience but also an interesting digital customer journey. This generates data that allow marketing to optimize the online presence of the sports organization to reach even more fans and customers with the digital presence and to provide existing target groups with attractive content and information. Likes, comments, conversation rates, and the analysis of website visits play a central role here.

Sponsorship and event or stadium management also generate important information for economic success. Sponsorship data include information on sponsorship contracts, agreements on services and consideration, activation campaigns, and impact analyses of sponsorship partnerships (Cornwell & Kwon, 2020). These data help to optimize and strategically align your own sponsorship strategy and cooperation with partners. The value of a sponsorship partnership is also derived from data on fans, reach, and digital opportunities and is therefore directly related to the marketing part of a sports organization. The event data make it possible to improve the spectator experience in the stadium or arena (Anderski et al., 2025). Absolute attendance figures, consumer behavior in the sports venue, and the overall stadium experience play an important role here. By optimizing the customer journey within the sports venue, the objective is to retain existing fans and attract new ones (Dolan, 2023).

Effective data management in all economic areas of a sports organization is essential to make well-founded strategic decisions, improve financial performance, and align the entire sports organization for the future. It is important to examine cross-connections with the sporting area and not to view these two areas as separate entities, but to recognize and make targeted use of synergies and mutually strengthening dynamics.

4.2 Organizational Level

From an organizational level, we can look at the scope of a single athlete (Sect. 4.2.1), the entire sports organization (Sect. 4.2.2), or beyond it, to issues that touch the whole sports system (Sect. 4.2.3) (see Fig. 4.4).

4.2.1 Athlete

At this organizational level, the focus is on the detailed analysis of the performance of individual athletes, as well as their health and athletic development. Data-based decisions ensure individualization of training plans and regeneration measures

Fig. 4.4 The organizational level can be differentiated between athletes, sports organizations, and the sports system. Figure created by the authors

Fig. 4.5 There are many sources to gain data from for individual athlete support. Figure created by the authors

(Pickering & Kiely, 2019). Optimal medical care can also be provided. Data also make it possible to identify the strengths and weaknesses of individual athletes and to counteract potential risk factors with preventive measures (Saragiotto et al., 2014). In this way, overload and susceptibility to injury can be avoided or minimized. This individual data-based support for athletes is beneficial not only for the sports organization but also for individual athletes. It provides them with optimal support for their individual goals and careers. This also benefits the sports organization.

There are many data sources relevant to the individual athlete's focus (see Fig. 4.5). These include both training data and competition performance data. Personal health and recovery data are also important. Furthermore, the subjective assessment of well-being and fatigue by the athlete also plays an important role. Thus, it is a mixture of objective and subjective data (Saw et al., 2016).

Numerous applications can be observed in this area of individual athlete support. The most obvious are personalized training plans. Real-time adjustment of workload based on current athlete data is also conceivable. Furthermore, movement patterns can be analyzed and optimized, for example, to prevent injuries. In addition, sleep quality can be examined, and its impact on performance can be determined. The task of the coaching and support team is to work with the athlete to identify the potential for improvement that will lead to optimal performance in the medium and long term.

At the individual athlete level, it is essential that individual data and analyses are combined and integrated (Jianjun et al., 2025). Data silos should be avoided. Protecting personal and sensitive health data is also challenging. However, overcoming these challenges offers the opportunity for precise and effective training and load control, as well as a reduction in the risk of injury.

Particularly important at the individual level are the implementation of systems for the central collection and integration of all relevant athlete data, ensuring the participation of athletes in the data management process, guidelines for handling sensitive data, and visualizations to make complex data easily accessible and understandable for athletes and coaches (Thornton et al., 2019).

4.2.2 Sports Organization

The level of the sports organization in data management involves comprehensive analysis of data from various areas. This can be both sports-related and business-related. The focus is on identifying trends and patterns at the organizational level to better allocate existing resources and lay the foundation for sound strategic decisions (Toma & Campobasso, 2023). This can improve the efficiency of processes and communication between different departments within the sports organization. The main goal of this level is to maximize the overall success of the sports organization through data-driven decisions, in both the purely sporting and business areas, as well as the interface between them (see Fig. 4.6).

The relevant data sources in this area are correspondingly diverse. They include aggregated training and performance data from all athletes or teams. At the economic level, the financial, marketing, fan, sponsorship, and event data mentioned above should be considered holistically and in combination. Data from administrative processes such as human resources and logistics are also included. These enable improvements to organizational and operational processes within the sports organization.

The application examples at this level are also diverse. For example, analyses are conceivable that reveal correlations between the training load at the team level and the frequency of injuries (Bache-Mathiesen et al., 2022). In the economic field, the effectiveness of marketing campaigns in ticket sales and fan growth can be analyzed. Furthermore, it would be possible to perform analyses of transfer expenditure and revenues to identify success factors in player transfers. In addition, especially in large sports organizations, there is the administrative organization of the utilization of training facilities and resource planning around coaching. Finally, data analysis also plays an important role in evaluating the success of sponsorship partnerships to continuously improve them and to seek contract extensions with existing partners

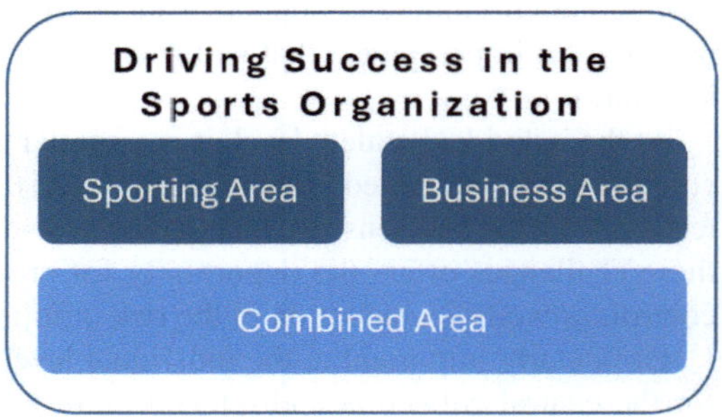

Fig. 4.6 Driving data success in sports organizations can either focus on the sporting area, the business area or on both. Figure created by the authors

or to acquire new sponsors (Walraven et al., 2016). Digitalization has created many new opportunities to provide meaningful key performance indicators (KPIs).

The data management application areas at the level of the entire sports organization are extremely diverse and complex (Bai & Bai, 2021). It is challenging to integrate data from different systems in such a way that they provide meaningful analyses that do not focus solely on one area, but rather improve the sports organization holistically. Generalists with a big picture perspective must recognize the potential of data management at this level, allowing them to make informed strategic decisions and ensure efficient resource allocation (Postma, 2023). It can be helpful to define KPIs throughout the organization for sports and business areas and track their development over time.

4.2.3 Sports System

Sometimes it can make sense in data management to look beyond one's own sports organization. Looking at other sports organizations allows for comparison and provides information about where one's own sports organization stands (see Fig. 4.7). In this context, this is called benchmarking. In addition, looking at other sports organizations in the sports system can provide information on trends and best practices. These represent an important element in the learning process. Furthermore, looking beyond one's own sports organization also reveals opportunities for cooperation, partnerships, and strategic alliances (BASPO, 2021). This is particularly interesting when several sports organizations form a common unit, for example, within a league. In this case, there are common interests that can be pursued in a deliberate manner through the targeted use of data (e.g., in the joint marketing of the league). Often, it also involves the further development of a sport on a broader level, for example, through the exchange of research results between sports organizations. Umbrella sports associations or leagues often play an important coordinating role at this level.

Public access to data is a hallmark of data management at the level of sports systems. Data from sports organizations represent an asset that is rarely shared voluntarily with the public. However, a league may occasionally collect data and statistics that are made available to all sports organizations and the public. In addition, there are industry reports and studies, often prepared by market research

Fig. 4.7 A sports system-wide comparison enables benchmarking, the identification of trends, and best practices. Figure created by the authors

institutes and made available to the public. Audience figures are also generally publicly accessible.

When looking at data beyond one's own sports organization, it is often about creating opportunities for comparison. How well does one's own sports organization perform in terms of athletics or business compared to other sports organizations? This creates the opportunity for bench learning. However, this means not only identifying particularly successful sports organizations but also analyzing the mechanisms behind their success (Ferguson, 2021). Furthermore, this allows for even better strategic decisions and increases the likelihood of success for one's own sports organization.

A particular challenge at this level is to access high-quality and truly comparable data from other sports organizations. Data protection regulations often prevent the sharing of data beyond one's own sports organization. In addition, individual sports organizations work with different formats and databases. This complicates integration and analysis at the level of the sports system. However, this option should be explored. It offers the opportunity to learn from the best and identify the potential for future competitive advantages. Furthermore, it provides the opportunity to develop one's own sport, from which the individual sports organizations also benefit. Therefore, professional associations and supra-organizational institutions play a central role in the networking and coordination between sports organizations in the sports system as a whole (Dowling et al., 2018).

4.3 Time Horizon

We distinguish between three different time horizons (see Fig. 4.8). First, the focus can be placed on a single sporting event (from several minutes to a few days) (see Sect. 4.3.1). Second, we can look at an entire season (around one year) (see Sect. 4.3.2) or, third, at an Olympic cycle of 4 years, the so-called Olympiad (see Sect. 4.3.3).

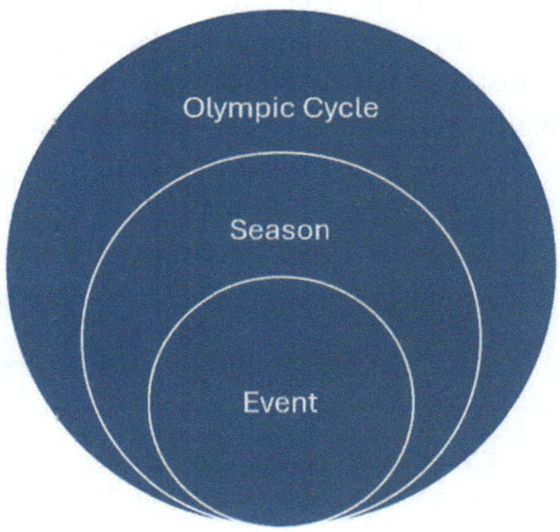

Fig. 4.8 Time horizon for analysis can focus on a single event, a whole season, or the Olympic cycle of 4 years. Figure created by the authors

Fig. 4.9 Simplified event-level data management with three core applications during sporting events. Figure created by the authors

4.3.1 Event

At this level, data management is considered in the context of a single sporting event (see Fig. 4.9). For example, this could be a single soccer game, an athletics meeting, a tennis match, or a triathlon. What these events have in common is that the time frame for the event is relatively short and the sporting intensity is high. Consequently, a lot of data are collected in a short time (Kovalchik, 2023) and are available for analysis and interpretation, either in real time or for evaluation after the event has taken place.

Consequently, different goals can be pursued in events on a single competition day. For example, performance analysis can be conducted in real time to immediately evaluate the data and make tactical adjustments during the event. The primary focus here is on the performance of the athletes and their evaluation and optimization during the competition. Coaches, support staff, and medical personnel play an important role in interpretation and decision-making in this context. By providing the right information, they can make data-based decisions and thus continuously optimize the performance of the athletes. Performance optimization can take place both at the individual athlete's level (Sect. 4.2.1) and throughout the sports organization (Sect. 4.2.2). Depending on the sport, different focus or a combination of these is required. For example, position data of players or athletes can be recorded using GPS tracking, statistics on ball possession and expected goals, passing rates, speeds, or running distances. Parameters such as heart rate and breathing rate can also be recorded, as can the technical executions of certain movements.

However, there are application areas not only in sports but also in business. For example, data can be collected that provide information about the fan experience and identify opportunities to optimally capitalize on consumers' willingness to pay, for example, when visiting a stadium. This is done by identifying needs and creating offers that generate high demand (Schmidt et al., 2024). The emotional bond between fans and the sports organization or individual athletes also plays a central role. A strong emotional bond creates good conditions for long-term fan or customer loyalty and lays the foundation for economic success (Loureiro et al., 2012). Data can also be used to optimize logistical processes in stadium utilization or access to and from the sports venue (Herold et al., 2019).

Another key area of consideration for the event is the technological tools used to ensure the integrity of the competition. These are both sporting and economic factors. In the sporting field, there are technologies, such as video assistant referee (VAR) in soccer or Hawk-Eye technology in tennis, that support the compliance and monitoring of the rules of the game. A distinction must be made between crystal clear decisions (e.g., offside and goal-line technology in soccer, in-out decisions in tennis, etc.) and decisions that leave room for interpretation by the referee (e.g., penalty decisions in soccer).

The integrity of the sporting event is also protected by data in the economic area. In particular, the monitoring of betting activities should be mentioned here (Forrest & McHale, 2019). There is a great potential for manipulation lurking here, which poses an existential threat to sports. Sports data providers monitor suspicious activities on the betting market on behalf of leagues and associations and report them to their clients. This ensures that undesirable developments are also curbed in the economic area of sporting events.

It becomes particularly interesting when sporting aspects are combined with economic elements to create a fan experience. For example, particularly interesting data-based events from a sporting event can be summarized in small video clips and prepared for fans almost in real time. Statistical data from the world of sports can also be an attractive accompanying element for fans if prepared and visualized appropriately (Perin et al., 2018).

Still, all of these fields of application described are associated with certain challenges during a sporting event. For example, there is great pressure to analyze the data and make decisions quickly and accurately. Nevertheless, the data should be reliable and accurate to draw the right and relevant conclusions even in a dynamic environment. In addition, different data streams often need to be linked in real time. However, if these challenges can be handled well, there is an opportunity to gain valuable insights that lead to increased performance and tactical optimization. At the economic level, there is an opportunity to improve fan experiences through live data and analyses and thus ensure attractive conditions for an economically viable sports organization in the long term. This can be done by responding to the needs of fans and customers and building a sustainable ecosystem around the sports organization. This ecosystem consists of strong elements such as fan culture, stadium experiences, merchandise articles, catering, and a digital fan journey, as well as many other factors.

To maximize all this potential, several important steps are required. First, it is essential to invest in reliable real-time data collection technologies. In addition, coaches and analysts must be trained for their respective application fields. It is also necessary to implement clear procedures and processes. These should ensure a rapid evaluation of the data during the event. Finally, ways must be found to prepare the data for the relevant stakeholders, and data should be communicated and visualized using meaningful stories.

In conclusion, it can be said that data management at the event level provides direct insights into current events and can therefore optimize both sporting and economic success in competition.

4.3.2 Season

This level looks at data management for the duration of an entire season, which in most sports covers around a year. The focus here is on the development, planning, and strategic alignment of medium- to long-term performance. This is in contrast to the real-time analyses in the previous event analysis (Sect. 4.3.1), which also deals with tactical issues, among other things.

One of the objectives of the seasonal review is the development of the performance of athletes over a certain period of time. The aim is to monitor and analyze the performance progress or setbacks of individual athletes and teams over the course of a season and to draw the right conclusions at the sporting level. During these longer periods of time, data management also creates new possibilities for load control and injury prevention by evaluating both training data and competition data. Data on rehabilitation and regeneration processes at the team and individual levels also contribute to minimizing injuries in the long term and optimizing athletes' performance. This should be in the interests of both the sports organization and individual athletes, at least if long-term career planning is assumed.

Another important goal lies in the area of tactical and strategic planning throughout the season. Data from previous seasons or ongoing operations are used to optimize future competitions and training sessions to meet the individual and collective needs of athletes (see Fig. 4.10).

In team sports, the optimization of the composition of the squad also plays a central role (Budak & Kara, 2021). During the course of an entire season, patterns can be identified as to which players particularly harmonize together and achieve top performances and where there are still deficits in the team structure. This makes it possible to identify potential for future player acquisitions and observe athlete development at an individual level, which goes beyond a purely tactical short-term view.

The seasonal view is also important on an economic level. The aim is to record financial performance and prepare it for stakeholders. However, data management in this area goes far beyond purely financial reporting. Rather, it is about creating a basis for controlling and steering strategic decisions at the management level. This offers the potential to critically review and improve the measures of fan loyalty or

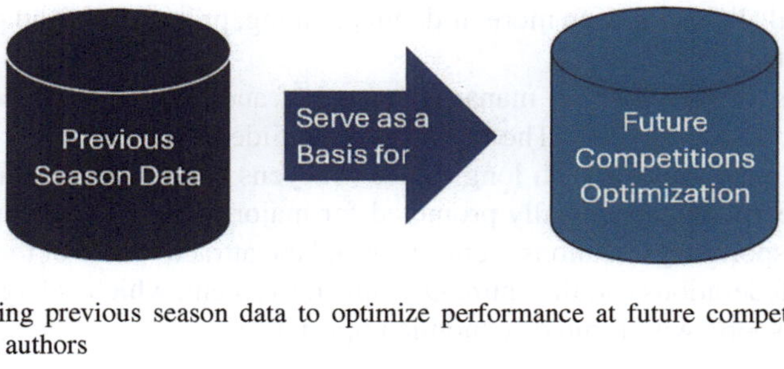

Fig. 4.10 Using previous season data to optimize performance at future competitions. Figure created by the authors

optimize the fan experience or generally to review the effectiveness of the marketing measures of a sports organization.

Concrete application possibilities arise in the sporting field, for example, when evaluating the effectiveness of different training methods over the course of the season. The development of players can also be closely monitored. Here again, there is a connection to the economic aspects, especially in sports with a player transfer system for money. Athletes also represent a kind of investment good, which becomes more valuable through the development of good performance and can potentially be sold again (Aprile et al., 2022). This adds an economic component to talent development and talent management.

Data management over the course of an entire season poses numerous challenges. During the course of a season, large amounts of data are collected over a long period of time. It is also essential to identify and correctly interpret the trends that are actually relevant in the long term within short-term fluctuations. Furthermore, data should remain consistent throughout the analysis period and ensure high data quality. If these conditions are met, there are great opportunities in terms of optimizing the use of resources at both the personnel and the financial level. In both the sporting and financial areas, the foundation is laid for making well-founded and strategically correct decisions to manage season planning in such a way that the sports organization can achieve success at both levels.

Data management at the seasonal level therefore allows a comprehensive evaluation of performance, strategies, and processes at the sporting and economic levels and at their interface (Taber et al., 2024). This enables a sports organization to continuously optimize an entire annual cycle in the form of a season through iterative processes and improvements, both within a season and beyond. The longer planning and analysis cycles will be discussed in the following section.

4.3.3 Olympic Cycle

This level is particularly relevant for sports that focus on the Olympic Games or similar major events that take place only every few years. This includes, for example, the World Championships in alpine skiing or freestyle, which are held every 2 years. An Olympiad refers to the 4-year period that begins with the Olympic Games. Data management therefore covers an even longer period than the seasonal approach and allows for even more in-depth planning, preparation, and performance development.

The focus is therefore on managing sporting and economic aspects over the entire cycle of several years. The factors of talent identification and promotion are particularly important for such long cycles (Vaeyens et al., 2009). Athletes can be discovered early and specifically promoted for major events. This is important not only for the sports organizations themselves and the attractiveness of their sports but also for the federations and the entire Olympic movement, which is largely made up of marginal sports with limited economic importance.

In addition, the periodization of training and the planning of different training phases over such long periods of time are particularly important. This is the only way to ensure that optimal form is achieved at the peak of the cycle (i.e., at the time of the World Championships or Olympic Games). In addition, such long-lasting cycles also offer great potential for sound scientific research. Long-term studies on performance optimization can provide important information on the future design of such training periods and ensure the development of even greater performance potential.

There are also goals in the economic area that can be pursued with targeted data management. This allows insights to be gained into long-term financial planning throughout the cycle. Realistic budgets can be drawn and optimally allocated to create the best conditions for athletes, coaches, and medical personnel in both economic and sporting areas.

The findings of previous cycles and experiences can also be incorporated. Therefore, knowledge management and institutionalized processes for sharing existing data in individual sports organizations and beyond are of great importance. Supra-organizational institutions such as federations and sports umbrella organizations (e.g., National Olympic Committees) have an important coordinating role to play here.

Such long-term observation and data processing require a long-term perspective, as well as a great deal of patience and perseverance in data management (Bai & Bai, 2021) (see Fig. 4.11). Despite the high input of resources, results in this area only become visible in the long term. This makes it even more important to ensure continuity in personnel and data collection processes when managing data with a long-term horizon. It can also be challenging to adequately take into account changes in the sporting environment, athletes, coaches, or support staff, as well as rules (i.e., the framework conditions under which the sport takes place), and still develop a consistent database.

However, if these conditions are met, there are also many opportunities. Long-term sound planning and sustainable performance development become possible. A valuable treasure trove of data can be built from which future generations will also benefit and that lays the foundation for competitive advantages for years to come. This also makes sports organizations attractive for coaches and trainers because they find a productive and promising environment for their work (Cushion et al., 2003).

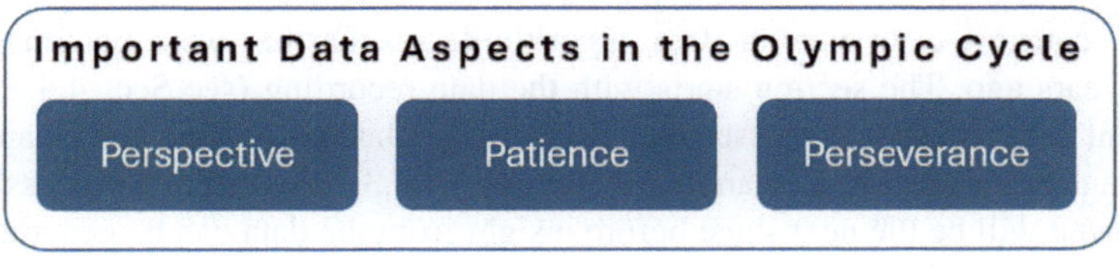

Fig. 4.11 Dealing with data in the Olympic cycle needs a clear perspective, patience, and perseverance. Figure created by the authors

Data management throughout the Olympic cycle allows a long-term strategic approach to performance (Nicholls et al., 2019) and economic development. This offers the potential for fundamental optimization and utilization of the existing potential in the sporting and economic spheres. It forms the basis for sustainable success in major sporting events, which for some fringe sports represent almost the only major stage in the multifaceted world of sport.

4.4 Sports Data Analytics

Sports data are exploited by many people in different domains, such as managers, associations, scouts, the media and broadcasting stations, but even by athletes themselves (Pascoal et al., 2019). The analytics of the data depends on the purposes that are the tasks at hand, for example, monitoring players or predicting some unforeseen events like injuries or performance problems (Zadeh et al., 2021). The results of the analyses can help to understand the behavior of the individual player, how a team performs, or what a trainer can do to improve the performance of this individual or team (Shi & Zou, 2024). However, the first stage always includes that the data are measured, recorded, and stored in nearly all areas of today's sports events, whether it be before, during, or after the events. Compared to the early days of sports events, today's data become more and more accurate and are present in steady data paces, for example, when recorded in real time, meaning every second or even millisecond a new data record has to be processed. These online data recording typically create a burden on algorithmic data processing since it requires algorithms that can quickly generate processed data, keeping pace with incoming data chunks, allowing users to quickly find answers to their problems at hand.

Figure 4.1 contains the part of sports analytics that includes the most important stages when working with sports data. Eble describes a three-stage model to record, process, and use sports data (Eble, 2016), but we extend this idea by including important data analysis concepts such as data cleaning, algorithmic processing, and structure, all of which lead to the input of interactive visualizations (Yi et al., 2007) or visual analytics tools (Keim et al., 2012). Those tools become increasingly overloaded with functionality and features, while additional technologies extend the earlier versions of the tools, including display technologies, as well as augmented, virtual, or mixed reality useful in immersive analytics. Artificial intelligence and machine and deep learning techniques are powerful concepts to quickly structure, cluster, categorize, or predict data, algorithmic results that were not imaginable many years ago. The section starts with the data recording (see Sect. 4.4.1). Then different data types are discussed (see Sect. 4.4.2). Data processing and cleaning are a prestage before data can be analyzed (see Sect. 4.4.3). Algorithmic processing and structuring will be the next stage before insight from the data can be generated (see Sect. 4.4.4). The algorithmic results can be monitored and observed using interactive visualizations and visual analytics tools (see Sect. 4.4.5).

4.4.1 Data Recording

There are various options to track athletes in sports and record, measure, and store their data (Karahanoglu et al., 2021). Not only are athletes of interest, but other people or objects related to sports or events are also observed, for example, trainers, supporters, or even weather-related aspects, such as wind directions and strengths, which are important issues in skiing (Ma et al., 2022) for example. No matter what kind of data is recorded, some kind of recording technology must be used, usually in the form of sensors, microphones, or cameras, replacing the early methods of manual observations that were typically very inaccurate and error-prone. To obtain more accurate measurements, such sensors take advantage of various outcomes from the environment and athletes, including air pressure, temperature, light, moisture, motion, sound, heart rate, oxygen saturation, and many more (Chang, 2021; Karahanoglu et al., 2021).

Tracking data might mean tracking a ball by placing a sensor inside it or monitoring soccer players on a field by placing cameras around the pitch to record several visual perspectives of the players giving detailed insights to build a dynamic scene. Typical performance metrics related to the behavior of athletes can be speed, position, heart rate (Djaoui et al., 2016), body temperature, oxygen saturation, or body poses, just to mention a few. These can also be tracked and monitored by wearable devices, mounted on athletes' bodies such as smart watches or vests, typically during physical activities such as running sports. The wearable technology is powerful enough to measure and record athletes' fitness levels while including location tracking with GPS, somewhat replacing mobile phones by even providing text messages. Moreover, the wearable and embedded character of these devices allows us to perform sports activities without being distracted by opening our pockets all the time and observing the current performance and metric values such as biomechanical, physiological, and environmental parameters.

Even more metrics are imaginable to augment the more traditional measurements, such as rest intervals, medical information, weather conditions, and many more. The number of recorded data sources and the type of data depend mainly on the task at hand that has to be solved by analyzing the recorded data which can quickly obtain large data when, for example, wearable devices record many variables, including health data (Zacheo et al., 2023). Apart from the health assessment the recorded data can even assist in recovery management, to return athletes to the performance level before they were injured. Therefore, the main goal of the tracked data is to avoid or predict injuries that are costly issues in professional sports.

In the following, we describe some data recording instruments (see Table 4.1) for different sports and discuss how and where they are installed, their purposes, benefits, and drawbacks. Moreover, we give some keywords on the kind of data they measure. We note that this list is far from complete. Our intention is to provide an overview of some sports and how they offer such instruments in certain scenarios such as before, during, and after a sports event (Bezuglov et al., 2021). The goal

Table 4.1 Data recording instruments in the three phases: before, during, and after. Some example sport scenarios are included with a perspective on used sensors, devices, and technologies

Before	During	After
☐ **Soccer** • GPS vests (Hennessy & Jeffreys, 2018) • Smart soccer shoe (Zhou et al., 2016)	☐ **Soccer** • Video assistant referee (Held et al., 2023) • Goal-line technology (Psiuk et al., 2014)	☐ **Soccer** • Monitor watch (He, 2020) • Foot massagers (Wang, 2023)
☐ **Running** • Treadmill (Singh et al., 2022) • GPS watch (Vorlícek et al., 2021)	☐ **Running** • STEPP (Promsri et al., 2024) • SmarTracks Timing (Wouda et al., 2018)	☐ **Running** • Footwear (Lacirignola et al., 2017) • Epidermal patch (Lee et al., 2024)
☐ **Tennis** • Smart racket (Jacquier & Gorce, 2024) • Portable serving machine (Ning et al., 2024)	☐ **Tennis** • Electronic line judge (Whitehurst, 2021) • Court monitoring system (Polk et al., 2020)	☐ **Tennis** • Electrical nerve stimulation (Ota et al., 2024) • Electro-muscular stimulation (Farbiz et al., 2007)
☐ **Basketball** • Cognitive training system (Madinabeitia et al., 2023) • Throwing trainer (Tharpe et al., 2021)	☐ **Basketball** • Inertial measurement unit (Nguyen et al., 2015) • Local positioning system (Alt et al., 2020)	☐ **Basketball** • Humero Tech C1 (Belotti et al., 2022) • Therabody PowerDot (Ticllacuri & Mio, 2021)
☐ **Ice Hockey** • Visuo-motor synergetics (Cui et al., 2024) • Office VR training (Lee & Kim, 2018)	☐ **Ice Hockey** • Puck tracking system (Cavallaro, 1997) • Goal sensor (Mrazek, 2008)	☐ **Ice Hockey** • Surface kinematic analysis (Ilham et al., 2024) • Wearable sensors (Khandan et al., 2023)

of the table is to emphasize how many technologies have been invented to support sports, no matter in which phase the sport is actually performed.

There are various data recording methods, which differ in the kind of sports and the phase in which they are installed. For example, in the World Cup 2022, the ball was equipped with a 6-axis motion sensor, a 3-axis magnetometer, a pressure sensor, and used ultra-wideband technology (Svensson et al., 2006). The idea behind this is that ball tracking can provide data on trajectories that help to identify hot spots during a soccer match and the way the match developed over time. A camera-based system can also be used to track the ball. Typically augmented by AI technology, several cameras close to the stadium roof are able to track the ball and individual players with their positions on the pitch over time. Also in soccer but before the match, it can be beneficial to measure the players' performance during training. This can be done efficiently using the so-called GPS vests. Such vests cannot be used in a real match scenario due to distractions during playing. However, during the training phase, the recorded data can be used to identify injuries, which means diagnosing them or even preventing them.

In the sports domain of running, for example, there are also measurement devices that record physiological and health-related data (Zacheo et al., 2023) like heart rate, oxygen level, blood pressure, etc. These values can be helpful in any of the three stages, be it in the training, competition, or rehabilitation phase. Fitness trackers or smart watches can be of great support here with already integrated simple miniature visualizations (Grioui et al., 2024). The STEPP system (Boyd, 2016) is equipped with sensors that help to monitor these values, and hence could prevent injuries, already in the training phase. The sensors are worn on each foot and attached to the athlete's waist. Several metrics are measured and recorded, like motion and acceleration being the most important ones, as well as other running variables including stride length, pronation, cadence, contact times, or impact force to mention some of a longer list. The variety of these measurements creates a data type that we refer to as multivariate data. These data are typically dynamic in the field of sports, i.e., varying over time and creating one of the most complex data types for a data analysis and visualization.

4.4.2 Data Types

The recorded data appear in a variety of data types that are typically important for the data analysis technique and for the interactive visualization, since they more or less guide which kind of algorithm should be chosen and which kind of diagram, plot, or chart is best suited to the tasks at hand. It should be noted that the type of data is independent of the format of the data, which just models how the data are stored and not what type it is. No matter what type of data it is, in most scenarios the data are transmitted to a server from which they can be accessed through API functions.

- **Quantitative data:** Arithmetic computations are the speciality of this type of data allowing numerical aggregations. Such data can be the number of points a team scored over a season or the monetary values of players. Both of them allow summing up, giving either the total score of a team or the value of a team in terms of money.
- **Ordered data:** As the name suggests, this kind of data allows some kind of ordering procedure to bring it into a well-defined structure. This kind of data occurs in nearly all types of sports due to the fact that athletes or teams must be ordered based on their performances, like a football table or a ranking after a skiing event.
- **Categorical/nominal data:** In the domain of sports we can find many names and categories, for example, for individual athletes or sports clubs. This kind of data cannot be computed with, nor can it be ordered in a meaningful way (apart from lexicographical ordering). However, the data are important since they provide additional detail views on the measurements, i.e., giving the numbers a name or a category.
- **Relational data:** Sports can be some kind of team activity, meaning athletes can be related to each other. For example, they can play in the same club, at the same positions on the pitch, or they pass the ball during a match. There are various types of relations in sports data, sometimes also attached to weights and strengths, expressing that some relations might be more important than others.
- **Hierarchical data:** In a typical league system we can find some kind of hierarchical structure. This means that there is a first league and typically also a second or a third league, while the deeper levels are split into several leagues on similar hierarchy levels. Moreover, a sports organization itself is composed of several hierarchy levels.
- **Multivariate data:** Various metrics are measured in sports that create some kind of tabular data consisting of rows (observations/cases) and columns (variables/attributes/metrics) which is called multivariate or hypervariate data. Such data might contain correlation effects between two or more variables, typically requiring advanced analysis techniques based on machine learning, dimensionality reductions, or projection methods.
- **Trajectory data:** In situations in which a behavior over space and time is of interest for an analysis, we are confronted by trajectory data. This can be important for soccer players' movements on a pitch over time to identify their playing strategies. Also the movement of a ball can be an application, as well as crowds of spectators who travel from home to a sports stadium.
- **Scalar data and vectors:** In a spatial environment it is of particular interest to examine how often and how long certain athletes stay at locations or regions. This creates scalar data that are typically visualized as some kind of heat map with hot spots.
- **3D or volumetric data:** In cases in which body movements are important, we have to deal with volumetric data. This could be interesting for VAR decisions to identify offside situations or in a medical situation in which body internal aspects are relevant like muscles with or without injuries.

- **Textual data:** Also verbal conversations like spoken words, interviews, reports in newspapers or online messages might be of interest. Textual data are also the player and team names, contracts, actually every kind of data that is word based and related to the domain of sports.

It may be noted that all data types can be combined and that all of them can be time dependent, that is, they can be dynamically changing in real time or they are passed already, but we have a (temporal) sequence of these data. Both scenarios refer to as the online or the offline data scenario.

4.4.3 Data Preprocessing and Cleaning

In many real-world scenarios the sports data that are originally recorded or manually written down are not in a form that allows data analyses. This is the case not only for sports-related applications but for any application in which data have to be explored and analyzed. Consequently, a first step before data analysis comes in the form of data preprocessing. This includes data-related techniques focusing on data cleaning (see Sect. 3.2.5) with error detection or gap filling, the linking and merging of data sources, as well as data augmentation. In addition, the data format plays a crucial role for data analysis tools since the proper reading of the data plays a key role when starting a data analysis or visualization tool. Figure 4.12 shows an example of a bivariate dataset in which one two-dimensional point might be an error or anomaly. This data point could be a candidate for data cleaning.

When cleaning data, we find several techniques that focus on removing errors or inconsistencies and identifying possible data gaps. The gaps can be found easily in most cases. However, whether or not a data element is an error is highly dependent on the application in which the data are recorded. For example, clear outliers might be errors, but there is always a small chance that such errors are actually measured values that have a realistic meaning about the data. Whether we have

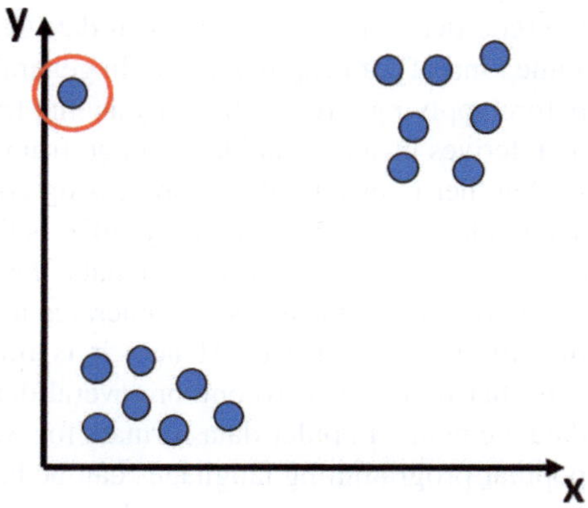

Fig. 4.12 A scatterplot showing two-dimensional data points. The point surrounded by a red circle is an anomaly, or it might be cleaned by a special algorithm or human interaction. Figure created by the authors

to deal with errors or gaps in the data, there are algorithmic approaches that can help. Interpolation, time series analysis, trend detection, or pattern recognition can be used to close a gap or change an erroneous value into a realistic one. But we have to keep in mind that whatever we do with a dataset, a modification will never show real data, and it is just a replacement with artificial data. Powerful algorithms can automatically process a dataset to remove it from gaps and errors, but human intuition, analytical reasoning, and decision-making may still be fairer solutions, but humans are slower and less accurate than computers, but typically more intelligent (Einstein, 1923).

Sports data come from various sources, for example, measured by several sensors, recorded by cameras, containing audio information, as well as manual tagging of the data, just to mention a few. These multiple perspectives on sports data can cause problems for a data analysis tool. Consequently, in the best case, the data have to be preprocessed in a way to link and merge it into a common data file or to store it in a common database to make it easier accessible by the analysis tool. In addition, in this stage, irrelevant data can be deleted to reduce the data access time and therefore the performance at runtime of the corresponding data analysis tool. Merging and linking data is sometimes not an easy stage in the data preprocessing since some kind of common key is required to allow a successful merging of the different data sources into one. In cases in which merging is difficult or impossible, the analysis tool might even work with several input data files, but proper reading and parsing of such data sources is definitely more challenging for a tool than just reading one standard file.

Moreover, data augmentation can be a powerful concept in this early stage since it allows adding more information pieces to the data to support more context-related analyses. This can be important in sports, since a given data source might be attached by events that provide further hints about why data elements are what they are. In sports, it might be possible to analyze real-time data of athletes while, at the same time, an algorithm computes special properties of the recorded data, from either static or dynamic data pieces, and annotates the original data. Apart from an algorithmic solution this can also happen manually by the human observers, but typically not in real time, rather as some kind of postprocess, after the data are recorded. All of the additional data included and annotated can be regarded as some kind of data augmentation. In general, data preprocessing describes any stages before applying a real data analysis that transforms the data into other structures or that derives meaning and knowledge from the data.

Another relevant data preprocessing concept, in addition to bringing the data in a suitable form to make it analyzable, is the transformation into a different kind of data format. This is important to make the data readable by analysis or visualization software. The field of sports generates a wealth of heterogeneous data consisting of various data formats. Hence, it is important to modify the data format in a way that it conforms to one or several data formats that allow proper parsing into data elements. Popular data formats for which parsing functionality exists in many popular programming languages can be based on comma separated values (CSVs), Newick format, or even extensible markup language (XML). In rare situations, the data format can also be a self-defined one but at the risk that a new data source has to be transformed into this data format before a data analysis tool can parse and read it properly. Note that the data type has nothing to do with the data format. The data type just describes the information chunks built on the data, and the data format describes how it is stored on the computer.

4.4.4 Algorithmic Processing and Structuring

After the data preprocessing stage, there are many more options to process the data. This time, the structure of the data can be modified, for example, to compute groups or clusters, to reduce the dimensionality, and to aggregate the data based on clusters, spatially or temporally, even spatiotemporally . Data mining could be a powerful approach to derive rules from data, for example, association or sequence rules. Neural networks could be used and models trained to classify new data elements or even predict new trends in the data. No matter what kind of algorithm is applied to a sports dataset, the goal is always the same. The data analyst is trying to find patterns, rules, correlations, trends, outliers, or anomalies in the data to answer a previously given research question. In some scenarios such answers can happen after the whole dataset is recorded, and in other scenarios the answer is required immediately, in real time. The first scenarios are typically referred to as an offline approach, while the second scenarios are called an online approach.

The goal of this stage is to transform the data into a usable form, typically one that the users-in-the-loop require for solving their tasks at hand and to confirm, reject, or refine the formerly stated hypotheses about the data. The structure of the data is typically given by relations between data elements, correlations between attributes, clusters or groups of connected and associated data elements, orders of data elements in any dimension, regression functions that express a strict mathematical model between two or more numerical attributes, or pure statistical metrics that describe data distributions, standard deviations, variances, or just medians and arithmetic means. Modern data science is equipped with a wealth of techniques to structure data in any kind of form, usually with the goal of finding insights and knowledge about the data. However, a great challenge with all of these concepts comes from the high runtime performances that some algorithms can have (see Sect. 4.7). In many situations, no optimal solution can be computed, but rather some kind of local minimum/maximum given by a heuristic approach, in particular when NP-hard problems have to be tackled that have a high degree of intractability (Garey & Johnson, 1979).

Sports data can have many forms, usually dynamic, which contain heterogeneous data varying in time, for example, videos, GPS, as well as additional metric values recorded by a multitude of sensors. All of this requires advanced techniques to eliminate the flood of data and to derive knowledge and insights, even in some situations, in real time. For example, the analysis of video data requires advanced algorithms that include computer vision methods to identify objects of interest (OOIs) or persons of interest (POIs) that are relevant data elements in sports

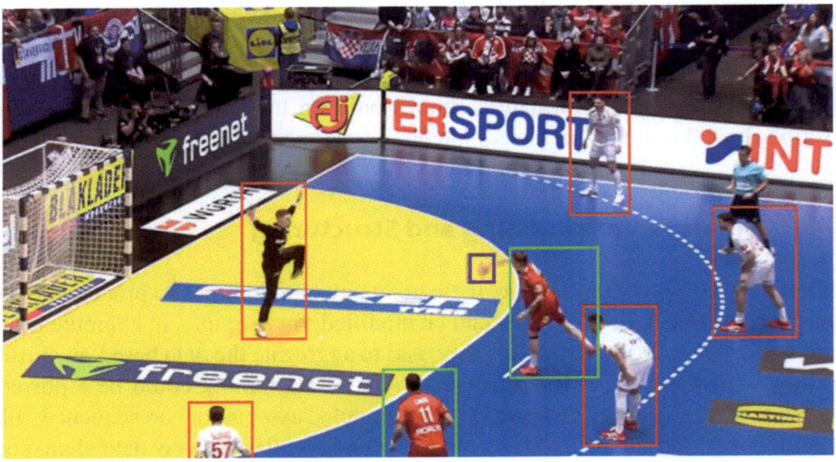

Fig. 4.13 Objects of interest (OOIs) and persons of interest (POIs) can be detected in videos and annotated by using computer vision and deep learning methods. Image created by the authors

events (see Fig. 4.13). These data elements are typically dynamically changing, for example, by varying their shapes and also suffering from occlusion effects, for example, a crowded scene in a football match during a corner kick situation where many players are located in front of a goal around the penalty area.

4.4.5 Interactive Visualization and Visual Analytics

To get the best out of the data analysis and exploration processes, it is quite efficient to provide a solution that supports visual, interactive, and algorithmic components (see Figs. 4.14 and 4.15, showing visualization and visual analytics pipelines created for sports data). Users-in-the-loop with their analytical reasoning abilities, perceptual abilities, and strengths in pattern recognition (Ware, 2004, 2008) apply such a visual analytics (Keim et al., 2012) tool to support the decision-making to solve their tasks at hand. Although this is a general approach for many data science problems, it is particularly useful for the domain of sports and sports management with large amounts of heterogeneous data and static, as well as dynamic, data. Such tools can be designed and implemented in the form of dashboards (Bach et al., 2023; Burch & Schmid, 2024) that provide several options including nonexperts' or experts' perspectives (see Sects. 4.5.2 and 4.5.3) on the data and different views for certain actors involved in sports such as athletes, trainers, managers, even newspapers, magazines, or online mass media.

Visual analytics (see Fig. 4.15 for a general pipeline focusing on sports data) can be based on at least two main concepts: pure data monitoring and a more predictive version that learns from the past to allow guessing what might probably happen in the future. Both concepts are useful for the domain of sports, as monitoring can

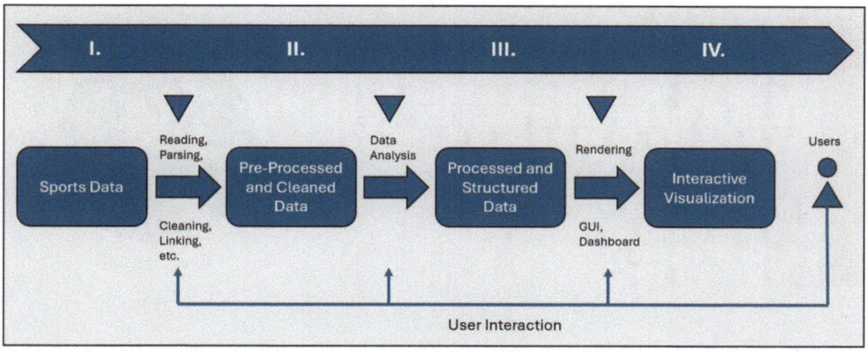

Fig. 4.14 The sports data visualization pipeline starts with raw data (I) that is read and parsed into preprocessed and cleaned data (II). A data analysis based on advanced algorithms brings the data into a processed and structured form (III). Finally, these data get visualized (IV), while users can interactively modify each of the subsequent stages in some kind of feedback loop. Figure created by the authors

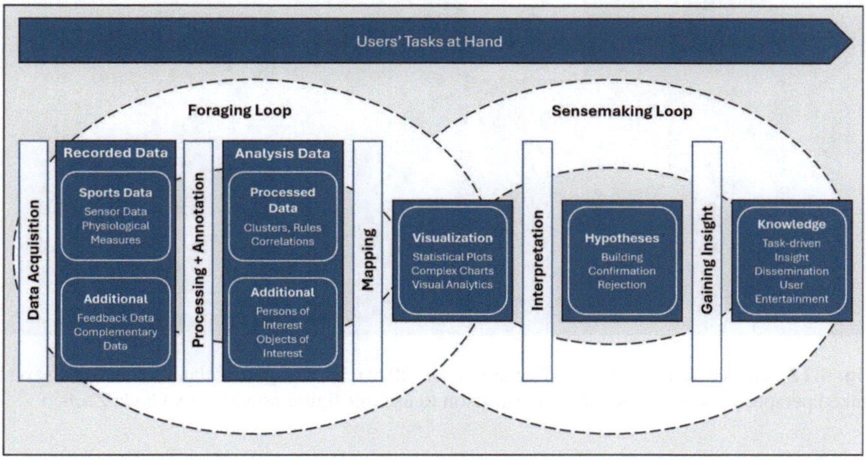

Fig. 4.15 The sports data visual analytics pipeline includes a foraging loop that ends in a visualization and a sense-making loop that supports interpretation, hypotheses building, confirmation, rejection, and knowledge generation, finally ending in decision-making integrating human users and algorithmic approaches. Figure created by the authors

help to understand, explore, and analyze current situations to compare them with past situations or those of other clubs or individual players. A predictive version of such a visual analytics tool might help people interested in sports to forecast what will happen next, for example, under certain training or match conditions. An athlete might suffer from an injury and analyzing past situations, and his/her medical parameters can give hints about further, even more serious, injuries under stress or hard training situations, for example, to adapt training or recovery plans. Moreover,

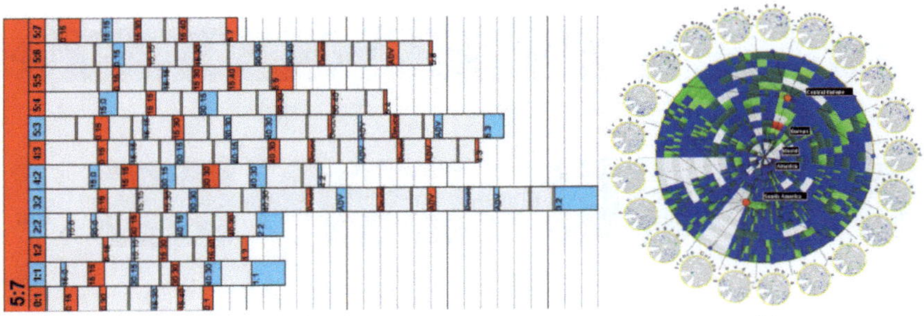

(a) (b)

Fig. 4.16 Example diagrams visualizing sports data from several perspectives: (**a**) Tennis match data shown as an icicle plot (Burch & Weiskopf, 2014). (**b**) Football match results visualized in a TimeRadarTrees technique (Burch & Diehl, 2008). Figures created by the authors

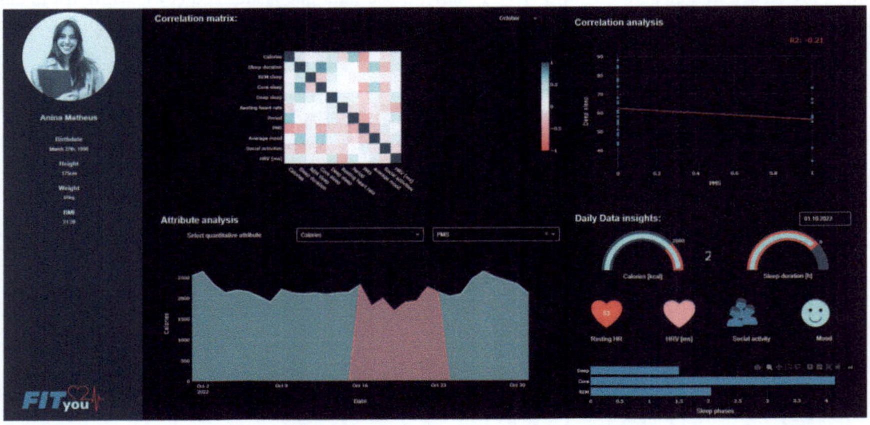

Fig. 4.17 The FitYou dashboard (Zacheo et al., 2023) shows sports-related data from several linked perspectives (Roberts, 2003). Permission to use this figure provided by Giada Zacheo

on a club level, it can be a valuable future insight to analyze financial aspects based on given facts and numbers from the past. No matter what kind of concept the tool is based on, the final decisions are still given by the end users, which is dependent on the tasks at hand.

The types of visualizations vary depending on the incorporated dataset and the users' tasks at hand. They range from simple statistical graphics including bar charts, histograms, box plots, line graphs, or even scatter plots to more advanced visualizations including stacked bar charts, icicle plots, dynamic graph visualizations, stream graphs, treemaps, and many more (see Fig. 4.16 for two prominent visualization techniques from the sports domain that are already quite complex). A visualization or visual analytics tool is typically composed of many visualization components in the so-called linked and multiple coordinated views (MCVs) (Roberts, 2003) showing the data from several perspectives (see Fig. 4.17

for an example of a tool's user interface consisting of several views on sports data). Complex charts and tools are mainly used for data analytics tasks, while simple charts are typically used to show some kind of sports statistics in a newspaper, on TV, or in a live broadcast on the world wide web. In addition, infographics (Purchase et al., 2018) and storytelling (Tong et al., 2018; Zhao & Elmqvist, 2023) are powerful concepts to illustrate certain events or outcomes of a game or even during an advertisement phase for a sports event.

Visual analytics is known to combine many visualizations—simple and complex—while using a variety of display and interaction technologies (Keim et al., 2012). This means that this inter- and multidisciplinary field is not only restricted to standard computer monitors, but it also provides solutions on small- and large-scale displays including mobile phones and large high-resolution displays (LHRDs) (Schmauder et al., 2015). Also the included technologies require a huge repertoire of interaction techniques in information visualization (Yi et al., 2007) and modalities (Lee et al., 2018), in particular if the system runs in augmented, virtual, or mixed reality (AR/VR/MR). A way to include such extended reality (XR) concepts in the domain of data analysis and interactive data visualization is known as immersive analytics (Levy et al., 2003), a relatively novel field of research that is quite useful for 3D sports scenes. Since sports data are often dynamic, visual representations of the data are accompanied by dynamic video scenes that require video analysis techniques (Höferlin, 2014; Höferlin et al., 2015) or video visualization (Höferlin et al., 2012). The dynamic aspect of sports data can be analyzed and visualized as a postprocess or in real time, making the requirements for the algorithms involved much higher.

4.5 Users and Users-in-the-Loop

The data analysis and interactive visualization techniques, tools, and systems created are only powerful when users are taken into account with their perceptual abilities to detect patterns and anomalies in data, maybe by visualization and based on analytical reasoning (Sect. 4.5.1). Such users can be nonexperts who are everyday users who like sports and are only interested in certain analytical or visual results, or they need it for entertainment purposes (Sect. 4.5.2). When building tools, we need the knowledge of real experts who are in the best case sports experts and also data analysts, data scientists, programmers and software engineers, or even visualization and visual analytics experts (Sect. 4.5.3). In general, user feedback, from nonexperts and experts, is recorded and integrated in the next iteration of the developed tool with the aim of improving the tool from time to time (Sect. 4.5.4). The integration of user feedback does not necessarily lead to improvement, but it must be evaluated over and over again. In the sports domain, there are always new technologies that need adaptations to such systems, even hardware and software technologies are further developed and require adaptations to a developed tool, and hence in the best case, benefits from the user side have to be taken into account to make the best out of it (Sect. 4.5.5).

Table 4.2 Several user types can play important roles not only for data analytics and visualization tools in the sports domain but also for advanced technologies

User type	Some roles
Sports performers	Athletes
Athlete supporters	Trainers, club managers, referees, medical staff
Event organizers	Planners, food sellers, cleaning team, security
Remote consumers	Spectators at home, TV and online stream watchers
On-site consumers	Spectators in a stadium, fans, mass media, journalists
Product users	Data analysts, sports equipment purchasers
Product developers	Software engineers, data scientists, statisticians

4.5.1 The Role of Users in Sports

By the term "user," we refer to people who consume sports either every day or a few times a year. These people watch sports events, but even more they are interested in patterns, rules, or correlations in sports, for example, who are the basketball players with the most ball contacts, which tennis player won Wimbledon most often, or which soccer team scored most goals in the last season. Users play an important role because their feedback helps improve sports as a whole. It not only benefits athletes but also supports the development of better tools, systems, and technologies. These tools again help athletes compete better with others, sometimes just as some kind of motivation.

Users can come in a variety of types (see Table 4.2). They can be professional users, for example, who know the latest technologies on the market, or they are just laymen looking from time to time and rarely using tools to explore data. No matter what type of user we take into account, they always provide feedback which is of great benefit if it is integrated to improve the tools developed. The role of users can be important at several stages during the development of a new tool or technology in sports. Either they are already involved during the design phase to guide the development process or they evaluate a tool or technology when it is ready to be published on the market. Both concepts are powerful, but including users during the design phase can reduce costs, since design flaws are detected immediately and therefore do not end up in the expensive implementation phase. However, in some scenarios, a developed tool is too complex to design with users first, in particular, when a real setting is impossible during the design phase. In such cases, users evaluate the tool or the technology with all their features and functionalities and the problematic issues when using it must be integrated in a new version or edition of the tool or technology.

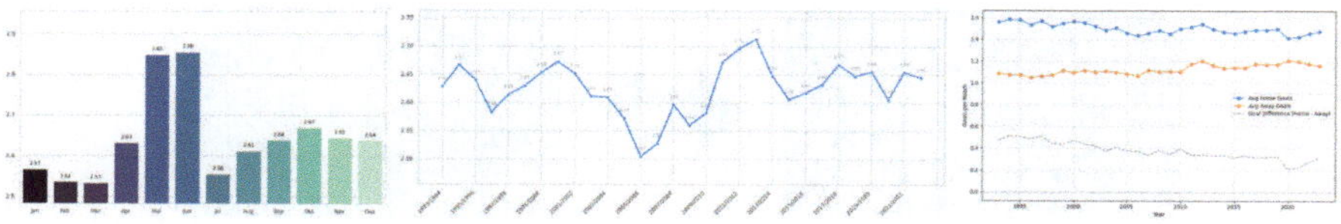

Fig. 4.18 Simple diagrams showing perspectives on statistical data in football: (**a**) Number of goals per month as a bar chart. (**b**) Number of goals per season as a line chart. (**c**) Number of home and away goals plus the difference of home minus away goals as line graphs. Permission to use the figures by Abdul Jamil Safi, Murat Arikan, and Leandro da Silva Pinto

4.5.2 Nonexperts

Nonexperts are typically people who are not very familiar with sports. They just watch sports occasionally and also do not need the right tools to analyze or visualize sports data. However, from time to time they get sports-related information, for example, statistical graphics in a newspaper or even during a sports event when a soccer scene is replayed or shown in slow motion augmented with additional graphical decorations. Those could be running paths, interplays between players, or even the trajectory of a tennis ball projected onto the scene. Even if those people are nonexperts, they might be able to understand the presented information due to the fact that these are very simple graphical enhancements, specifically made for the everyday user (see Fig. 4.18).

One might argue that nonexperts are not important, but they make up the largest part of people who consume sports, and it is a wise decision not to overwhelm them with information but to step by step lead them to more complex scenarios. Maybe one day the nonexperts will become experts. There can be a learning effect that makes nonexperts understand more and more data analysis and visualization techniques. The goal is not to lose those nonexperts right from the beginning but to carefully support them to keep them entertained. There is a huge amount of money involved in sports, and consumers pay for the services provided. There are even platforms that allow us to find many more sports-related visual analytics tools. For example, YouTube can dynamically annotate sports events with corresponding visual decorations that entertain us even more and let us understand when, where, and why during a sports event.

4.5.3 Domain Experts

In sports data analytics, there are actually at least two major types of domain experts. The first type is created by sports experts who are familiar with almost any kind of sports or are domain experts of a specific type of sports. However, they have great knowledge and expertise of the facts, events, and athletes in sports, both present and past. Those people typically know each sportsperson from each club and also

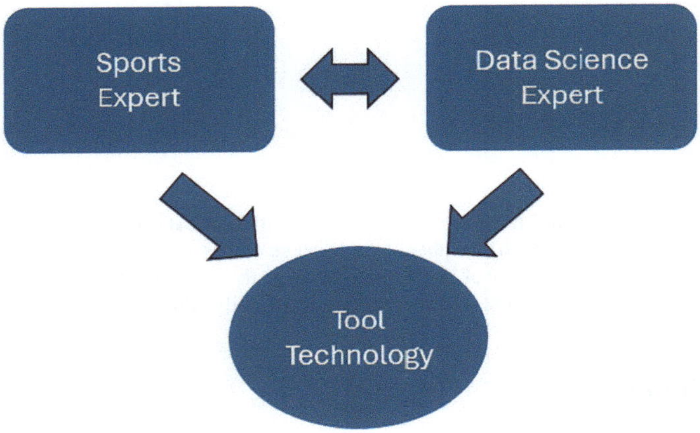

Fig. 4.19 Two types of domain experts are required to create a powerful data analytics tool of a new technology. Figure created by the authors

where and when he or she played. Furthermore, additional information about each athlete, such as injuries, trophies, special events, or even family circumstances, is of particular interest and well known by experts in this domain. The other type of domain expert is given by people who are familiar and experts in the field of data science and technology. They do not know each sports event and each athlete with additional information, but they know the latest version of a sports analytics tool or a new technology, be it a new hardware or a new software. Those experts are important, as they can help improve the available systems to explore and analyze sports data.

Including only one type of domain expert will not take full advantage of the domain knowledge available. The design and construction of a powerful tool for sports data analysis requires the knowledge of experts in both camps (see Fig. 4.19). Sports experts can provide typical sports-related knowledge, while data scientists provide the technologies that are required to build such a tool in a well-performing environment. Even if both types of experts are available, it is quite difficult to link the expertise of both into a running system with which we can analyze and visualize sports data in an interactive way. Domain-specific research questions and tasks should be provided by experts in the sports domain and even usability aspects, since they reflect a group of users of such a tool. The algorithmic, visual, interactive, and usability aspects must be designed and developed by data science experts. This process can be done side by side and synchronously by taking into account both opinions from time to time. However, including experts is a time-consuming and expensive procedure but will ultimately lead to powerful solutions from which the whole sports community can benefit.

Table 4.3 Various feedback types exist that could flow into the design and development of a sports data analytics tool or a technology

Feedback type	Recording type	Data type	References
Interview	Interview session	Textual	(Golemati et al., 2008)
Voting	Likert scale	Categorical	(Silhavy et al., 2014)
Questionnaire	Q&A	Textual	(Díaz-Oreiro et al., 2019)
Multiple choice	Check boxes	Vector	(Tilly, 2015)
Written Feedback	Social media	Textual	(Dalip et al., 2013)
Think-aloud	During experiment	Verbal, textual	(Cutler et al., 2025)
Performance test	Errors, response time	Quantities	(Burch et al., 2011)
Physiology	Sensors	Time series	(Blascheck et al., 2015)
Workload	Task load index (TLX)	Categorical	(Mancini et al., 2021)
Cognitive effort	EEG	Time series	(Kuo et al., 2009)
Eye movements	Eye tracker	Spatio-temporal	(Burch, 2022)
Mouse movements	Computer mouse	Spatio-temporal	(Weisgarber et al., 2024)
Mood, Emotion	Camera	Categorical	(Greca et al., 2024)
Facial expression	Camera	Categorical	(Ortmann et al., 2024)
Body movement	Camera	Video data	(Huang et al., 2023)

4.5.4 Integrating User Feedback

User feedback can come in a variety of forms (see Table 4.3), be it quantitative measures in a quantitative user evaluation (see Sect. 4.6), qualitative feedback in the form of spoken words, from interviews or even from feedback on social networks. A relatively novel approach in the domain of usability is eye tracking technology (Burch, 2022) that allows us to record eye movements over space and time. The generated spatiotemporal data are useful since they describe where and when a user, a nonexpert or expert, has problems in solving given tasks. Industrial projects focusing on data analysis and visualization typically have their own domain experts who evaluate their tools and provide feedback.

No matter what kind of user feedback is available, it can be taken into account to improve the tool or technology. Feedback is collected over time, and finally, it is discussed if it makes sense to integrate the feedback into a new version of the tool or technology. After the integration has been completed, the whole process starts from the beginning. Users work with the latest software or hardware and provide feedback in various forms. All of it is collected and again integrated into the current version, a process that steadily improves the tool and extends the functionality. This process is important because otherwise a tool could not keep up with the rapidly evolving sports market. However, this evolution does not come for free. The question of user feedback and the integration of such feedback is a time-consuming process, but competition on the market makes it unavoidable.

Fig. 4.20 The integration of real users can generate many benefits for data analytics tools and technologies. Figure created by the authors

4.5.5 Benefits from the Users

Software or hardware for sports data analytics can be powerful and can include various features related to algorithms, visualizations, interactions, display technologies, even including concepts like VR, AR, or MR such as immersive technologies. However, it is always questionable whether user feedback is relevant at all. In cases in which the user group is split and undecided on a certain feature, it is a bad idea to just integrate the desired feature into the tool. In this case, it might happen that the other half of the user group is no longer confident in the tool and will buy the tool from another competing company. The question from a design and development perspective is always if there is a benefit based on user feedback. This is the most difficult part of developing tools for the sports market. As an option, a tool can be developed in different styles or variants, but this creates even more costs. These costs have to be outweighed by the benefits.

The greatest benefit comes from the identified design flaws or poor functionality and features. Improvements for everyone are always welcome. If the tool runs smoothly and the functionality is useful for solving certain tasks, the chance is high that the tool will be sold many times. This again covers the implementation costs, and the benefit on the company side is making money. However, the sport side also has many benefits. Tools that run properly and are used by many users create an opportunity to explore and analyze sports and therefore improve the athletes' performances. The focus can be on all available sports-related data metrics, either for an individual athlete or even the entire team, and how it communicates and collaborates, i.e., how it performs and how it is prepared for the opponent. Such benefits can come in a postprocess that is after a sports event or it can happen in real time that is during a sports event as a way to rapidly react on some issues. To sum up, there are lots of benefits from integrating real users that end in user satisfaction, improved tool development, better user experience (UX), reduced costs, and also a larger number of products sold (see Fig. 4.20).

4.6 User Evaluation

Taking into account the user's experience and knowledge can result in additional data that can support the improvement of a tool or system. In this section, we describe the evaluation of a tool (see Fig. 4.21) or technology during the design phase (Sect. 4.6.1), the implementation phase (Sect. 4.6.2), and the testing phase (Sect. 4.6.3). General user experiments can come in various forms (Sect. 4.6.4).

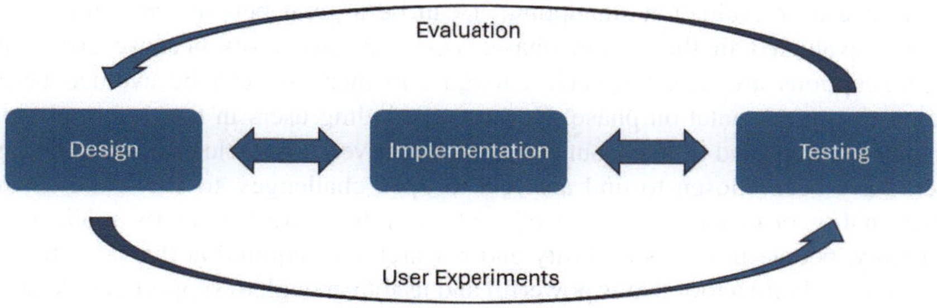

Fig. 4.21 A user evaluation must include domain experts and nonexperts in all important stages including design, implementation, and testing. Figure created by the authors

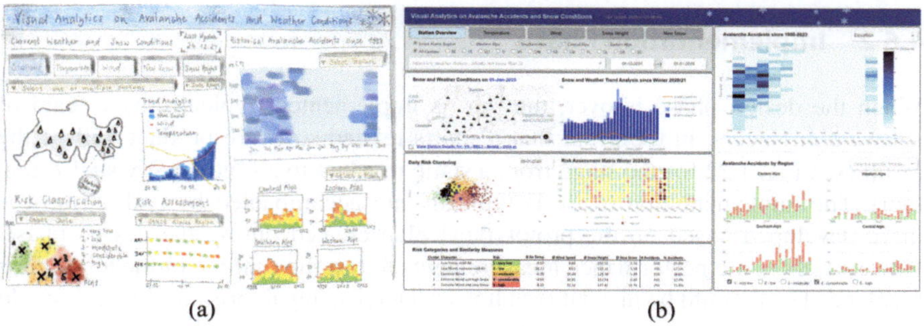

Fig. 4.22 Creating a sports data analytics tool for skiing and hiking athletes that computes spatiotemporal avalanche risk categories (Nyffeler & Burch, 2025). A static mockup (**a**) can help during the design phase to create the final version of a visual analytics tool (**b**). Permission to use these images by Tamara Nyffeler

All user experiments create different types of data that have to be analyzed, either statistically or visually (Sect. 4.6.5).

4.6.1 Design Phase

The first stage after a brainstorming with experts or nonexperts, which are people involved in the tool building process, is the design phase. In this phase, a first mockup or plan of the tool is created, maybe sketched on a piece of paper or by using some kind of prototyping tool (see Fig. 4.22). The design phase is very important because it creates some kind of starting point for the development and implementation phase. Resources are also checked, that is, how many implementers are required to build a software or a new technology. The environment in which the tool should run and the number of users at the same time are also of special importance. Many parameters must be fixed; also, features and functionality must be defined and described in enough detail to allow the implementers to understand all the required components and processes.

From a user evaluation standpoint, it can be a great benefit when the tool is already evaluated in the design phase. This can save costs because errors and misconceptions are detected early enough and therefore can be avoided before the costly implementation phase. However, including users in the design phase is already a tedious and time-consuming task. Moreover, it is unclear whether the right users have been chosen to find answers to open challenges, to check the desired functionality, or to set the features of the tool in the context of sports applications. In reality, people in sports usability and research are required at the same time to successfully build a tool that is powerful and usable enough to support people doing sports research or just people who use such tools as an additional entertainment option.

4.6.2 Implementation Phase

When the design phase is over, the tool is implemented, typically by a team of software engineers, in the event that a sports-related software product will be the result (see Fig. 4.22 for the stage from a static mockup to a functional visualization tool). The implementation phase is typically not accompanied by real users; it is more developed based on the prototypical plan created during the design phase. However, there are performance measurements to test the runtime of the algorithms involved. Those could be just data reading or data parsing algorithms, but they could also be more data processing and data structuring algorithms. For example, high-dimensional data might be projected to a lower dimension using dimensionality reduction techniques such as principal component analysis (PCA) or stochastic neighbor embedding distributed by t (t-SNE). Time series data might be analyzed for trends and countertrends. Unstructured data might be clustered to identify group patterns and related objects or persons in a dataset. All of these algorithms have a runtime, and if not implemented properly, there is a chance that they will not perform well, leading to a performance degradation. Poor performance can slow down a tool, and interaction techniques will suffer from that, leading to poor interactive responsiveness and poor usability.

Performance can be measured as a function of two variables, an input variable and an output variable. The input variable can be the size of the dataset, and the output variable the time it takes to read, parse, or algorithmically process the dataset of the given size. The dependency of the size of the dataset on the output variable generates a characteristic mathematical function that can be linear, polynomial, or even exponential, just to mention a few (see Fig. 4.23 for example runtime functions visualized as line plots). By inspecting this function, we can say for which dataset size the tool is still useful and scalable. Moreover, we might identify an algorithmic issue that can be reimplemented to get better performance at runtime. The evaluation during the implementation phase consequently typically takes into account runtime issues and tries to eliminate slow algorithms, in case there exist some. In some scenarios, there is no well-performing algorithm, for example, when the algorithmic problems are NP-hard (Garey & Johnson, 1979) and heuristics must be applied to

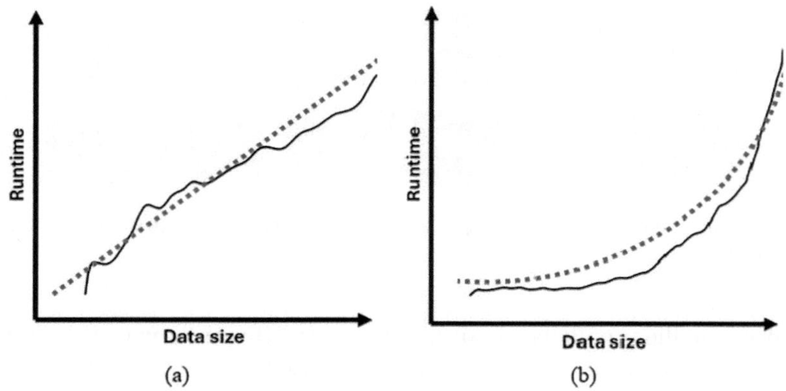

Fig. 4.23 A comparison of two different types of algorithmic runtimes for growing dataset sizes. (**a**) Linear runtime complexity. (**b**) Exponential runtime complexity. Figure created by the authors

compute good but not optimal solutions to a given algorithmic problem. Lack of experience in data science can lead to real big issues; hence a domain expert is definitely required to build such complex sports data-related tools.

4.6.3 Testing Phase

After the implementation phase is complete, a developed sports analytics tool must be tested. It will be provided to real users, experts, and nonexperts who work with the tool. They test the functionality, features, algorithms, interactions, and many more aspects related to the sports data analytics tool (see Fig. 4.24). They typically have one or more tasks-in-mind that they are going to solve by applying the tool. Users also try to crash the tool by confronting it with some kind of stress test in which huge datasets are loaded, different environments are used, and a variety of display technologies are checked. For example, a tool might run on a small-scale display on a smart phone, a medium-scale display on a laptop computer, or even on a large-scale display like a large high-resolution display (LHRD). It may be noted that a sports analytics tool typically does not run in all scenarios, and it is developed for one or more specific scenarios.

Each tool and technology are different and require another kind of test setting. For example, a sports data analytics tool that is provided as a wearable technology typically makes use of small-scale miniature visualizations that are integrable in small-scale displays provided by a watch. If sports data have to be analyzed as a postprocess, after a sports event, maybe with many people at the same time, the tool can be offered on a large-scale display like a power wall. Even immersive technologies are imaginable using augmented, virtual, or mixed reality (AR/VR/MR), but we must admit that these technologies are still not dominating the market and can only be found in rare situations, for example, in a lab of a company

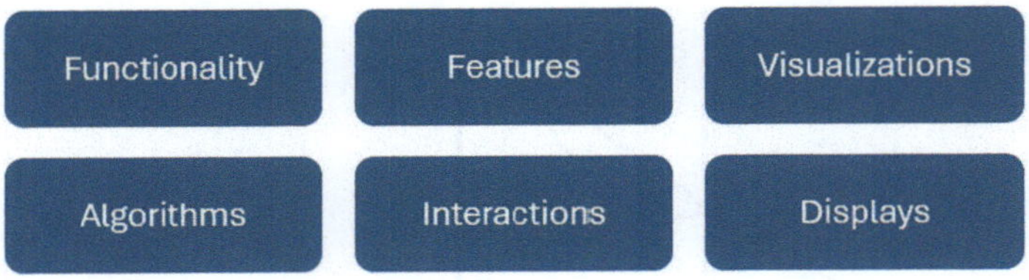

Fig. 4.24 The testing phase includes many aspects of a sports data analytics tool. Figure created by the authors

that invests millions of dollars in such technologies. However, no matter what kind of tool or technology is developed, it has to be tested and such user testing usually occurs after the development phase or at least when large portions of such a tool are already implemented, that is, featurewise testing.

4.6.4 User Experiments

Testing a tool after the design and implementation phase is a powerful idea, but such a tool is typically tested as a whole with all its features and functions. To obtain more detailed feedback, be it quantitative or qualitative, we should only evaluate small components of the tool. This can be done by varying some kind of independent variable to measure its impact on the dependent variables. Dependent variables can be error rates, response times, eye movements, physiological measures such as galvanic skin response (GSR), stress, pupil dilation, blood pressure, brain activity, and many more (Blascheck et al., 2015; Burch et al., 2025). Such experiments are very fine granular and require hypotheses prior to study design and execution. These hypotheses are then taken into account to design and set up a study, invite the right and appropriate number of study participants, and fix the number of stimuli, tasks, and duration of the experiment, for example.

User experiments can be controlled or uncontrolled. In a controlled setting, participants can come to a laboratory and be monitored all the time while answering tasks using the functions and the features of the evaluated tool (see Fig. 4.25 for a study participant sitting in front of an eye tracking device). In an uncontrolled setting, users might sit in a remote location and just use their web browsers to answer given tasks in a remotely accessible version of the sports analytics tool. The big difference between these two setups is that we typically have fewer study participants in a controlled user study than in an uncontrolled one. However, the uncontrolled one can be used as some kind of pilot test to create specific hypotheses that are then tested in a more controlled setting by fewer participants. No matter what kind of setting is used, it generates new types of user data, in the case of eye tracking, even spatiotemporal visual attention data which are quite challenging to analyze (see Sect. 4.6.5).

Fig. 4.25 A study participant in an eye tracking study sitting in front of a remote eye tracking device. Permission to use this image given by image creator Kuno Kurzhals. Permission to use the stimulus content on the eye tracking monitor given by Anna Kuriger

4.6.5 Statistical and Visual Evaluation

Data recorded in a user experiment can take a variety of forms (see Table 4.3). It can be quantitative data coming in the form of error rates or response times. It can also be qualitative data in the form of verbal feedback, facial expressions and moods, or interviews. Qualitative data are typically summarized in some way, while quantitative data are statistically evaluated to confirm or reject formerly stated hypotheses. To do this in a reliable way, the data are evaluated using statistical methods including ANOVA, the t-test, the chi-square test, Pearson's correlation, or the Mann-Whitney U test. These tests typically aggregate data and produce results that are visually depicted as box plots or other simple statistical graphics

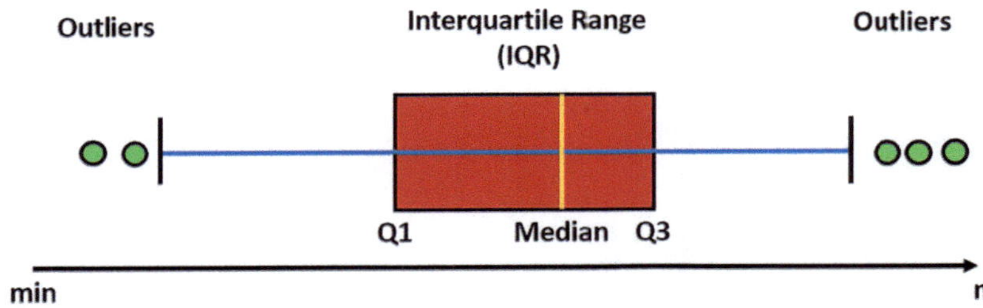

Fig. 4.26 A box plot is a simple statistical graphic that can show the distribution of a measured quantity from a user experiment, for example, the error rate or response times. Figure created by the authors

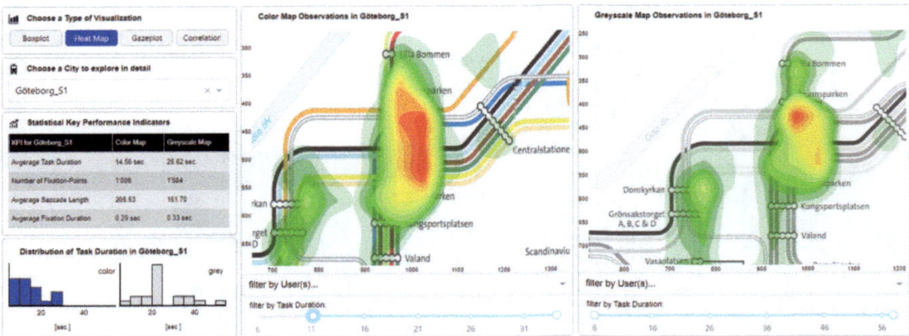

Fig. 4.27 A visual attention map is useful to show eye movement data overlaid on a visual stimulus. Here we see a visual analytics tool that can compute visual attention results and that can generate visual representations of the processed eye movement data with visual attention maps among them. Permission to use this image by Tamara Nyffeler, Sharon Reiser, and Serge Pellegatta

(see Fig. 4.26). However, even if tests are properly executed, experts in the domain are required to apply them and interpret the results.

In addition to the textual summary and statistical data aggregation, we can also rely on visual representations of user evaluation data. This makes in particular sense when an eye tracking technology is applied that generates spatiotemporal data. This kind of data can be split into several pieces of data, but a greater benefit is achieved when the pieces of data can be monitored in a linked fashion, for example, to explore the data for correlations. A pure statistical approach aggregates the data too much and usually looks at the data pieces. Visualization, on the other hand, tries to show the whole dataset, for example, as scatter plots to explore correlations, as line charts to see dynamic trends, as adjacency matrices to see weighted relations, or even as heat maps or visual attention maps (see Fig. 4.27, for example, visual attention maps) in the case of eye movement data (Blascheck et al., 2017) to explore the data for visual attention hot spots. Statistics and textual summaries are not bad but combined with interactive visualizations they become even more powerful.

4.7 Scalability Issues

Keeping up with the growing datasets is a big challenge, not only in general data science but also in sports data analytics. There are several scalability aspects that can be considered, such as data scalability (Sect. 4.7.1). Software, hardware, and environment must also be scalable for growing datasets (Sect. 4.7.2). Typical algorithmic approaches with their runtime performances suffer from scalability issues (Sect. 4.7.3). The results of data analyses are mainly visually represented in the corresponding visualization techniques integrated in dynamic user interfaces (Sect. 4.7.4). Human perceptual systems are important to rapidly detect patterns in a visualization, but perception also has scalability problems (Sect. 4.7.5).

4.7.1 Data Scalability

In modern times, datasets are growing at incredible rates (Sect. 2.1.1). This also holds for the field of sports. There are various heterogeneous data sources that consist of several data types and are stored at different locations. The datasets exceed sizes that we could not imagine. Currently, data can still be stored in various formats in files and databases, local and remote. Even real-time data can be of interest in the sports field, which requires even larger storage space due to their finer granularity of time. However, if we are only interested in the current data point, the storage might not be the challenge, but rather the fast algorithmic processing of the data. This requires fast access to each data point or time period that is needed for an algorithm to work, while the results of the algorithms must be stored again somewhere, generating even more data.

The question is if all sports data, static, dynamic, and real-time data, can still be stored in a few years or if this whole storage process becomes a scalability problem. Moreover, not the storage itself but rather the access time can be an even bigger problem. Data must be stored in a way that allows for fast access times. Otherwise, algorithmic processing would suffer, and, consequently, a sports data analytics tool would have poor interactive responsiveness, or it would freeze or crash completely. The data scalability problem will definitely become a huge problem in the future. We must be careful about the kind of data that that stored to avoid serious problems.

4.7.2 Software, Hardware, and Environment Scalability

Several interactive tools are already available that focus on sports data analysis (Zacheo et al., 2023). Some older ones already reached their capacities and do not really scale with the growing datasets anymore. This shows that modern tools must be able to keep up with the increased complexity and size of today's datasets. In addition, hardware, including processors, central processing units (CPUs), and graphics processing units (GPUs), must be able to handle growing amounts of data. For example, more and more data must be kept in memory to allow fast computations, especially if modern data science concepts are applied to analyze sports-related data. This is mainly problematic for real-time data that must be processed in a fraction of a second to inform users about the latest changes in the data and to react on circumstances in a running sports event, for example. This is in particular beneficial for survival in a highly competitive sports world with a lot of money involved.

The final result, whether software or hardware, is not the only critical issue. How the software is built, where it is installed, and where it runs also has a major impact on the success of such tools. Each software is typically based on one or more programming languages with available libraries that provide the required functionality. This also holds for interactive visualization techniques that must follow modern design rules and integrated algorithmic approaches that focus on interactive responsiveness. Such libraries are further developed, and from time to time they might reach their limits due to scalability issues. Improvements and updates must be integrated that, on the negative side, can cause runtime problems due to deprecated functionality. In addition, available environments, including operating systems or web browsers for online tools, can cause problems from time to time. A tool that ran smoothly in the beginning can suddenly become a poor performing tool from many perspectives. If developers cannot foresee or detect such issues, the role of users should not be neglected in such cases.

4.7.3 Algorithmic Scalability

To analyze and visualize sports data, there are many algorithms involved. Those can be based on static or dynamic data, on structured or unstructured data, or even on homogeneous or heterogeneous data. Depending on the tasks-in-mind, there are different types of algorithms that typically take an input dataset or several of them, transform them in some way, and output another kind of data that tries to provide a solution to the users' tasks-in-mind. The data output is typically large enough so that pure observation in a text file or on the console is a challenging, even impossible task. Consequently, the data output is prepared in a graphical form to hint the users to specific data patterns or anomalies in the data. For example, a previously unstructured dataset might be clustered by a k-means or hierarchical clustering algorithm to bring structure to the data. A time series and a dynamic dataset might contain trend and countertrend patterns that are difficult to find. Hence, trend analysis detection can quickly identify those patterns. However, the cluster and also the trend patterns are difficult to describe by textual and value-based output. A visual representation of such data is much better, as users can understand visualizations to derive patterns. Visual communication is very important for making such algorithms useful in detecting patterns and outliers.

Many algorithms are easy to implement, or there exist libraries that provide efficient and effective algorithmic solutions. However, some algorithms have high runtime complexity, although they are easy to implement and integrate. This class of algorithms that are denoted by NP-hard or NP-complete problems (Garey & Johnson, 1979) make data analysis a tedious task. Heuristic approaches can help at least obtain a locally minimal or maximal solution instead of the optimal solution with the benefit that runtime is still acceptable and allows interactive responsiveness in a data analytics tool. The NP-hardness is actually not a big issue for small-scale datasets, but it quickly becomes serious when the size of the dataset increases just slightly. Another major scalability issue is that popular languages like Python, JavaScript, Java, and C++ have so many libraries that developers often don't understand the underlying algorithms anymore and treat them as black boxes. This again makes maintaining such computer programs a challenging endeavor.

4.7.4 Visual Scalability

Even if the data can be quickly processed and transformed, it can still be a challenging problem to visualize the output data in a scalable way. The problem is that there are typically many visual elements that overlap or cross each other, leading to occlusion effects, a problem that is denoted by the term visual clutter (Rosenholtz et al., 2005). There are a few ways to eliminate that problem, for example, by aggregating the data, using a different visual metaphor, or filtering the data for the most relevant ones. All of these approaches lead to an information loss and mostly do not show the same information as in the original visual representation. Statistical approaches can work in this direction. They can work with huge datasets, but as a negative consequence they strongly aggregate the data and do not show the details anymore. Visualization should show all the data in the best case or, as Tufte pointed out, "Above all else show the data" (Tufte, 1992).

In addition to visual clutter, we can easily run into other design-dependent visualization problems. The lie factor or chart junk (Tufte, 1992) can lead to misinterpretations of data or even missing scales or different scales and no legends and meta data. If there are large variations in the quantitative data, logarithmic transformations or even normalizations can modify the data in a way that is difficult to interpret at first sight. In general, a visualization, created for small- or large-scale datasets, is typically based on a composition of visual variables that include color, size, length, area, or position to mention the most important ones (Bertin, 1967, 1981, 2010). Most of the interactive visualization tools follow the visual information seeker mantra (Shneiderman, 1996) stating overview first, zoom and filter, and then details on demand. This means that no matter how large the data are, there should always be an overview about most of the data, and then the users decide where to put the focus on and finally look for specific visual elements. This concept is also useful for sports data analytics applications in which an overview is often missing to find an entry point into more advanced, even more complex, data exploration tasks.

4.7.5 Perceptual Scalability

Even if a visualization follows all possible design rules, it can run into another problematic challenge which is caused by the humans' perception. Perceptual abilities are useful for rapidly detecting visual patterns (Ware, 2004, 2008), but this is not possible in all visual situations. There are also scalability issues and limitations, caused by inherent visual acuity or color deficiency problems. This means that visual elements cannot be as small as possible; there is a smallest visual element that can be seen on a display. This also depends on the human eye and the distance to the display. Color coding can also be a problematic visual variable, since the human visual system is only able to distinguish a small number of different colors. Even the field of view is limited and cannot get all the information displayed in one glance, especially if it is displayed on a large high-resolution display (LHRD).

Humans also have limited short-term memory, which is actually important in visualization. For example, when doing a comparison task, several visual elements or visual patterns have to be stored for a short time and then recalled after a fraction of a second to visually compare it with another part of a visual scene. If short-term memory would not work properly, such comparison tasks would be difficult or even impossible to solve. In fact, humans solve comparison tasks all the time. We look at something, detect a visual pattern, store it for a moment, recall if there is a similar or the same pattern, and then decide if the new pattern is familiar or new that we cannot categorize and that we must first learn. This effect is related to change blindness (Healey & Enns, 2012) stating that we cannot easily detect differences between two visual scenes, even if they are placed next to each other. Inattentional blindness can also occur when we focus on any other task that distracts us from the original task. A powerful perceptual concept denoted by preattentive processing can help identify outliers in a huge dataset, making the outlier data elements visually different from all other (distracting) visual elements, and hence the task of finding and locating a specific data element becomes easy and even scales with a growing dataset size.

References

Alt, P. S., Baumgart, C., Ueberschär, O., Freiwald, J., & Hoppe, M. W. (2020). Validity of a local positioning system during outdoor and indoor conditions for team sports. *Sensors, 20*(20), 5733.

Anderski, M., Fortagne, M. A., Kapfer, K., Lis, B., & Ströbel, T. (2025). Navigating fan reactions: The role of innovation resistance and acceptance in smart stadium technology use. In *Proceedings of the 58th Hawaii International Conference on System Sciences* (pp. 4313–4322). University of Hawai'i at Mānoa.

Aprile, R., Nicoliello, M., & Durst, S. (2022). Intellectual capital (IC) framework for elite athletes: Connecting sport performance and economic value. *Journal of Intellectual Capital, 23*(7), 1596–1612.

Bach, B., Freeman, E., Abdul-Rahman, A., Turkay, C., Khan, S., Fan, Y., & Chen, M. (2023). Dashboard design patterns. *IEEE Transactions on Visualization and Computer Graphics, 29*(1), 342–352.

Bache-Mathiesen, L. K., Andersen, T. E., Dalen-Lorentsen, T., Clarsen, B., & Fagerland, M. W. (2022). Assessing the cumulative effect of long-term training load on the risk of injury in team sports. *BMJ Open Sport & Exercise Medicine, 8*(2), e001342.

Bai, Z., & Bai, X. (2021). Sports big data: Management, analysis, applications, and challenges. *Complexity, 2021*, 6676297.

BASPO. (2021). Zukunftsorientierte Breitensportförderung. Bericht des Bundesamts für Sport BASPO.

Belkacem, I., Tominski, C., Médoc, N., Knudsen, S., Dachselt, R., & Ghoniem, M. (2024). Interactive visualization on large high-resolution displays: A survey. *Computer Graphics Forum, 43*(6), e15001.

Belotti, N., Bonfanti, S., Locatelli, A., Rota, L., Ghidotti, A., & Vitali, A. (2022). A telerehabilitation platform for shoulder motor function recovery using serious games and an Azure Kinect device. In G. Schreier, B. Pfeifer, M. Baumgartner & D. Hayn (Eds.), *Proceedings of the 16th Health Informatics Meets Digital Health Conference, dHealth*, volume 293 of *Studies in Health Technology and Informatics* (pp. 145–152). IOS Press.

Bengoa, A. B., & Méndez-Zorrilla, A. (2021). A systematic review of the application of camera-based human pose estimation in the field of sport and physical exercise. *Sensors, 21*(18), 5996.

Bertin, J. (1967). *Semiology of graphics: Diagrams, networks, maps*. Wisconsin: University of Wisconsin Press, (first published in French in 1967 translated by William J. Berg in 1983).

Bertin, J. (1981). *Graphics and graphic information processing*. De Gruyter. Translation: William J. Berg, Paul Scott.

Bertin, J. (2010). *Semiology of graphics—diagrams, networks, maps*. ESRI.

Bezuglov, E., Lazarev, A., Khaitin, V. Y., Chegin, S., Tikhonova, A., Talibov, O., Gerasimuk, D., & Waśkiewicz, Z. (2021). The prevalence of use of various post-exercise recovery methods after training among elite endurance athletes. *International Journal of Environmental Research and Public Health (IJERPH), 18*(21), 11698.

Blascheck, T., Burch, M., Raschke, M., & Weiskopf, D. (2015). Challenges and perspectives in big eye-movement data visual analytics. In *Proceedings of the Symposium on Big Data Visual Analytics, BDVA* (pp. 17–24). IEEE.

Blascheck, T., Kurzhals, K., Raschke, M., Burch, M., Weiskopf, D., & Ertl, T. (2017). Visualization of eye tracking data: A taxonomy and survey. *Computer Graphics Forum, 36*(8), 260–284.

Bouman, R., Bukhsh, Z., & Heskes, T. (2024). Unsupervised anomaly detection algorithms on real-world data: How many do we need? *Journal of Machine Learning Research, 25*, 105:1–105:34.

Boyd, N. (2016). Stepp, running sensor. Retrieved August 25, 2025, from https://officeforproductdesign.com/projects/RunningSensor/

Brink, M. S., Visscher, C., Arends, S., Zwerver, J., Post, W. J., & Lemmink, K. A. P. M. (2021). Load monitoring practice in European elite football and the impact of club financial resources. *Frontiers in Sports and Active Living, 3*, 679824.

Budak, G., & Kara, I. (2021). A multiobjective mathematical model to form the best team at sports clubs: Team harmony and player performance objectives. *Team Performance Management, 28*(3–4), 145–159.

Burch, M. (2022). *Eye tracking and visual analytics*. River Publishers.

Burch, M., & Diehl, S. (2008). TimeRadarTrees: Visualizing dynamic compound digraphs. *Computer Graphics Forum, 27*(3), 823–830.

Burch, M., Kurzhals, K., & Weiskopf, D. (2025). Eye tracking studies in visualization: Phases, guidelines, and checklist. In *Proceedings of the Symposium on Eye Tracking Research and Applications, ETRA*.

Burch, M., & Schmid, M. (2024). *Dashboard design*. River Publishers.

Burch, M., Vehlow, C., Konevtsova, N., & Weiskopf, D. (2011). Evaluating partially drawn links for directed graph edges. In M. J. van Kreveld & B. Speckmann (Eds.), *Proceedings of the 19th International Symposium on Graph Drawing, GD*, volume 7034 of Lecture notes in computer science (pp. 226–237). Springer.

Burch, M., & Weiskopf, D. (2014). Tennis plots: Game, set, and match. In T. Dwyer, H. C. Purchase & A. J. Delaney (Eds.), *Proceedings of the 8th International Conference on Diagrammatic*

Representation and Inference, Diagrams, volume 8578 of Lecture notes in computer science (pp. 38–44). Springer.
Cavallaro, R. (1997). The FoxTrax hockey puck tracking system. *IEEE Computer Graphics and Applications, 17*(2), 6–12.
Chang, B. (2021). Application of heart rate acceleration motion wireless sensor fusion in individual special competitive sports. *Journal of Sensors, 2021*, 1–11.
Cornwell, T. B., & Kwon, Y. (2020). Sponsorship-linked marketing: Research surpluses and shortages. *Journal of the Academy of Marketing Science, 48*(4), 607–629.
Cui, Z. J., Pan, H., Iyer, A., Haldar, S., & Pinto, L. (2024). Dynamo: In-domain dynamics pretraining for visuo-motor control. In A. Globersons, L. Mackey, D. Belgrave, A. Fan, U. Paquet, J. M. Tomczak & C. Zhang (Eds.), *Proceedings of Advances in Neural Information Processing Systems 38: Annual Conference on Neural Information Processing System, NeurIPS.*
Cushion, C. J., Armour, K. M., & Jones, R. L. (2003). Coach education and continuing professional development: Experience and learning to coach. *Quest, 55*(3), 215–230.
Cutler, Z., Harrison, L., Nobre, C., & Lex, A. (2025). Crowdsourced think-aloud studies. In N. Yamashita, V. Evers, K. Yatani, S. X. Ding, B. Lee, M. Chetty & P. O. T. Dugas (Eds.), *Proceedings of the CHI Conference on Human Factors in Computing Systems* (pp. 207:1–207:23). ACM.
Dalip, D. H., Gonçalves, M. A., Cristo, M., & Calado, P. (2013). Exploiting user feedback to learn to rank answers in Q&A forums: A case study with stack overflow. In G. J. F. Jones, P. Sheridan, D. Kelly, M. de Rijke & T. Sakai (Eds.), *Proceedings of the 36th International ACM SIGIR Conference on Research and Development in Information Retrieval, SIGIR* (pp. 543–552). ACM.
Díaz-Oreiro, I., López, G., Quesada, L., & Guerrero, L. A. (2019). Standardized questionnaires for user experience evaluation: A systematic literature review. In J. Bravo, & I. González (Eds.), *Proceedings of the 13th International Conference on Ubiquitous Computing and Ambient Intelligence, UCAmI*, volume 31 of *MDPI Proceedings* (p. 14). MDPI.
Dijkstra, H. P., Pollock, R., Chakraverty, J., & Alonso, N. M. (2014). Managing the health of the elite athlete: A new integrated performance health management and coaching model. *British Journal of Sports Medicine, 48*(7), 523–531.
Djaoui, L., Garcia, J. D.-C., Hautier, C., & Dellal, A. (2016). Kinetic post-match fatigue in professional and youth soccer players during the competitive period. *Asian Journal of Sports Medicine, 7*(1), e28267.
Dolan, S. (2023). How technology and digital experiences in the customer journey enhance fan engagement in professional sports. *Journal of Undergraduate Research, 23.*
Dowling, M., Leopkey, B., & Smith, L. (2018). Governance in sport: A scoping review. *Journal of Sport Management, 32*(5), 438–451.
Eble, M. (2016). *Öffentlichkeiten im Social Web: Strukturen, Dynamiken und analytische Zugänge in Zeiten von Big Data, . In I. E. Kastens & A. Busch (Hrsg.), Handbuch Wirtschaftskommunikation: Interdisziplinäre Zugänge zur Unternehmenskommunikation*. Francke Verlag.
Einstein, A. (1923). Die Grundlage der allgemeinen Relativitätstheorie. In *Das Relativitätsprinzip. Fortschritte der Mathematischen Wissenschaften in Monographien*. Vieweg+Teubner Verlag.
Farbiz, F., Yu, Z. H., Manders, C., & Ahmad, W. (2007). An electrical muscle stimulation haptic feedback for mixed reality tennis game. In M. Alexa & A. Finkelstein (Eds.), *Proceedings of the International Conference on Computer Graphics and Interactive Techniques, SIGGRAPH* (p. 140). ACM.
Ferguson, J. (2021). Effective sporting organisations: A practitioner's perspective. *Open Journal of Social Sciences, 9*, 167–211.
Forrest, D., & McHale, I. G. (2019). Using statistics to detect match fixing in sport. *IMA Journal of Management Mathematics, 30*(4), 431–449.
Garey, M. R., & Johnson, D. S. (1979). *Computers and Intractability: A Guide to the Theory of NP-Completeness*. W. H. Freeman.
Gümüşdağ, H. (2024). Sport economics and financial management. *Journal of Business Management and Economic Research, 8*(4), 155–166.

Golemati, M., Katifori, A., Giannopoulou, E. G., Daradimos, I., Vassilakis, C., Lepouras, G., & Halatsis, C. (2008). An interview-based user study on the use of visualizations for folder browsing. In *Proceedings of the 12th International Conference on Information Visualisation, IV* (pp. 106–112). IEEE Computer Society.

Greca, A. D., Amaro, I., Tucci, C., Frugieri, N., & Tortora, G. (2024). A user study on the relationship between empathy and facial-based emotion simulation in virtual reality. In C. Conati, G. Volpe & I. Torre (Eds.), *Proceedings of the International Conference on Advanced Visual Interfaces, AVI* (pp. 17:1–17:9). ACM.

Grioui, F., Blascheck, T., Yao, L., & Isenberg, P. (2024). Micro visualizations on a smartwatch: Assessing reading performance while walking. CoRR (pp. 46–50).

Guo, X., Li, X., & Guo, M. (2024). Diversifying configurational paths for athlete data protection. *Scientific Reports, 14*, 32053.

He, L. (2020). Application of biomedical signal acquisition equipment in human sport heart rate monitoring. *Journal of Medical Imaging Health Informatics, 10*(4), 877–883.

Healey, C. G., & Enns, J. T. (2012). Attention and visual memory in visualization and computer graphics. *IEEE Transaction on Visualization and Computer Graphics, 18*(7), 1170–1188.

Held, J., Cioppa, A., Giancola, S., Hamdi, A., Ghanem, B., & Droogenbroeck, M. V. (2023). VARS: Video assistant referee system for automated soccer decision making from multiple views. In *Proceedings of the IEEE/CVF Conference on Computer Vision and Pattern Recognition, CVPR* (pp. 5086–5097). IEEE.

Hennessy, L., & Jeffreys, I. (2018). The current use of GPS, its potential, and limitations in soccer. *Strength & Conditioning Journal, 40*(3), 83–94.

Herold, D. M., Breitbarth, T., Schulenkorf, N., & Kummer, S. (2019). Sport logistics research: Reviewing and line marking of a new field. *The International Journal of Logistics Management, 31*(2), 357–379.

Höferlin, B. (2014). *Scalable visual analytics for video surveillance*. PhD thesis, University of Stuttgart.

Höferlin, B., Höferlin, M., Heidemann, G., & Weiskopf, D. (2015). Scalable video visual analytics. *Information Visualization, 14*(1), 10–26.

Höferlin, B., Netzel, R., Höferlin, M., Weiskopf, D., & Heidemann, G. (2012). Inter-active learning of ad-hoc classifiers for video visual analytics. In *Proceedings of 7th IEEE Conference on Visual Analytics Science and Technology, IEEE VAST* (pp. 23–32). IEEE Computer Society.

Houtmeyers, K. C., Jaspers, A., & Figueiredo, P. (2021). Managing the training process in elite sports: From descriptive to prescriptive data analytics. *International Journal of Sports Physiology and Performance, 16*(11), 1719–1723.

Huang, Y., Richter, E., Kleickmann, T., Scheiter, K., & Richter, D. (2023). Body in motion, attention in focus: A virtual reality study on teachers' movement patterns and noticing. *Computers & Education, 206*, 104912.

Ilham, J., Nakamura, Y., Ito, T., Kondo, K., An, Q., Akita, J., & Toda, M. (2024). Improving repeatability of surface electromyography measurement of sit-to-stand motions by using muscle synergy. *Biomedical Signal Processing and Control, 93*, 106185.

Jacquier, J., & Gorce, P. (2024). Kinematics of the tennis serve using an optoelectronic motion capture system: Are there correlations between joint angles and racket velocity? *Sensors, 24*(11), 3292.

Jianjun, Q., Isleem, H. F., Almoghayer, W. J. K., & Khishe, M. (2025). Predictive athlete performance modeling with machine learning and biometric data integration. *Scientific Reports, 15*, 16365.

Karahanoglu, A., Gouveia, R., Reenalda, J., & Ludden, G. D. S. (2021). How are sports-trackers used by runners? Running-related data, personal goals, and self-tracking in running. *Sensors, 21*(11), 3687.

Keim, D. A., Zhang, L., Krstajic, M., & Simon, S. (2012). Solving problems with visual analytics: Challenges and applications. *Journal of Multimedia Processing and Technologies, 3*(1), 1–11.

Khandan, A., Fathian, R., Carey, J. P., & Rouhani, H. (2023). Assessment of three-dimensional kinematics of high- and low-calibre hockey skaters on synthetic ice using wearable sensors. *Sensors, 23*(1), 334.
Kim, W., & Kim, M. (2017). Sports motion analysis system using wearable sensors and video cameras. In *Proceedings of the International Conference on Information and Communication Technology Convergence, ICTC* (pp. 1089–1091). IEEE.
Kovalchik, S. A. (2023). Player tracking data in sports. *Annual Review of Statistics and Its Application, 10*, 677–697.
Koyama, Y., Nishiyama, M., & Watanabe, K. (2015). Actual running performance monitoring for personal trainer system based on perceptive sportswear. In *Proceedings of the IEEE 4th Global Conference on Consumer Electronics, GCCE* (pp. 260–261). IEEE.
Kuo, F., Hsu, C., & Day, R. (2009). An exploratory study of cognitive effort involved in decision under framing—an application of the eye-tracking technology. *Decision Support Systems, 48*(1), 81–91.
Lacirignola, J., Weston, C., Byrd, K., Metzger, E., Singh, N., Davis, S., Maurer, D., Young, W., Collins, P., Balcius, J., Richter, M., & Palmer, J. (2017). Instrumented footwear inserts: A new tool for measuring forces and biomechanical state changes during dynamic movements. In *Proceedings of the 14th IEEE International Conference on Wearable and Implantable Body Sensor Networks, BSN* (pp. 119–124). IEEE.
Lalić, S., & Lučić, R. (2023). Cost management in sports organizations. *Journal of Faculty of Economics Brcko, 17*(1), 32–41.
Lee, B., Srinivasan, A., Stasko, J. T., Tory, M., & Setlur, V. (2018). Multimodal interaction for data visualization. In T. Catarci, K. L. Norman & M. Mecella (Eds.), *Proceedings of the 2018 International Conference on Advanced Visual Interfaces, AVI* (pp. 11:1–11:3). ACM.
Lee, E. C., Fragala, M. S., Kavouras, S. A., Queen, R. M., Pryor, J. L., & Casa, D. J. (2017). Biomarkers in sports and exercise: Tracking health, performance, and recovery in athletes. *Journal of Strength and Conditioning Research, 31*(10), 2920–2937.
Lee, H. T., & Kim, Y. S. (2018). The effect of sports VR training for improving human body composition. *EURASIP Journal on Image and Video Processing, 2018*, 148.
Lee, Y. Y., Asaduzzaman, M., Samad, A. A., & Park, J. Y. (2024). A MXene@Pt nanocomposite-based wearable epidermal patch for real-time glucose and pH monitoring. In *Proceedings of the IEEE SENSORS* (pp. 1–4). IEEE.
Levy, R., Katz, L., Sorrentino, R. M., & Peng, X. (2003). Virtual reality: Visualization for athletic competition. *International Journal of Computer Science in Sport, 2*(1).
Loureiro, S. M. C., Ruediger, K. H., & Demetris, V. (2012). Brand emotional connection and loyalty. *Journal of Brand Management, 20*(1), 13–27.
Ma, Z., Yu, Y., Wang, H., & Deng, G. (2022). Wind tunnel test research on the flight style of ski jumping. In *Proceedings of the 3rd Asia-Pacific Conference on Image Processing, Electronics and Computers, IPEC* (pp. 557–562). ACM.
Madinabeitia, I., Alarcón-López, F., Chirosa-Ríos, L. J., Pelayo-Tejo, I., & Cárdenas-Vélez, D. (2023). The cognitive benefits of basketball training compared to a combined endurance and resistance training regimen: A four-month intervention study. *Scientific Reports, 13*, 11132.
Mancini, M., Spreadborough, J., Maye, L., Biancardi, B., & Varni, G. (2021). Interaction fidelity vs user's workload in a VR environment: A pilot study. In M. D. Marsico, D. Gadia, L. A. Ripamonti, D. Maggiorini, I. Mariani, M. Mancini, G. Varni, D. Murphy, F. Pellacini, L. Maye & P. O'Toole (Eds.), *Joint Proceedings of 4th Workshop on Games-Human Interaction (GHItaly21) & 1st Workshop on Multi-party Interaction in eXtended Reality (MIXR) in conjunction with CHITALY - Biannual Conference of the Italian SIGCHI Chapter*, volume 2934 of *CEUR Workshop Proceedings*. CEUR-WS.org.
Mrazek, J. (2008). Development of an ice hockey goal sensor.
Nguyen, L. N. N., Martín, D. R., Català, A., Pérez-López, C., Samà, A., & Cavallaro, A. (2015). Basketball activity recognition using wearable inertial measurement units. In P. Ponsa & D. Guasch (Eds.), *Proceedings of the XVI International Conference on Human Computer Interaction, Interacción* (pp. 60:1–60:6). ACM.

Nicholls, S., James, N., Bryant, E., & Wells, J. (2019). The implementation of performance analysis and feedback within Olympic sport: The performance analyst's perspective. *International Journal of Sports Science & Coaching, 14*(1), 63–71.
Ning, T., Fu, M., Wang, Y., Duan, X., & Abedin, M. Z. (2024). Application of deep learning for automatic detection of table tennis balls from an intelligent serving machine. *Applied Soft Computing, 167*, 112329.
Nyffeler, T., & Burch, M. (2025). Avalanche risks in the Swiss mountains. In *Proceedings of the Swiss Data Science Conference, SDS*.
Obi, O. C., Dawodu, S. O., Onwusinkwue, S., Osasona, F., Atadoga, A., & Daraojimba, A. I. (2024). Data science in sports analytics: A review of performance optimization and fan engagement. *World Journal of Advanced Research and Reviews, 21*(1), 2663–2670.
Ortmann, T., Wang, Q., & Putzar, L. (2024). EmojiHeroVR: A study on facial expression recognition under partial occlusion from head-mounted displays. In *Proceedings of the 12th International Conference on Affective Computing and Intelligent Interaction, ACII* (pp. 80–88). IEEE.
Ota, T., Amemiya, T., Kuzuoka, H., & Aoyama, K. (2024). Electrical stimulation of nerve bundles in the lower leg generates tactile sensations on the plantar and dorsal foot. *IEEE Access, 12*, 188914–188925.
Pascoal, R. M., de Almeida, A., & Sofia, R. C. (2019). Activity recognition in outdoor sports environments: Smart data for end-users involving mobile pervasive augmented reality systems. In R. Harle, K. Farrahi & N. D. Lane (Eds.), *Proceedings of the ACM International Joint Conference on Pervasive and Ubiquitous Computing and Proceedings of the ACM International Symposium on Wearable Computers, UbiComp/ISWC* (pp. 446–453). ACM.
Perin, C., Vuillemot, R., Stolper, C., Stasko, J., Wood, J., & Carpendale, S. (2018). State of the art of sports data visualization. *Computer Graphics Forum, 37*(3), 663–686.
Pickering, C., & Kiely, J. (2019). The development of a personalised training framework: Implementation of emerging technologies for performance. *Sports Medicine - Open, 5*(1), 1–14.
Polk, T., Jäckle, D., Häußler, J., & Yang, J. (2020). CourtTime: Generating actionable insights into tennis matches using visual analytics. *IEEE Transactions on Visualization and Computer Graphics, 26*(1), 397–406.
Postma, M. (2023). *Best practices for big data management in the sports industry* (pp. 1–8). TScIT 39, University of Twente. Accessed July 10, 2025.
Pradhan, T., Rao, K. N., & Tiwari, K. (2025). Winning with data: Exploring advanced statistical methods in sports performance analysis. *International Research Journal of Modernization in Engineering Technology and Science, 7*(3).
Promsri, A., Deedphimai, S., Promthep, P., & Champamuang, C. (2024). Impacts of wearable resistance placement on running efficiency assessed by wearable sensors: A pilot study. *Sensors, 24*(13), 4399.
Psiuk, R., Seidl, T., Strauß, W., & Bernhard, J. (2014). Analysis of goal line technology from the perspective of an electromagnetic field based approach. *Procedia Engineering, 72*, 279–284.
Purchase, H. C., Isaacs, K., Bueti, T., Hastings, B., Kassam, A., Kim, A., & van Hoesen, S. (2018). A classification of infographics. In P. Chapman, G. Stapleton, A. Moktefi, S. Pérez-Kriz & F. Bellucci (Eds.), *Proceedings of the 10th International Conference on Diagrammatic Representation and Inference, Diagrams*, volume 10871 of Lecture notes in computer science (pp. 210–218). Springer.
Roberts, J. C. (2003). Guest editor's introduction: Special issue on coordinated and multiple views in exploratory visualization. *Information Visualization, 2*(4), 199–200.
Rosenholtz, R., Li, Y., Mansfield, J., & Jin, Z. (2005). Feature congestion: A measure of display clutter. In G. C. van der Veer & C. Gale (Eds.), *Proceedings of the Conference on Human Factors in Computing Systems, CHI* (pp. 761–770).
Rüger, S. M. (2005). Putting the user in the loop: Visual resource discovery. In M. Detyniecki, J. M. Jose, A. Nürnberger & van C. J. Rijsbergen (Eds.), *Proceedings of the Third International*

Workshop on Adaptive Multimedia Retrieval: User, Context, and Feedback, AMR, volume 3877 of Lecture notes in computer science (pp. 1–18). Springer.

Saragiotto, B. T., Pierro, L. G. D., Lopes, L. M., Costa, F. A., Cabral, C. D., & Lopes, A. D. (2014). Risk factors and injury prevention in elite athletes. *Brazilian Journal of Physical Therapy, 18*(2), 142–149.

Saw, A. E., Main, L. C., & Gastin, P. B. (2016). Monitoring the athlete training response: Subjective self-reported measures trump commonly used objective measures: A systematic review. *British Journal of Sports Medicine, 50*(5), 281–291.

Schmauder, H., Burch, M., Müller, C., & Weiskopf, D. (2015). Distributed visual analytics on large-scale high-resolution displays. In *Proceedings of the Symposium on Big Data Visual Analytics, BDVA* (pp. 33–40). IEEE.

Schmidt, J., Priem, R., & Zanella, P. (2024). Customers, markets, and five archetypical value creation logics: A review of demand-side research in strategic management. *Journal of Management, 50*(6), 2309–2342.

Shi, X., & Zou, H. (2024). Data collection and analysis based on sensor technology in sports training. *Scalable Computing: Practice and Experience, 25*(5), 4399–4406.

Shneiderman, B. (1996). The eyes have it: A task by data type taxonomy for information visualizations. In *Proceedings of the IEEE Symposium on Visual Languages* (pp. 336–343). IEEE Computer Society.

Silhavy, P., Silhavy, R., & Prokopova, Z. (2014). User testing and trustworthy electronic voting system design. In R. Silhavy, R. Senkerik, Z. K. Oplatková, P. Silhavy & Z. Prokopova (Eds.), *Proceedings of the 3rd Computer Science Online Conference on Modern Trends and Techniques in Computer Science, CSOC*, volume 285 of *Advances in Intelligent Systems and Computing* (pp. 619–629). Springer.

Singh, G., Kushwah, G., Singh, T., Ramírez-Campillo, R., & Thapa, R. K. (2022). Effects of six weeks outdoor versus treadmill running on physical fitness and body composition in recreationally active young males: A pilot study. *PeerJ, 10*, e13791.

Svensson, A., Nallanathan, A., & Tewfik, A. H. (2006). Ultra-wideband communication systems: Technology and applications. *EURASIP Journal on Wireless Communications and Networking, 2006*(1), 016497.

Taber, C. B., Sharma, S., Raval, M. S., Senbel, S., Keefe, A., Shah, J., Patterson, E., Nolan, J., Artan, N. S., & Kaya, T. (2024). A holistic approach to performance prediction in collegiate athletics: Player, team, and conference perspectives. *Scientific Reports, 14*, 1162.

Tharpe, B., Bourgeois, A. G., & Ashok, A. (2021). A do-it-yourself computer vision based robotic ball throw trainer. In S. Banerjee, L. Mottola & X. Zhou (Eds.), *Proceedings of the 19th Annual International Conference on Mobile Systems, Applications, and Services, MobiSys, Virtual Event* (pp. 505–506). ACM.

Thornton, H. R., Delaney, J. A., Duthie, G. M., & Dascombe, B. J. (2019). Developing athlete monitoring systems in team sports: Data analysis and visualization. *International Journal of Sports Physiology and Performance, 14*(6), 698–705.

Ticllacuri, V., & Mio, R. (2021). Design and simulation of a soft robotic device for muscle rehabilitation and blood flow stimulation therapy. In *Proceedings of the 43rd Annual International Conference of the IEEE Engineering in Medicine & Biology Society, EMBC* (pp. 1588–1592). IEEE.

Tilly, R. (2015). An approach to derive user preferences from multiple-choice questions in online reviews. In J. Becker, J. vom Brocke & M. de Marco (Eds.), *Proceedings of the 23rd European Conference on Information Systems, ECIS*.

Toma, P., & Campobasso, F. (2023). Using data analytics to capture the strategic and financial decision-making of Europe's top football club. *Technological Forecasting and Social Change, 189*, 122340.

Tong, C., Roberts, R. C., Borgo, R., Walton, S. P., Laramee, R. S., Wegba, K., Lu, A., Wang, Y., Qu, H., Luo, Q., & Ma, X. (2018). Storytelling and visualization: An extended survey. *Information, 9*(3), 65.

Tufte, E. R. (1992). *The visual display of quantitative information*. Graphics Press.

Vaeyens, R., Güllich, A., Warr, C. R., & Philippaerts, R. (2009). Talent identification and promotion programmes of Olympic athletes. *Journal of Sports Sciences, 27*(13), 1367–1380.

Vorlícek, M., Stewart, T., Schipperijn, J., Burian, J., Rubín, L., Dygrýn, J., Mitás, J., & Duncan, S. (2021). Smart watch versus classic receivers: Static validity of three GPS devices in different types of built environments. *Sensors, 21*(21), 7232.

Walraven, M., Koning, R. H., Bijmolt, T. H. A., & Los, B. (2016). Benchmarking sports sponsorship performance: Efficiency assessment with data envelopment analysis. *Journal of Sport Management, 30*(4), 411–426.

Wang, C. (2023). Artificial neural network based image detection applied to foot massage machines. *Journal of Robotics, Networking, and Artificial Life, 10*(1), 39–42.

Wang, Z. (2024). Research on sports marketing and personalized recommendation algorithms for precise targeting and promotion strategies for target groups. *Applied Mathematics and Nonlinear Sciences, 9*(2).

Ware, C. (2004). *Information visualization: Perception for design*. Morgan Kaufmann.

Ware, C. (2008). *Visual thinking: For design*. Morgan Kaufmann Series in Interactive Technologies, Paperback.

Weisgarber, P., Valacich, J. S., Jenkins, J. L., Kim, D., & Kumar, M. (2024). Detecting social desirability bias with human-computer interaction: A mouse-tracking study. In T. X. Bui (Ed.), *Proceedings of the 57th Hawaii International Conference on System Sciences, HICSS* (pp. 4673–4682). ScholarSpace.

Whitehurst, B. (2021). BallCaller: A computer vision line caller for tennis. In K. Rahman & E. Gamess (Eds.), *ACM Southeast Conference, Virtual Event* (pp. 249–251). ACM.

Wouda, F. J., Giuberti, M., Bellusci, G., Maartens, E., Reenalda, J., van Beijnum, B., & Veltink, P. H. (2018). On the validity of different motion capture technologies for the analysis of running. In *Proceedings of the 7th IEEE International Conference on Biomedical Robotics and Biomechatronics, BioRob* (pp. 1175–1180). IEEE.

Yi, J. S., ah Kang, Y., Stasko, J. T., & Jacko, J. A. (2007). Toward a deeper understanding of the role of interaction in information visualization. *IEEE Transactions on Visualization and Computer Graphics, 13*(6), 1224–1231.

Yiapanas, G. (2025). The application of big data analytics in sports as a tool for personalized fan experience, operations efficiency, and fan engagement strategy. *Business and Management Theory and Practice, 2*(1), 3075.

Zacheo, G., Buzimkic, A., Roi, A. L., van Schie, A., Staudt, Y., & Burch, M. (2023). FitYou: A personalized dashboard for health data. In R. Malina, K. Zhang, W. Zeng & G. Wallner (Eds.), *Proceedings of the 16th International Symposium on Visual Information Communication and Interaction, VINCI* (pp. 4:1–4:5). ACM.

Zadeh, A. H., Taylor, D., Bertsos, M., Tillman, T., Nosoudi, N., & Bruce, S. (2021). Predicting sports injuries with wearable technology and data analysis. *Information Systems Frontiers, 23*(4), 1023–1037.

Zhao, Z., & Elmqvist, N. (2023). The stories we tell about data: Surveying data-driven storytelling using visualization. *IEEE Computer Graphics and Applications, 43*(4), 97–110.

Zhou, B., Koerger, H., Wirth, M., Zwick, C., Martindale, C., Cruz, H., Eskofier, B. M., & Lukowicz, P. (2016). Smart soccer shoe: Monitoring foot-ball interaction with shoe integrated textile pressure sensor matrix. In M. Beigl, P. Lukowicz, U. Blanke, K. Kunze & S. C. Lee (Eds.), *Proceedings of the ACM International Symposium on Wearable Computers, ISWC* (pp. 64–71). ACM.

Zhou, X., & Huang, F. (2018). Study of the sports precision marketing model under big data environment. In *Proceedings of the 2018 International Conference on Information Technology and Management Engineering (ICITME 2018)* (pp. 22–26).

Best Practices in Sports Data Management 5

The following case studies serve as a bridge between the data challenges (see Chap. 3) and the Sports Data Management Framework presented (see Chap. 4) and its concrete implementation in the real world of sports (see Fig. 5.1). This shows how sports organizations use data to address specific challenges, create real added value, and enable continuous learning. The first case study (Sect. 5.1) focuses on Sportian, a company that provides digital platform solutions for sports organizations to overcome challenges driven by data in sports and business. The case study on FC Bayern Munich (Sect. 5.2) deals with professionalization in both sports and business. As one of the leading clubs in the world, FC Bayern Munich can be described as an outstanding example of best practice when it comes to data-driven approaches. The case study on the International Olympic Committee (Sect. 5.3) highlights aspects of data management in a sports umbrella organization. It focuses on data-driven personalization of fan engagement in the context of the Olympic Games and beyond. The case study on the Premier League (Sect. 5.4) focuses on the aspect of commercialization. As one of the most commercially successful leagues in the world, the Premier League wants to further strengthen its position as the most lucrative league in the world with data-based strategies. The case studies conclude with UEFA (Sect. 5.5) and its long-term sustainability strategy, in which data play an important role.

The case studies are uniformly structured. First, the context in which the data-based strategies are pursued is briefly described. Then concrete examples are used to illustrate the tools and solutions that the respective player uses to address the challenges. Finally, an overall assessment is made with reference to the Sports Data Management Framework.

D. Schwizer, M. Burch, *Data Excellence in Sports*, Management for Professionals,
https://doi.org/10.1007/978-3-032-10993-4_5

Fig. 5.1 Five exemplary case studies illustrate how sports organizations solve their data challenges in different areas. Figure created by the authors

5.1 Digital Platform Solutions in Sports and Business

Digitalization is changing sports organizations on many different levels. This includes competitive situations, organizational problems, and the relationship with spectators and fans. Data management and digital platforms are becoming key success factors. Today, many sports organizations face the challenge of optimizing both athletic and commercial processes. External technology partners such as Sportian offer scalable and modular solutions for various data-driven challenges in sports. The first case study therefore does not deal with a sports organization itself but rather highlights how such an organization can obtain support from external partners to overcome challenges in data management. The example of Sportian shows how data analysis, fan engagement, and the protection of commercial rights can be integrated.

5.1.1 Sports Data Ecosystem

Sportian was founded in 2021 under the name LaLiga Tech as a subsidiary of the Spanish soccer league LaLiga. The company offers projects of digital transformation projects in sports, although its focus is not exclusively on soccer. It covers both sporting and commercial processes by creating its own technology platforms (LaLiga, 2021; SportBusiness, 2021).

The company aims to achieve this through its strategic approach (LaLiga, 2021). In its external communications, Sportian relies on a modular product portfolio with three different product lines (see Fig. 5.2): *Ignite Your Fan Experience*, *Empower Your Sports Teams*, and *Supercharge Your Organization* (Sportian, nd). This enables the company to maintain a modular ecosystem for its customers, which allows for a gradual deepening of cooperation.

In 2023, the company underwent a rebranding. It was renamed Sportian so that its offerings would be perceived more strongly as those of an independent technology provider. This is intended to appeal even more effectively to international customers (SportsPro, 2023).

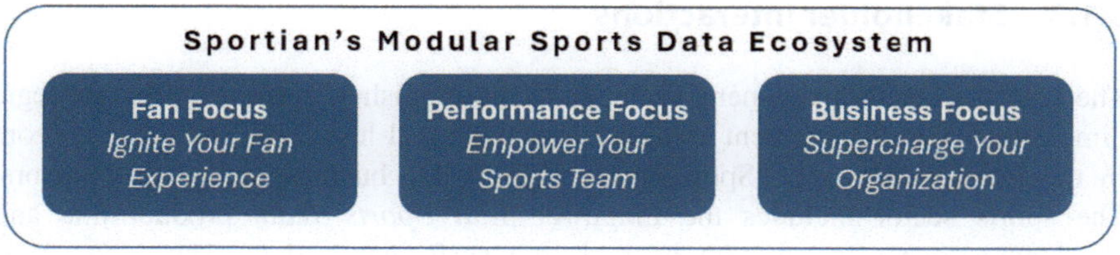

Fig. 5.2 Sportian's modular sports data ecosystem consisting of three main services. Figure created by the authors

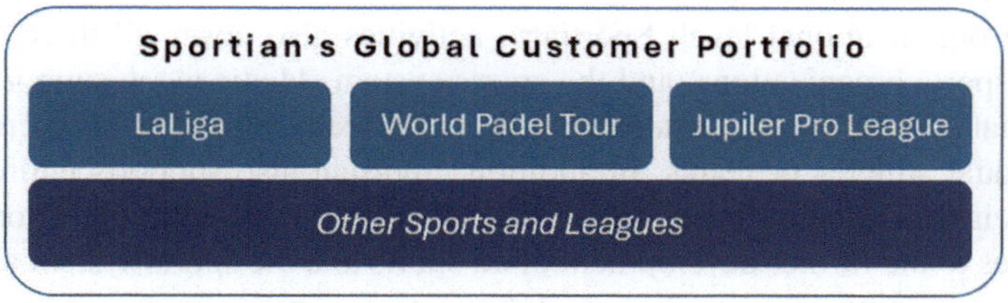

Fig. 5.3 Sportian's global customer portfolio includes LaLiga, World Padel Tour, and Belgian Jupiler Pro League. Figure created by the authors

5.1.2 Multilevel Solutions

Sportian offers its customers a wide range of services and solutions. In the area of performance analysis, *Mediacoach* provides detailed performance data in real time. This generates more than 3.5 million data points per game recorded (Reuters, 2025). The analysis uses 3D visualizations and tactical evaluations for various target groups such as analysts, media partners, and coaches.

Furthermore, Sportian also offers solutions for content protection and anti-piracy. The anti-piracy platform relies on a round-the-clock monitoring of the Internet and tracks down unauthorized streams. This prevents illegal broadcasts of sporting events, protecting the media rights of leagues and partners (SVG Europe, 2023).

Sportian is constantly expanding its network of partners. The company works closely with Microsoft, using Azure cloud services to store large amounts of data and process them in a secure environment. AI applications are also used to optimize content for fans and support data-driven decision-making in sports organizations (Microsoft, 2024, 2025a).

The solutions presented are not used exclusively in LaLiga but are available to a wide range of customers. Other sports and leagues are also among Sportian's customers. These include the World Padel Tour and the Belgian Jupiler Pro League (see Fig. 5.3). This demonstrates the diverse range of applications for Sportian's services (SportBusiness, 2021).

Sportian's business model is scalable. The company relies on a specialized team and proven technologies to offer global solutions for sports and business. Its modular architecture enables rapid adaptation to customer needs, taking into account the specific requirements of certain markets and target groups (SportBusiness, 2021).

5.1.3 Stakeholder Interactions

The Sports Data Management Framework distinguishes between three strategic dimensions: the management area, the organizational level, and the time horizon. In the management area, Sportian covers both the business and sports sectors. The sports sector includes the *Empower Your Sports Team* product line and the *Mediacoach* offering with its real-time performance data. The *Ignite Your Fan Experience* and *Supercharge Your Organization* products, on the other hand, illustrate Sportian's focus on commercial aspects as well. This also includes the company's anti-piracy solution.

At the organizational level, Sportian's activities also cover all three elements: athletes, sports organizations, and the sports system. *Mediacoach* supports performance analysis and tactical evaluation. This is directly related to the performance of individual athletes or teams. In addition, Sportian also supports entire leagues and associations in improving organizational processes. Implicitly, Sportian also contributes to the further development of all sports and the sports system as a whole by improving commercial processes, optimizing fan engagement, and striving for the further development of sports in general.

Finally, Sportian's solutions cover different time horizons. *Mediacoach*'s real-time data analysis is an example of how data management is applied during a single sporting event. The company also offers solutions that can be used throughout the season or even beyond.

Within the scope of sports data analytics components, numerous elements of the framework are covered by the activities described. An example of efficient data recording is the *Mediacoach* application, which captures several million data points per game. The company's analysis applications cover various types of data, ranging from quantitative performance data to 3D visualizations. Algorithmic processing also plays an important role. AI applications are used to optimize content or enable data-based decisions. Finally, interactive visualizations ensure that findings are presented in a way that is tailored to the target audience.

5.2 Professionalization Through Data-Driven Strategies

Leading international soccer clubs represent strong brands in sport with a global fan base. Data management and digitalization have a particularly high leverage effect in such sports organizations. FC Bayern Munich is already well advanced in this area. The club has long been integrating state-of-the-art technologies into scouting and training, knows a lot about its fans thanks to data, and also relies on a strong database for internal processes such as ticketing and HR procedures. As a result of strong partnerships with renowned technology companies such as SAP, the club has access to comprehensive platform solutions. The example of FC Bayern Munich shows how data contribute to efficient and targeted club management in many different areas and can also be used strategically in many ways.

5.2.1 Need for Professionalization

FC Bayern Munich is a leading global club with an extremely large fan base and an internationally renowned brand. Data-driven decisions therefore play an important role and have a significant leverage effect (SAP, 2025). The club has a long-standing strategic technology partnership with SAP in various areas of sports and business processes (SAP, 2023, 2024). The club not only strives to improve its performance on the pitch but also has a strong focus on expanding monetization in the economic sphere, such as increasing fan engagement, merchandising, and ticketing (Emarsys, 2025). Bayern Munich not only maintains international activities but also has offices and active branding in markets such as Asia and the United States, increasing the requirements for scalable and flawless data management (SAP, 2024). In 2024, the club underwent a restructuring and new appointments in the performance area to link sports and data functions even more effectively (FC Bayern Munich, 2024b). This shows that the club's data management, which is already highly professionalized, needs to be continuously reviewed and, in some cases, adapted. This is not least because the club collects millions of fan contacts and faces the constant challenge of consolidating data silos and generally cleaning up data (Emarsys, 2025). In addition, the club is investing in scouting and the professionalization of data support for talent processes (FCB Inside, 2025b). When recruiting new employees in the economic sector, the club also relies on modern cloud-based HR systems from SAP, which also use AI technologies (FC Bayern Munich, 2024a).

5.2.2 Management Approaches

FC Bayern Munich uses a variety of different digital tools to approach its challenges (see Fig. 5.4). With *SAP Sports One*, FC Bayern Munich is relying on a unified platform for training planning, game and player data, and scouting workflows, allowing real-time data analysis on match days (SAP, 2023). For example, the company is already using AI enhancements in SAP for scouting, integrating automatic summaries, and prioritizing scouting reports and has also participated in the development of prototypes (SAP, 2024, 2025). In addition, FC Bayern Munich is pushing forward with the further development of CRM for ticketing and fan data consolidation. This involves, in particular, the centralization of ticketing, the strengthening of e-commerce, and the improvement of individual fan journeys (Emarsys, 2025). FC Bayern Munich is not only a club with global appeal but also employs many people in various locations. That is why the club relies on cloud-based HR data management via *SAP SuccessFactors* for recruiting, onboarding, and employee analytics (FC Bayern Munich, 2024a). However, the club does not rely solely on internal scouting but also depends on external analytics providers (e.g., SciSports) to supplement its internal data (SciSports, 2019). The club uses match tracking and video feeds for real-time monitoring in training management and for tactical decisions during a game (SAP, 2023). Data-based processes are also used

Fig. 5.4 FC Bayern Munich uses different tools to address issues in sports, for the fans, and in business. Figure created by the authors

Fig. 5.5 FC Bayern Munich influences the sports systems and its actors on different levels. Figure created by the authors

in stadium management. Data from different cash register systems are consolidated and converted to standardized formats to further improve service quality and overall experience of fans (Emarsys, 2025). It is also interesting to note that FC Bayern Munich is now using a hybrid strategy in its scouting activities. The club relies on a combination of data-driven preselection and live observation on site (FCB Inside, 2025a).

5.2.3 Collaboration

FC Bayern Munich is a prime example of how data management can be used in both the sporting and economic spheres. With the applications it uses, Bayern Munich operates at both the organizational level of individual athletes and the entire sports organization, and with its high degree of professionalism, it also sets standards for the entire league, even if other clubs benefit from this only indirectly at most (see Fig. 5.5). However, the club's highly professional data management also has an influence on developments in the sports system. In this case, this mainly concerns not only the Bundesliga but also the development of soccer on a global level. Nevertheless, it should be noted that the gap between clubs such as FC Bayern Munich and smaller, less financially powerful sports organizations tends to widen. The applications described, which are used on match days, focus on a single event. Approaches such as the HR platform or scouting, on the other hand, represent long-term ongoing processes that are not tied to a specific point in time. In terms of the time horizon, all periods are covered. For tracking and video recording, Bayern Munich uses a central data platform for preprocessing to later create dashboards for application target groups in the data processing workflow. Numerous stages of the data cycle are also covered in between. In the data applications mentioned, the HR team, coaches, scouts, and performance teams are particularly relevant as users in the loop. They work with the generated outputs, and players, employees, or fans ideally benefit from the results but are not directly involved in the data processes. User evaluation also plays an important role. It forms the basis for iterative improvements because tools are developed more in response to user feedback. Cloud HR, event ticketing, and global data integration are key scalability issues. However, it is also important to maintain data quality and overcome governance challenges. One thing that really stands out at Bayern Munich is that they use both internally generated data and third-party tools, such as for scouting. This creates an integrated data ecosystem with many specific benefits from individual applications. Data governance and data protection are of great importance here. For example, the consolidation of POS systems and CRM requires targeted policies and clean rights management to maintain high quality and comply with the specified data protection guidelines.

5.3 Personalized Fan Engagement Through Data

As the global umbrella organization for sport, the International Olympic Committee (IOC) has a unique appeal. However, the sports umbrella organization faces the challenge that the attention of fans and spectators is focused on a few major events, primarily the Summer and Winter Olympic Games. It therefore makes sense that the IOC is seeking to use a solid database to increase fan interaction between the Games to ensure lasting loyalty to the Olympic movement. Digital transformation is being used to reduce mass communication and instead create more personalized fan experiences. Data platforms and artificial intelligence are designed to help reach a young, digitally savvy target group in particular. With partners such as Alibaba and Deloitte, the IOC also brings external technology and data expertise to the organization. It is clear that even, or perhaps especially, traditional organizations such as the IOC need data-driven approaches to remain attractive and economically successful in the long term.

5.3.1 Personalized Experience

The IOC is striving for a complete digital transformation. The IOC faces the challenge of receiving particularly high attention when the Olympic Games are taking place. However, these are only held every 4 years. The IOC therefore has the vision of not only focusing on the main event that takes place every 2 (or 4) years for fans but also transforming the time between the Olympic Games into a data-driven experience throughout the year. The aim is to maintain the attention of the Olympic movement between two major events. The increasingly fragmented media landscape makes this a real challenge. The IOC has realized that it is no longer enough to simply broadcast sporting competitions. In some cases, this is already

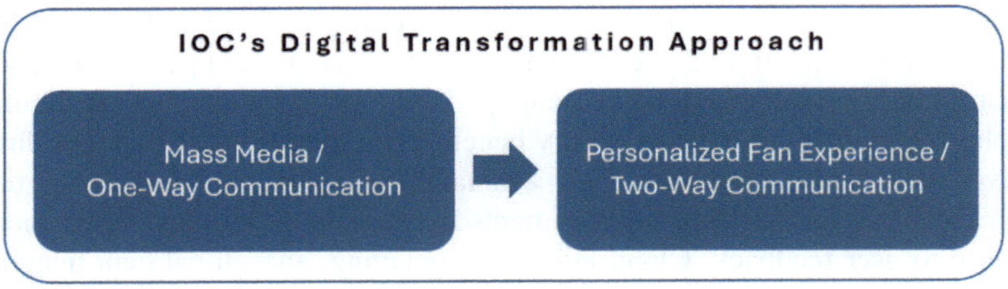

Fig. 5.6 The IOC is using data to create personalized fan experiences. Figure created by the authors

insufficient to reach young target groups in particular. This target group is especially digitally savvy and expects interactive and personalized content. The transformation is intended to enable these young fans to interact continuously with content related to the Olympic movement and Olympic athletes. This is notably important because young target groups represent future consumers of the Olympic Games. This project is therefore of great significance for the entire Olympic movement (Doerer, 2024).

With this approach, the IOC aims to move away from mass media communication and toward individualization (see Fig. 5.6). Unidirectional communication is becoming increasingly obsolete. Instead of distributing uniform content to a broad target group, the focus is now on enabling modern and individual fan journeys. Each fan is a unique individual whose behavior and interests determine what content and services are displayed on the platforms. However, this requires having data about these fans and knowing their preferences. Preferences can relate to various elements, such as athletes, countries, or sports. This type of communication is about transforming passive viewers into active members of a global community who are interested in this type of content even outside of the Olympic Games (IOC, 2024a).

To manage this complex digital transformation, the IOC relies on strategic partnerships. Leading technology companies such as Alibaba Cloud and Deloitte are playing a central role in this. Alibaba provides the technological cloud infrastructure for the IOC, which is essential to process such large amounts of data. The company also supplies innovative AI technologies to keep up with the latest developments. Deloitte, on the other hand, acts as a strategic advisor and supports the IOC with implementation. The company was instrumental in the design and development of the central fan data platform. Alibaba and Deloitte are therefore important partners for the IOC in further developing the digital transformation and individualization of fan engagement at a high level and within a reasonable time frame (IOC, 2024b, 2025a).

5.3.2 Digital Solution Tools

The real heart of digital transformation is the central fan data platform, which was developed in collaboration with Deloitte. All data from the IOC's digital channels

Fig. 5.7 The IOC uses several elements to boost fan engagement. Figure created by the authors

are consolidated on the platform. This includes data from the official website, social media channels, the mobile app, and the e-commerce platform. Consolidating all this data enables the creation of comprehensive fan profiles. However, these fan profiles are not based solely on demographic data and also include behavioral data. These data show which content fans have interacted with, which content they have viewed, which sports and athletes they prefer, and which items they have purchased in the past. This enables a personalized approach to fans, which is available in 12 languages (IOC, 2025b).

The fan data platform is the basis for hyper-personalization of content (see Fig. 5.7). It enables personalized and dynamic feeds on the Olympic app and other digital IOC platforms. For example, if a fan has a keen interest in athletics and the British team, their feed will automatically display more news, videos, and live results based on these interests. This type of hyper-personalization ensures that fans see the content that is most relevant to them. The IOC hopes that this will lead to higher interaction rates and longer dwell times on platforms, as well as a greater emotional attachment to the Olympic Games as a brand. Initial experiences at the 2024 Olympic Games in Paris have shown that the approach works and that the relevant figures have increased (Doerer, 2024).

AI applications also play an increasingly important role in targeted personalization, individualization, and segmentation. The IOC's partnership with Alibaba Cloud provides access to innovative AI tools. These AI tools enable the creation of novel and interactive experiences. For example, there is an AI-supported media search and a function to create automated highlights. This not only generates clips from the current Olympic Games but also captures memorable moments from the past and makes them available to fans via digital channels. AI-based tools were also used to colorize and reprocess historical footage. At the Olympic Games in Paris, there was also an activation on site that made the merchandising experience even more interesting for fans (Alibaba, 2024).

Therefore, data from fan engagement are used exclusively not only to optimize content for fans but also to improve commercial processes. Fans can purchase official Olympic Games merchandise on e-commerce platforms such as *AliExpress*. Data from these purchasing processes are also fed into the fan data platform. This enables the IOC and its partners to target fans and customers even more specifically, for example, by displaying personalized product recommendations. Various marketing campaigns can also be targeted based on these data. The IOC hopes that this will lead to higher sales and greater overall economic value creation. In summary, data-driven monetization is a central element of the IOC and the Olympic movement's strategy to strengthen their brand and become even more relevant to fans. This also reduces the dependence on traditional sources of income, such as media rights and sponsorship (IOC, 2024).

5.3.3 Actors in Fan Engagement

In the IOC case study, content from the world of sports is used for commercial purposes. Therefore, the focus is on the economic aspect, with sport and the emotions associated with it. Improving the fan experience and targeting fans according to their interests create new monetization potential, for example, in merchandising or marketing. The central fan data platform serves as a link between commerce and sport. The data platform links the needs of fans with the commercial goals of the IOC.

At the organizational level, the focus here is on sports organizations. It should be noted that the IOC is a global umbrella organization for sports. However, individual athletes also play a role. By personalizing the content for fans, athletes gain an even better and larger platform and thus attention for their achievements. The sports system as a whole also benefits from the IOC's activities and strategies. Together with its technology partners, the IOC makes sports and its emotions even more accessible and, with its data-driven solutions, also creates benefits for the National Olympic Committees and their partners.

In terms of time frame, the IOC addresses the issue of a single major event every 4 years when considering the Summer and Winter Olympic Games. The fan data platform is designed to generate personalized content based on real-time data during the event, but it also aims to extend the event beyond the actual competition times (see Fig. 5.8). Fans should be inspired by individual Olympic Games to support the Olympic movement, thus opening up new commercial potential for the IOC. The aim is to continuously engage the fans and create a lasting community. In addition, data can also be used to design future marketing strategies and digital products.

Algorithmic processing also plays an important role. The proprietary algorithms usually come from partners such as Deloitte or Alibaba Cloud. These algorithms

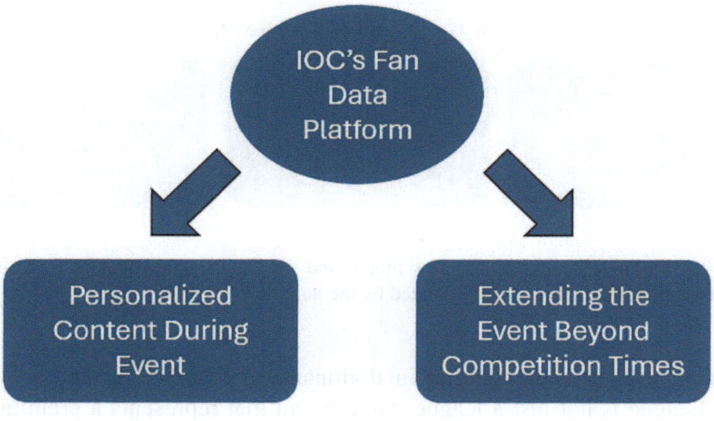

Fig. 5.8 IOC's fan data platform creates personalized content and extends the event beyond the Olympic Games. Figure created by the authors

process the data to segment fan groups, identify specific behavior patterns, and compile individually tailored recommendations for content or products.

Finally, interactive visualization elements also play a role. The results of the data analyses are distributed in real time via the official Olympic app or other digital channels of the IOC and its partners to provide fans with a personalized, interactive, and visually appealing experience.

5.4 Data-Driven Commercialization on a Global Scale

The English Premier League is not only a leading global league in all sports but also a brand in its own right with considerable international reach. The league recognized the potential of digital transformation to maintain and expand its commercial dominance at an early stage. Among other things, the league aims to engage and interact with fans not only on match days but also throughout the year and between games via its digital channels. The Premier League works with external providers to commercialize its data. This ensures maximum monetization for betting providers, media, and analysts. The Premier League also relies on close technology partnerships with companies such as Microsoft as a partner for AI and cloud solutions. This creates innovative platform solutions with enormous economic potential.

5.4.1 Commercialization Through Data

The Premier League is one of the most commercially successful leagues in the world, even beyond soccer. It recognized early on that digital transformation would

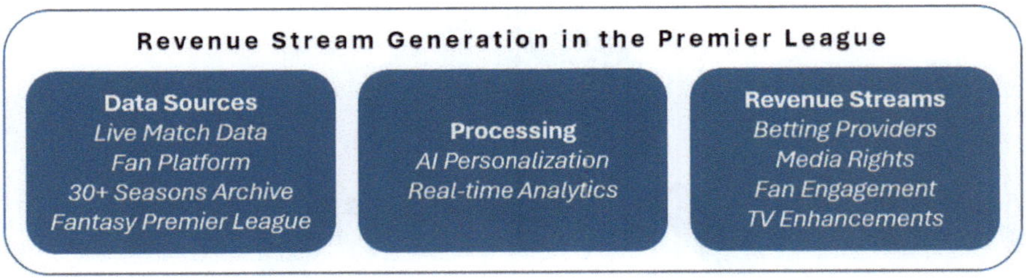

Fig. 5.9 The Premier League transforms match and fan data into diversified revenue streams through strategic partnerships. Figure created by the authors

help cement its position of commercial dominance and further promote growth. The Premier League is not just a league, but a brand that represents a premium sports product. The league sees digital transformation as an opportunity to better reach its global fan base and offer personalized fan experiences throughout the year (see Fig. 5.9). This strategy aims to increase fan loyalty and reach new target groups. These target groups should not only engage with the league and its teams on match days but also remain connected through digital channels between match days or even seasons. The launch of a new app and the collaboration with Microsoft are intended to bring the Premier League a big step forward in this regard (Premier League, 2025).

In addition, the Premier League has recognized that the match data is not only relevant to the interaction with fans but also represents an independent commercial asset. Many companies associated with the Premier League, particularly betting providers, have been able to increase their revenues in recent years and expand their business activities. Premier League clubs are becoming increasingly aware of the value of their data and in some cases demand a new revenue distribution (Sim, 2024).

To benefit even more from digital transformation and the data generated in the future, the Premier League is cooperating with renowned technology partners such as Genius Sports and Microsoft. Microsoft is the official cloud and AI partner, providing the infrastructure for new digital products and services. Genius Sports acts as the official data partner, responsible for collecting and distributing live game data to media outlets and betting providers. These partnerships are of paramount importance to the Premier League's commercially oriented data strategy. In particular, they are intended to strengthen the following areas: fan engagement, cloud transformation, organizational productivity, and match insights and analysis (Microsoft, 2025b).

5.4.2 Marketing and Monetization

To make the most of the digital transformation commercially, the Premier League focuses on a central fan platform with hyper-personalization. The new mobile app and the website are the heart of this fan platform. The primary goal is to create personalized experiences. Thanks to collaboration with Microsoft and AI technology ("Premier League Companion"), data from more than 30 seasons, 300,000 articles, and 9000 videos are used to compile relevant content. Fans benefit from live updates, analyses, and stories that are continuously tailored to their interests, clubs, and players (SportsPro, 2025).

The Premier League is working with Genius Sports to monetize live data and betting information. The company is responsible not only for collecting but also for distributing real-time match data, serving a global network of betting providers. This data is important for them so that they can offer live betting during matches. It also represents an important source of revenue for the Premier League. Data are also needed for the use of semi-automated offside technology (Hughes, 2025).

In addition, the Premier League also offers its fans the opportunity to participate in the Fantasy Premier League (FPL). This format of games is extremely popular and is now enhanced by AI tools. Fans can use the AI Assistant Manager to obtain data-driven decision-making support to build their fantasy teams (Schlosser, 2025).

Finally, the Premier League also uses the data to enhance the experience for home television viewers. This is achieved, among other things, through collaborations with technology providers that offer real-time statistics and integrate data overlays into live broadcasts. An example of this is the Data Zone, which provides fans with insight into game statistics, player performance, and tactical elements (NBC Sports, 2023).

5.4.3 Sports, Media, and Business

In this case study, the focus is primarily on the management level and less directly on the sport itself due to commercialization. However, the sport also benefits from this because, for example, even more accurate data are made available. In addition, overall revenues are increased, which should have a positive effect on the further development and quality of the league. The Premier League uses its data rights to monetize and personalize content. It is a good example of how a league can tap into and expand data-based revenue streams while maximizing value creation for its partners.

In terms of organizational level, the Premier League operates primarily at the level of the sports organization, that is, the league itself. However, it also influences the sports data ecosystem of individual clubs within the league. Therefore, it could be argued that the Premier League also influences the sports system, at least that of the clubs and partners. Although data help clubs strengthen their bond with fans and provide them with unique experiences, the league retains control over the central data strategy and its commercialization.

The Premier League is aware that its content and entertainment elements should not be limited to game days or seasons, but that relevant content should be made available on an ongoing basis. However, the event-based approach is still an important component. This applies in particular to visualizations for TV viewers and data provision for betting providers. Data are also collected throughout the season to observe trends and developments in fan behavior. Thus, the Premier League has a comprehensive view: from individual match days throughout the season and beyond.

With regard to sports data analytics, the Premier League illustrates the entire analytics data pipeline in a commercial context. Some aspects are particularly noteworthy. Data recording is of essential importance. During games, the technology partner Genius Sports collects a lot of data in real time. In addition, user data are collected from the league's digital platforms (website, app, and Fantasy Premier League). Various types of data are used, including live statistics, tracking data, clickstream data, user preferences, and demographic information. For algorithmic processing, the Premier League and its partners rely on artificial intelligence and machine learning algorithms. Those process the data in such a way that patterns can be recognized. In addition, this also ensures personalized content and recommendations for fans. Finally, interactive visualizations ensure that the results of the data analyses are made available in an understandable form through the official platforms and on TV broadcasts. This can take various forms, such as dashboards, overlays, or interactive tools, and allows for an intuitive and appealing presentation.

5.5 Enhancing Sustainability Through Data

As the continent's leading football organization, UEFA bears a great deal of responsibility for the development of sport in the narrower sense and the football ecosystem in the broader sense. Sustainability at various levels is a key challenge that all sports organizations must address today. Digital and data-based approaches are increasingly ensuring the transparency and verifiability of existing or lacking progress. UEFA is right not to focus only on its own structures and processes. It also involves national associations, clubs, fans, and partners. This ensures a systemic effect. An example of this is EURO 2024, where data were used to manage environmental and social impacts. In its sustainability efforts, UEFA relies on close cooperation with various stakeholders and technology partners to standardize and professionalize data collection and processing. The example of UEFA demonstrates an approach by which sports organizations can assume social responsibility through data-driven sustainability strategies, thus contributing to their own credibility and positioning themselves for the future.

5.5.1 Sustainability Challenges

UEFA is aware that sustainability is an issue that goes beyond sport and finance and will shape the long-term future of the association and its members. That is why UEFA is striving for a strategic realignment toward applicable ESG standards in terms of sustainability. ESG refers to the three areas of environmental, social, and governance in which sustainability is to be promoted and ensured. In its initiatives,

Fig. 5.10 UEFA's ESG-driven sustainability strategy integrates data-based approaches with comprehensive stakeholder cooperation to achieve measurable environmental, social, and governance improvements across European football. Figure created by the authors

UEFA focuses not only on its own business activities but also on the entire European football ecosystem. It sets out its vision in various documents, such as the *UEFA Football Sustainability Strategy 2030*. In it, it describes how football can be used to drive positive change through sustainability and meet the growing expectations of society, politics, fans, and partners (UEFA, 2025).

The example of UEFA shows that sustainability does not have to be merely a PR strategy, but that a data-based approach enables real and verifiable improvements (see Fig. 5.10). The approach goes beyond simply announcing intentions and sets measurable goals. The achievement of these goals can be reviewed at regular intervals. An example of this is EURO 2024, where UEFA relied on a comprehensive database to assess both the environmental and social footprint of the tournament (Ewing, 2024).

Cooperation with various stakeholders is extremely important in data-based sustainability projects. UEFA has recognized that it cannot achieve its sustainability goals alone. That is why the association's sustainability strategy focuses on close cooperation with various relevant players. These include national associations, clubs, fans, venues, and technology partners. UEFA requires national associations, in particular, to employ sustainability officers within their own structures to develop strategies and coordinate data work in this area. This ensures that data from the entire football ecosystem are incorporated into the sustainability strategy (UEFA, 2024).

5.5.2 Sustainability Strategies

With the UEFA Carbon Footprint Calculator (see Fig. 5.11), UEFA has created a central tool for data-based traceability of measures to increase environmental sustainability. This is an online tool that enables football organizations at various levels to record their CO_2 emissions in a uniform way and make them transparent. Various areas such as mobility, facilities, logistics, and purchased goods and services are taken into account. This enables consistent data collection that is consistent with global standards (UEFA, nd).

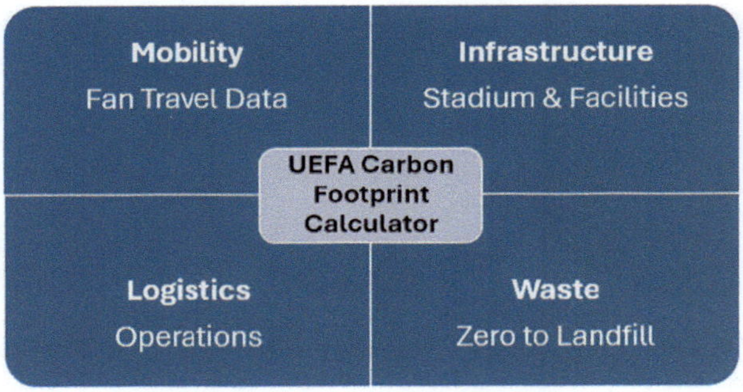

Fig. 5.11 UEFA's comprehensive data-driven sustainability framework leverages the Carbon Footprint Calculator as a central tool to systematically measure, monitor, and reduce environmental impact across mobility, infrastructure, logistics, and waste management while ensuring transparency through independent verification and ESG reporting. Figure created by the authors

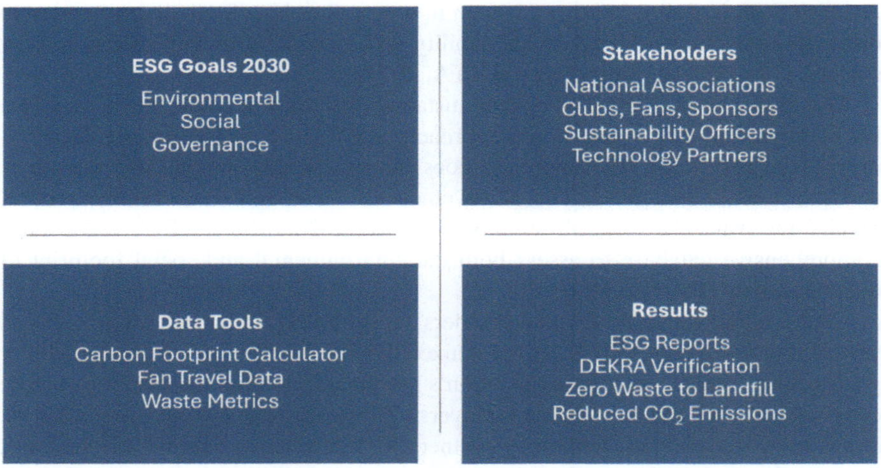

Fig. 5.12 UEFA's data-driven sustainability framework combines ESG goals with stakeholder collaboration and systematic monitoring for measurable environmental and social impact. Figure created by the authors

In addition, UEFA places a specific focus on sustainable mobility. It collects data on fan travel to reduce the carbon footprint of its events. For example, data on fan travel behavior were collected during EURO 2024. Through a partnership with Deutsche Bahn, fans were encouraged to travel by public transport. An analysis of ticketholder data showed that this resulted in demonstrable success in reducing greenhouse gases (UEFA, 2024b).

UEFA also relies on data-based strategies in the areas of infrastructure and waste management (see Fig. 5.12). For example, UEFA uses data to improve the sustainability of training facilities and stadiums. In its *Sustainable Infrastructure Guidelines*, the association provides advice and recommendations for the construction and operation of infrastructure and uses best practices to highlight areas where particularly significant positive effects on sustainability can be achieved. As part of EURO 2024, data on the amount of waste generated at the venues were explicitly collected to achieve the goal of "zero percent waste to landfill." This means that waste does not end up in a landfill or waste disposal site but is reused, recycled, converted to energy, or processed otherwise (UEFA, 2024a).

Data-driven sustainability strategies are also subject to critical scrutiny. This is why transparent reporting and external monitoring are so important. UEFA regularly publishes ESG reports to highlight progress and disclose measurement data. An example of such a report is the *UEFA EURO 2024 ESG Report*. In addition, independent bodies such as DEKRA check whether data collection is being carried out adequately. This is intended to contribute to credibility and transparency (UEFA, 2024c).

5.5.3 Stakeholder Roles

The case study on UEFA's sustainability efforts focuses on the interface between sport (sporting events) and economic aspects. In this case, UEFA is strengthening its long-term raison d'être through measurable, data-based sustainability measures by fulfilling its social responsibility beyond sports. The sustainability data lead to more environmentally friendly practices or modern mobility solutions being used during sporting events or in planning and use of infrastructure. Compliance with sustainability standards and verification through concrete data create a solid foundation for UEFA to place its business activities on a long-term footing together with its partners and sponsors (see Fig. 5.13). The measures also strengthen the brand.

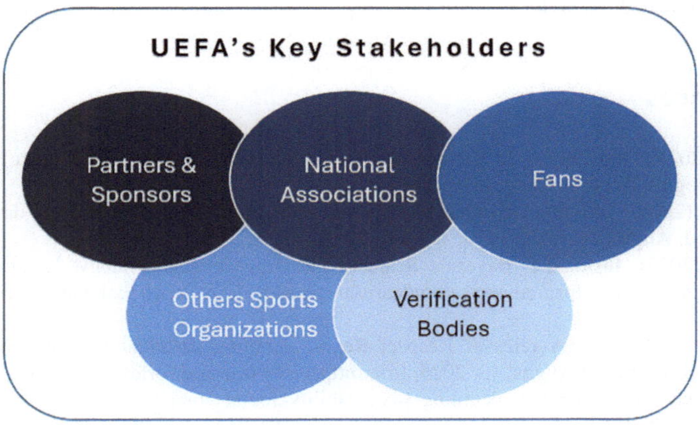

Fig. 5.13 UEFA's comprehensive sustainability analytics pipeline transforms multisource data collection through standardized processing into actionable insights, engaging key stakeholders including partners and sponsors, national associations, fans, other sports organizations, and verification bodies. Figure created by the authors

UEFA's data-based sustainability measures primarily affect individual sports organizations, UEFA itself as an association and umbrella organization, and the entire European football ecosystem as part of the global sports system. Due to its size and importance, UEFA's data-based approach to sustainability also influences other associations and sports organizations and provides valuable experience. Individuals also play a role in the UEFA sustainability strategy. However, in this case, the focus is not primarily on individual players but on the much larger number of fans whose mobility behavior can make a significant contribution to achieving sustainability goals.

In terms of time frame, UEFA is focused on both specific individual events such as EURO 2024 and the long-term orientation of its sustainability strategy in the coming years. UEFA collects data in real time during an event, thus laying the foundation for the measurability of individual actions. On this basis, the time between events is used to make future tournaments even more sustainable. The long-term orientation is also evident in the association's strategic documents that contain plans and visions until 2030.

Several components from the Sports Data Analytics section are also visible in the data analytics pipeline. Data recording is carried out using specialized instruments such as the Carbon Footprint Calculator, fan surveys (e.g., on travel behavior), and reports from individual national associations and their sustainability officers. UEFA and its partners process various types of data. These range from quantitative metrics (CO_2 emissions, waste volumes) to qualitative behavioral data (fan mobility behavior) and governance metrics such as compliance with guidelines. UEFA uses standardized methods for algorithmic processing to calculate the carbon footprint and classify performance. Finally, results are visually presented in reports, graphics, and high-profile campaigns using modern interactive visualization techniques to make progress transparent and raise awareness of the importance of the sustainability strategy.

References

Alibaba. (2024). Alibaba Cloud Elevates Paris 2024's Games Viewing Experience with Cloud Technologies. Accessed August 11, 2025.

Doerer, K. (2024). To boost Olympics engagement, the IOC turned to a customer data platform. Accessed: August 11, 2025.

Emarsys. (2025). Inside FC Bayern's Scalable Fan Engagement Strategy. Retrieved August 11, 2025, from https://emarsys.com/learn/blog/inside-fc-bayerns-scalable-fan-engagement-strategy/

Ewing, H. (2024). UEFA releases Respect Report detailing sustainability and social impact initiatives. Retrieved August 13, 2025, from https://www.insideworldfootball.com/2024/12/20/uefa-releases-respect-report-detailing-sustainability-social-impact-initiatives/

FC Bayern Munich. (2024a). FC Bayern elevates their HR strategy with SAP Success Factors and AI-enabled recruiting. Retrieved August 11, 2025, from https://fcbayern.com/en/news/2024/05/fc-bayern-elevates-their-hr-strategy-with-sap-successfactors-and-ai-enabled-recruiting

FC Bayern Munich. (2024b). Realignment of sport board division. Retrieved August 11, 2025, from https://fcbayern.com/en/news/2024/06/personnel-realignment-of-sport-board-division

FCB Inside. (2025a). Live-Scouting statt Datenanalyse: Bayern ändert Scouting-Strategie. Retrieved August 11, 2025, from https://fcbinside.de/2025/04/19/live-scouting-statt-datenanalyse-bayern-aendert-scouting-strategie/

FCB Inside. (2025b). Schattenteams und Spieler-Rankings: Bayerns Scouting-Revolution. Retrieved August 11, 2025, from https://fcbinside.de/2025/05/21/schattenteams-und-spieler-rankings-das-steckt-hinter-bayerns-scouting-revolution/

Hughes, M. (2025). Exclusive: Premier League data partner Genius expands portfolio. Accessed August 12, 2025.

IOC. (2024). Alibaba opens interactive "Wonder Avenue" AI experience to engage fans during Paris 2024. Retrieved August 11 2025, from https://www.olympics.com/ioc/news/alibaba-opens-interactive-wonder-avenue-ai-experience-to-engage-fans-during-paris-2024

IOC. (2024a). How the IOC and Deloitte are using data and technology to help enhance fan experiences. Retrieved August 11 2025, from https://www.olympics.com/ioc/news/how-the-ioc-and-deloitte-are-using-data-and-technology-to-help-enhance-fan-experiences

IOC. (2024b). IOC and Deloitte announce expansion of Worldwide Olympic Partnership. Retrieved August 11 2025, from https://www.olympics.com/ioc/news/ioc-and-deloitte-announce-expansion-of-worldwide-olympic-partnership

IOC. (2025a). Alibaba Cloud to provide core digital services for Dakar 2026. Retrieved August 11 2025, from https://www.olympics.com/ioc/news/alibaba-cloud-to-provide-core-digital-services-for-dakar-2026

IOC. (2025b). How the IOC and Deloitte are using data and technology to help enhance fan experiences. Retrieved August 11 2025, from https://www.olympics.com/ioc/news/how-the-ioc-and-deloitte-are-using-data-and-technology-to-help-enhance-fan-experiences

LaLiga. (2021). LaLiga Tech introduces its suite of technology solutions, designed for the digital era of sports and entertainment. Retrieved August 8, 2025, from https://www.laliga.com/en-GB/news/laliga-tech-introduces-its-suite-of-technology-solutions-designed-for-the-digital-era-of-sports-and-entertainment

Microsoft. (2024). LaLiga delivers seamless fan experience and AI insights with Azure Arc. Accessed: August 8, 2025.

Microsoft. (2025a). How Microsoft is transforming sports with cutting-edge technology. Accessed: August 8, 2025.

Microsoft. (2025b). Premier League and Microsoft announce five-year strategic partnership to personalize the fan experience with AI for 1.8 billion people. Accessed August 12, 2025.

NBC Sports. (2023). Premier League Data Zone enhanced viewing experience debuts exclusively on Peacock for this Sunday's Arsenal-Liverpool match. Accessed August 12, 2025.

Premier League. (2025). Premier League launches fan-facing platforms as part of digital transformation. Retrieved August 12, 2025, from https://www.premierleague.com/en/news/4337361/premier-league-launches-new-fan-facing-platforms-as-part-of-digital-transformation

Reuters. (2025). LaLiga leads AI evolution with global outreach. Retrieved August 8, 2025, from https://www.reuters.com/sports/soccer/laliga-leads-ai-evolution-with-global-outreach-2025-04-02/

SAP. (2023). FC Bayern: Optimizing fan engagement, scouting decisions, and match-day operations. Retrieved August 11, 2025, from https://www.sap.com/documents/2023/11/f4e29848-9b7e-0010-bca6-c68f7e60039b.html

SAP. (2024). FC Bayern Scores Big with SAP. Retrieved August 11, 2025, from https://news.sap.com/2024/09/fc-bayern-scores-big-with-sap/

SAP. (2025). SAP and FC Bayern Success Story. Retrieved August 11, 2025, from https://www.sap.com/about/customer-stories/fcbayern.html

Schlosser, K. (2025). Microsoft teaming with Premier League to enhance soccer fans' digital experience using AI. Retrieved August 12, 2025, from https://www.geekwire.com/2025/microsoft-teaming-with-premier-league-to-enhance-soccer-fans-digital-experience-using-ai/

SciSports. (2019). FC Bayern Munich: Using data to rebuild the Rekordmeister. Retrieved August 11, 2025, from https://www.scisports.com/fc-bayern-munich-a-data-driven-approach-to-rebuild-the-rekordmeister/

Sim, J. (2024). Premier League clubs 'lobbying' for bigger share of data deal. Retrieved August 12, 2025, from https://www.sportspro.com/news/premier-league-efl-data-rights-revenue-apt-vote-aston-villa-offside-delay-november-2024/

SportBusiness. (2021). LaLiga Tech's digital transformation opportunity. Retrieved August 8, 2025, from https://www.sportbusiness.com/2021/09/laliga-techs-digital-transformation-opportunity/

Sportian. (n.d.). Sportian: Empowering sports & entertainment. Retrieved August 8, 2025, from https://www.sportian.com/

SportsPro. (2023). LaLiga Tech rebrands as Sportian to accelerate sports tech mission. Retrieved August 8, 2025, from https://www.sportspro.com/news/laliga-tech-globant-sportian-rebrand/

SportsPro. (2025). How the Premier League, Microsoft and AI will change the way fans consume English soccer. Retrieved August 12, 2025, from https://www.sportspro.com/broadcast-ott/media-rights/premier-league-microsoft-technology-sponsor-app-ai-fpl-dtc-radio/

SVG Europe. (2023). Inside LaLiga: Digital transformation triggers new era with global outlook. Retrieved August 8, 2025, from https://www.svgeurope.org/blog/headlines/inside-laliga-digital-transformation-triggers-new-era-with-global-outlook/

UEFA. (2024). How UEFA social and environmental sustainability requirements are catalysing change across Europe. Accessed August 13, 2025.

UEFA. (2024a). Sustainable Infrastructure Guidelines. Accessed August 13, 2025.

UEFA. (2024b). UEFA EURO 2024 champions sustainability and social responsibility. Accessed August 13, 2025.

UEFA. (2024c). UEFA EURO 2024 Environmental, Social and Governance (ESG) Report. Accessed August 13, 2025.

UEFA. (2025). UEFA Women's EURO 2025: Sustainability in action. Accessed August 13, 2025.

UEFA. (n.d.). Climate advocacy. Retrieved August 25, 2025, from https://www.uefa.com/sustainability/environment/climate-advocacy/

Conclusion

6

In this chapter, we discuss some challenges, limitations, and future directions. Challenges (Sect. 6.1) can occur in various places, including technical, organizational, and ethical aspects. They can lead to limitations that could hinder us in creating solutions to the analytics tasks at hand (Sect. 6.2) or even make it impossible to find a good solution. Although we do not really know how the field will develop in the future, we can discuss some possible upcoming directions (Sect. 6.3), for example, considering novel concepts from artificial intelligence or even display technologies. In addition, ethical concerns can play a crucial role in the future, especially for data access and publication and dissemination of the analysis results.

6.1 Challenges

This section addresses the challenges sports organizations face in data management and data analysis (see Fig. 6.1). The section begins with technical-specific aspects (Sect. 6.1.1) and then moves on to organizational topics (Sect. 6.1.2). The challenge topic ends with the ethical and social aspects of data management in sports organizations (Sect. 6.1.3).

6.1.1 Technical Aspects

Sports organizations face concrete challenges at the technical level. These include various parts and are interrelated. Only when technical requirements are met can there be a solid foundation for making data-driven decisions. A particularly challenging aspect in this area is that technologies and applications are constantly evolving at a rapid pace, necessitating constant adaptation.

D. Schwizer, M. Burch, *Data Excellence in Sports*, Management for Professionals,
https://doi.org/10.1007/978-3-032-10993-4_6

Fig. 6.1 The challenges in the conclusion focus on technical, organizational, and ethical aspects. Figure created by the authors

Challenge 1: Ensure the Integration and Compatibility of the Data Sources
Sports organizations collect data from a variety of different sources (e.g., wearables, results databases, training data, etc.). The data are available in various formats. To guarantee efficient and targeted data processing, it is essential to ensure the integration of the data into a single system and the corresponding compatibility is critical (Jianjun et al., 2025). This ensures that data from different areas (e.g., sports and business domains within the sports organization) can be viewed holistically. Only in this way can potential cross-connections be identified. It also prevents silo mentality within the sports organization. Data management in sports organizations is a cross-departmental and cross-functional effort, ideally based on well-thought-out data processing (Postma, 2023).

Challenge 2: Providing Real-Time Data Appropriately
Real-time data are particularly important for sports organizations. For example, to make tactical adjustments based on data during a match, it is necessary to be able to access and process data quickly and reliably (Hussain et al., 2024). Automated analysis methods can also be an important element here. High data processing capacities and frequencies are prerequisites for not only providing data within a reasonable time frame but also evaluating it. Decision-making should not be delayed by excessive latency (the time between data collection and its availability for use). Therefore, the stability of IT systems is of central importance. Robust systems also ensure a high degree of data security and availability. These elements are essential to strengthen trust in real-time data collection and to ensure a solid basis for decision-making.

Challenge 3: Ensuring Data Security and Protection Against Cyberattacks
Ensuring data security and protection against cyberattacks is one of the most important challenges facing sports organizations (Bongiovanni et al., 2024). Sports organizations store a wealth of information from various sources and process it in different systems. These data, some of which are personal and organization-specific, are valuable and require appropriate protection. Data have personal, strategic, or tactical values that must be preserved. Therefore, these data must be well protected not only during collection but also during storage. This includes protection against hacker attacks. Both the server infrastructure and the cloud services must be

encrypted. In addition, access rights must be defined and controlled (Li & Guo, 2024). In addition, security protocols must be established not only at the technical level but also at the organizational level. Furthermore, software must always be up-to-date. It is important to install updates in a timely manner and to continuously review and update the software. Particular attention should be paid to protecting the privacy of the affected stakeholders. This protection goes beyond purely legal standards.

Challenge 4: Ensure Availability and Scalability of the IT Infrastructure
The IT infrastructures of sports organizations are typically constantly changing (Postma, 2023). Frequent adjustments to the IT infrastructure are necessary to remain able to process large amounts of data in a short period of time. The challenge for sports organizations is to align the IT infrastructure for peak periods. This could, for example, involve using the infrastructure during a game or competition to provide real-time data within a useful time frame. It can be advantageous to use cloud-based solutions. This allows resources to be adapted as needed without having to make huge initial investments. In addition, the IT infrastructure of sports organizations must usually be available around the clock. Emergency systems must also be implemented to bridge system interruptions. Technological changes mean that IT systems must be continuously adapted and tested for full functionality. Furthermore, systems should be continuously optimized in an iterative process.

Challenge 5: Ensure the Quality and Accuracy of the Collected Data
The quality and precision of the collected data is vital for having a reliable and well-founded basis for decision-making, in both the sporting and business sectors. Only with a good database can incorrect conclusions be avoided (Obi et al., 2024). However, achieving this high level of data quality and accuracy is challenging due to the variety of data formats and different data sources (e.g., sensors, videos, etc.). Incorrect or inaccurate data can lead to misinterpretations, which, in turn, can have a negative impact on teams, careers, or economic developments. However, it is not only the accuracy and quality that are essential but also the relevance and usefulness of the data used. Unnecessary data can distort the analysis and lead to misinterpretations (Davis et al., 2022). As a result, data lose accuracy over time. Therefore, it is crucial that the data are cleaned and validated before being incorporated into the analysis. Data management processes must also be constantly monitored. Technical expertise, precise collection methods, and regular maintenance are essential to ensure the long-term quality and precision of the collected data.

Challenge 6: Enable Automated and Efficient Data Processing
Automated systems, data analysis, and preparation processes are critical to data management success. Sports organizations face diverse data in different formats that need to be processed (Bai & Bai, 2021). A partially automated approach helps to complete the preparatory process steps. However, data preparation and evaluation can rarely be fully automated; manual intervention is necessary. This

Fig. 6.2 There are several aspects that influence future success in sports data management. Figure created by the authors

ensures that data preparation is appropriate and flexible in the situation. This guarantees that no important information is lost. A particular challenge for sports organizations is that time and resources for manual interventions are used sparingly. In addition, automated and manual processes must be transparent and traceable. Potential sources of error must be identified and eliminated early on. Therefore, systems must be regularly reviewed in this regard.

6.1.2 Organizational Aspects

At the organizational level, there are numerous opportunities to promote effective and efficient data management in sports organizations (see Fig. 6.2). A data-friendly organizational culture contributes significantly to smooth data management. In addition, an attractive environment for talented individuals and specialists, as well as opportunities for continuing education, should be ensured. Interdisciplinary collaboration helps integrate diverse perspectives and package data analyses into relevant narratives (Burns & Collins, 2023). This can counteract the resistance of selected stakeholders.

Challenge 1: Creating a Data-Friendly Organizational Culture

Sports organizations face the challenge of finding a good balance between data-based decisions and the appropriate consideration of intuition and experience. An employee-centric organizational culture is important for this. Open communication must be encouraged so that ideas and concerns are shared confidently among employees. As several specialists are often involved in data-based decisions, trust-based cooperation is essential. A positive error culture promotes learning within a sports organization. Mistakes should be seen as learning opportunities that help individual employees and the sports organization as a whole move forward. Psychological safety is therefore an important factor in learning from mistakes and addressing them openly to drive innovation within the sports organization (Saxe & Hardin, 2022). The quality of managers and their exemplary actions in daily life also contribute to the establishment of a data-friendly organizational culture. It is also important to promote agility and flexibility in organizational culture to be able to react and adapt quickly to changing circumstances. Finally, mutual trust and the integration of different perspectives help to foster collaboration within the team and ensure creative and innovative solutions based on data.

Challenge 2: Attracting Talent and Specialists

The targeted handling of data in sports organizations poses a significant difficulty. Specialists are therefore often required to adequately address the issues that arise. Consequently, it is essential for sports organizations to recruit and retain talented individuals who are ideally familiar with both sports and data analysis. Targeted recruitment strategies are necessary to be perceived as an attractive employer. Partnerships with universities and research institutions are also worth considering. These not only facilitate access to current research but also to up-and-coming talent and university graduates. As data specialists are in high demand in many industries (Büchel et al., 2023), competitive remuneration and career development opportunities within the sports organization are important not only to attract these specialists but also to retain them in the long term. As this is a challenge for many sports organizations due to their financial situation and limited size, the aspect of organizational culture should also be considered here. This can also be an important element of employee retention.

Challenge 3: Promote Continuous Training

Although time and resources are often scarce in sports organizations, it is still essential for effective data management that the skills and competencies of the employees in data analysis are always up-to-date (Zhang et al., 2023). Training and further education help not only to keep track of new developments but also to put them into practice. For smaller sports organizations, it can be important to invest in employees' communication skills. These are particularly important when working with external data specialists. This is because the challenges to be solved with the data must be appropriately formulated to achieve efficient solutions. Added to this are the changing legal requirements regarding data protection. Employees should be informed about sensitive issues and the legally compliant handling of data. Internal security guidelines and the handling of access rights also play a key role here. All of this contributes to proactive risk management. The implementation of knowledge management systems can also support organizational learning.

Challenge 4: Strengthening Interdisciplinary Collaboration

Collaboration between different specialists is essential to ensure sound data-based decisions (Fattah & Mts, 2023). Sports organizations always include both a training science component and an economic science component. To effectively manage these two areas, interdisciplinary collaboration is required in certain areas. In many cases, specialists from different departments are involved in data-based decisions: IT, sport, economics, law, etc. Through good interdisciplinary cooperation, sports organizations can create synergies and come to better solutions. Therefore, it is not only about being familiar with certain tools as an individual employee and using them in the right place but also about making the right strategic decisions in collaboration with others. As the field of data management in sport is constantly changing, cooperation also requires constant improvements and adjustments to keep pace with technological progress.

Challenge 5: Translating Data into Stories
Only a few recipients of data-based decisions are familiar with data management and data analysis. However, to ensure the effectiveness of data-based decisions, the results of analyses must be translated into convincing stories or visualizations (Neifer et al., 2020). In any case, the data should be prepared in an understandable format and translated to suit the target group. The key messages should be clearly identified and presented. It is important to maintain objectivity and build trust with the addressees by not manipulating the data at any time. It is also important to obtain feedback from those affected by data-based decisions, thus iteratively refining the data story. This is the only way to maintain long-term relevance and impact.

Challenge 6: Anticipate Resistance of Selected Stakeholders
Sports organizations must prepare for an increase in resistance to the free availability of athlete, coach, trainer, and consultant data to the sports organization. These stakeholders are likely to become increasingly aware of the value and importance of these data. Therefore, special attention must be paid to responsible and transparent data handling (Stoudt et al., 2024). Only ethically sound use can ensure that there is long-term acceptance for the utilization of their data. It would also make sense for the sports system to consider how data handling is regulated and standardized not only within a sports organization, a sport, a league, or an association but also in an international context. However, these are issues that go far beyond the sphere of influence of a single sports organization.

6.1.3 Ethical Aspects

Sports organizations are part of an entire sports ecosystem with many participants and interest groups. Their data-driven decisions not only influence their own sports organization but also directly impact individual stakeholders within it, such as coaches, support staff, medical personnel, players, athletes, etc. In addition, they influence the entire sports ecosystem (see Fig. 6.3). Therefore, the ethical challenges of data management in sports organizations are particularly important (Kim et al., 2025).

Challenge 1: Ensure Fairness and Transparency
Sports organizations should maintain a fair and transparent approach to data management. This ensures that both internal stakeholders and the public can build trust. Those directly affected by data-based decisions should have insight into data processing procedures to ensure their traceability. This applies to both data collection and analysis. This ensures transparency, fair data handling, and the avoidance of discriminatory models and processes. In summary, fairness and transparency contribute to ethically sound data management within a sports organization (Costa et al., 2025).

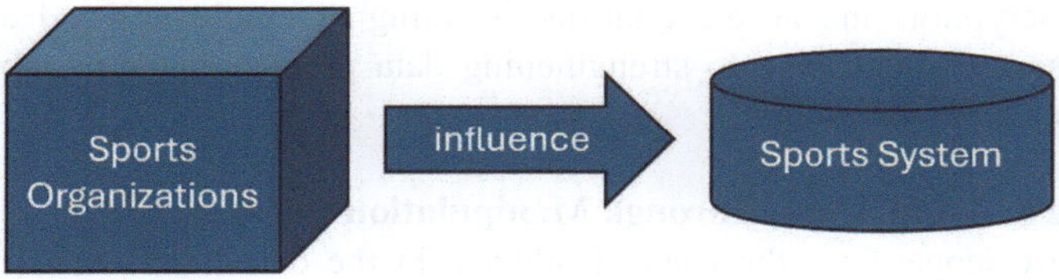

Fig. 6.3 How ethical aspects are dealt with in sports organizations influences the entire sports system. Figure created by the authors

Challenge 2: Maintain Responsible Handling of Data

Responsible data handling also always includes avoiding unlawful discrimination (Kim et al., 2025). Ensuring the quality of data processing and data protection are important prerequisites. Furthermore, each sports organization should specifically define what constitutes responsible data handling. Responsible data handling contributes significantly to ensure that data management is widely accepted in sports organizations and that those directly affected build trust in data-based decisions.

Challenge 3: Consider the Impact of Data Decisions on Athletes and Teams

Data-based decisions in sports organizations have specific consequences for the athletes and teams involved. Therefore, it is essential that sports organizations make their data-based decisions fairly and in a situation-specific manner. On the one hand, the positive impacts for all involved should be maximized. On the other hand, negative impacts should be minimized as much as possible. Data-based decisions can significantly or even decisively affect the careers of individual athletes (Reddy, 2023). Therefore, data-based decisions should always be made with care and foresight, as well as with awareness of those affected.

Challenge 4: Strengthening Athletes' Data Sovereignty

Sports organizations should pay close attention to who within the organization generates, owns, and evaluates the data (Bowles & McGee, 2023). Athletes and their advisors are expected to become increasingly aware of the value of their own data and may demand more control over them. Data are an extremely valuable resource in sports and can lead to disputes over distribution. Therefore, sports organizations should consider early how to strengthen athletes' data sovereignty. This means giving athletes more control over which data is collected and how and why it is used. This is the only way to ensure that the data are used for the benefit of both the sports organization and the athletes.

Challenge 5: Ensure Privacy Protection

The basis for privacy protection is clear guidelines for the collection, storage, and use of data within a sports organization (Li & Guo, 2024). This applies not only to the organization's athletes and members but also to the data of fans. All those affected by data management must explicitly consent to the processing of their data. Furthermore, the privacy of those affected must be protected by additional measures, such as encryption and access controls. Training of employees and awareness-raising measures contribute to strengthening data protection for members of the sports organization and fans.

Challenge 6: Avoid Abuse Through Manipulation

Data misuse jeopardizes the trust of athletes in the data-based decision-making system (Guo et al., 2024). Therefore, it should be avoided whenever possible. A key element in preventing misuse through manipulation is clear responsibilities within the sports organization. Clear guidelines should ensure that the data are not manipulated or misused. Training and awareness-raising measures among employees can play an important role in this. Furthermore, monitoring mechanisms and control mechanisms should also be integrated. These ensure that data are used exclusively in a permissible manner and that any misuse is detected at an early stage. In larger sports organizations, the definition of a code of ethics is also conceivable. This serves as a guide for the responsible handling of data.

6.2 Limitations

In addition to the challenges mentioned above, there are also various limitations that must be addressed in the field of sports management and data analysis. Challenges are typically solvable but hard problems, while limitations mean some kind of problem that makes a complete solution impossible. Sect. 6.2.1 addresses the lack of access to existing technologies that would otherwise support sports management and data analysis. In the days of artificial intelligence, there is always the option to create tools that make use of AI components, but in some cases, we are far from tapping the full potential of this novel technology (see Sect. 6.2.2). In addition, prohibited technologies that would hinder athletes from their sports activities are imaginable (see Sect. 6.2.3). Data science in sports is a huge and interdisciplinary topic, but not each subtopic is researched equally well (Sect. 6.2.4). In addition to all the technologies we can use in sports, there are still critical decisions that cannot be resolved with the best available technologies (Sect. 6.2.5).

6.2.1 Missing Access to Technologies

As in many areas related to data science, there are also missing and underdeveloped concepts and technologies in sports-related domains. For example, sports itself in its pure natural way is a cheap activity. Almost everyone can do it. However, when data science technologies come into play, sports can be quite expensive, making them accessible only to rich people (Khurana et al., 2021). The typical costs for data management and data analysis tools depend on the number of consumers and the number of software and hardware features included. This means that for niche sport activities or people who do not have access to these technologies, there can be extreme costs that make it difficult to use and develop them (see Fig. 6.4).

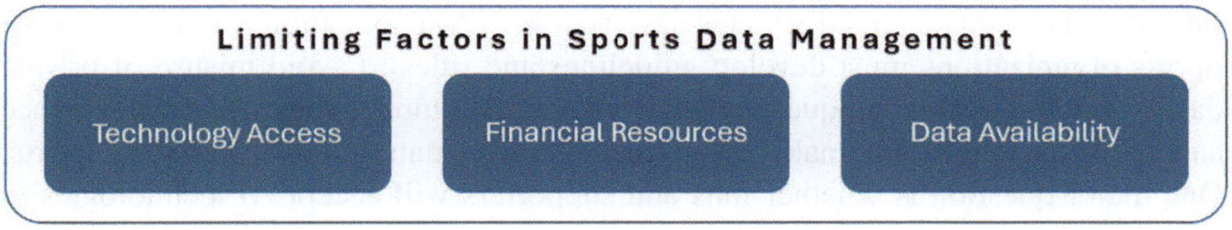

Fig. 6.4 Not only lacking access to technology can cause problems but also financial constraints and lack of data availability. Figure created by the authors

In addition, not all regions of the world are equally supported. Poor regions in the world might have less access to modern tools, systems, and technologies, while less educated people or people who earn less might not have access to tools that help improve their sports activities. This creates some kind of unfair situation in the world of sports. Furthermore, this could be one of many reasons why even for countries with a large population such as Indonesia it is difficult to qualify for the FIFA World Cup with their soccer team.

Another general problem is missing data, which means that data cannot be measured, recorded, or stored for some reason. Even the best technology or the data analysis system cannot run successfully without an adequate amount of data, for example, to evaluate the efficiency of a tool or to use the data to train a model to make predictions on existing data. Even privacy issues and data protection are limitations these days, as they hinder the development of software and hardware or even modern AI applications to run successfully.

6.2.2 Questionable AI Support

AI methods are becoming more important due to technological advances not only in the data science domain in general but also in sports data science and sports data management (Glebova et al., 2024). Due to growing datasets and changing user requirements, sports data can also be taken as input of popular algorithmic methods, for example, for deep learning applications that try to predict new results based on labeled data. However, the results of such neural networks and trained models are questionable, as they typically rely on input data that can miss some very important features for an accurate prediction. Consequently, there is a high probability that wrong predictions cause doubtful decisions before or during a sports event and typically result in less success and therefore a loss of money.

Although AI applications have some benefits for data analysis, training, team formation, talent identification, medicine, or prediction of match results, people related to sports should be aware that it is not the perfect solution to any kind of problem. It must be applied with care and by consulting a data science and AI expert who informs about critical issues when applying techniques from this novel application field. Not only do ethical issues play crucial roles here, meaning that sensitive biometric data about athletes must be protected, but fairness can also be a limitation here, since not all athletes have access to AI applications in the same way. Sports organizations must develop guidelines and rules to avoid misuse of private data by applying AI techniques, which is one of the future challenges in data science and in all disciplines that make use of concepts from data science, including sports. One major question is whether fans and supporters will accept AI technologies to be a part of sports as they might have a big impact on fans' enthusiasm.

6.2.3 Forbidden Technologies

Not all available technologies must be applied in sports management. In some situations, it does not make sense to apply them, but in other scenarios, the technique can lead to distractions or even to unfair results that are not just caused by the performance of athletes. Similarly to doping, there could be some kind of external impact on improving performance, improvements that are strictly forbidden in sports. However, there are gray zones missing a clear definition of what is allowed and what is not. Defining these standards is one role for the World Anti-Doping Agency (WADA).

A popular term in this context is technology doping (Khan & Shafeek, 2024), which describes a way for athletes to obtain any kind of advantage or benefit during a sports competition, either by using medical treatment, including doping, or by applying advanced sports technologies, tools, or equipment. However, clearly defining what doping is in sports and what is not remains a challenging problem that also causes many limitations for sports organizations and athletes. New technologies must first be tested before they are allowed and do not threaten integrity (see Table 6.1 for some examples). The problem of rich countries having a benefit over poor countries can also be related to the advancement in new technologies in sports.

In 1971, Werner Fischer developed tennis rackets with double-string construction. This allowed players to achieve exceptional spin values with their shots. The trajectories of the balls became unpredictable. Spaghetti stringing only became well

Table 6.1 Technologies and sport equipment that fall into the category of technology doping

Technology	Year	Prominent features and advantages
Recumbent bicycle	1930	Faster than upright bicycles (Hadland & Lessing, 2021)
"Spaghetti" racket	1978	Extreme spin, unpredictable trajectory (Tennis Museum, 2025)
"Stickum" adhesive	1981	Improved grip on the ball (NFL, 2025)
Spinaci bars	1997	Dangerous aerodynamic positions (Rouleur, 2025)
Electronic sign stealing	2001	Allowed teams to decode catcher signs illegally (Wikipedia, 2025)
Ionized shirts	2007	Negatively charged electron field, blood flow (Barkham, 2007)
LZR racer swimsuit	2008	Similar to shark skin, enhance oxygen flow (Andreoni et al., 2022)
Mechanical doping	2010	Cycling, secret motor to propel the bike
Vaporfly shoes	2017	Special foam, faster running (Young et al., 2020)
Telemetry hacking	2020	Gliding, real tracking

known in 1977, when US player Michael Fishbach advanced to the third round of the US Open with it. However, the technology was banned shortly after (Tennis Museum, 2025).

During the so-called Stickum era in the late 1970s and early 1980s, players in the National Football League (NFL) used a sticky substance to catch an unusually high number of balls. The most famous player was Lester Hayes, who was named Defensive Player of the Year in 1980, in part because of this adhesive. Stickum was quickly deemed an unsportsmanlike advantage, which is why it was banned by the NFL in 1981. However, the basic idea remains in the sport to this day with the development of sticky gloves, which are now part of standard equipment (NFL, 2025).

In the 1990s, many professional road cycling teams relied on Spinaci bars. These were mini aero handlebars that were mounted as attachments. On the one hand, the handlebars enabled an aerodynamically advantageous position. On the other hand, it was impossible to stop in this position. This led to dangerous situations, which is why the UCI banned the use of Spinaci bars in 1997 (Rouleur, 2025).

In Major League Baseball (MLB), sign stealing refers to deciphering the opposing catcher's hand signals to select pitches. This is permitted by the rules if it is done without tools. However, there have been repeated cases of sign stealing with tools, for example, in 1951 with the New York Giants. In 1961, MLB finally banned mechanical and electronic aids, as they were considered unsportsmanlike. Not all teams complied with the bans. For example, the Boston Red Sox and the Houston Astros used high-tech systems such as cameras and smart watches to cheat (Wikipedia, 2025).

In addition to forbidden technologies, there are also innovations that have made their way to sports, although they appear to be a candidate for the forbidden list. What they typically have in common is standardization, which means that everyone must use them in a similar way to avoid unfair advantages during competition. Such standards involve weight, size, dimension, and many more. Popular examples are tennis rackets or baseball bats. For example, general AI technologies could be seen as such examples, starting in 1997 with the popular IBM's Deep Blue that won against world chess champion Garry Kasparov. It is questionable whether such AI technologies will continue to be allowed in the way they are allowed today.

6.2.4 Under-researched Fields

Although data science seems to be the holy grail for sports-related disciplines, there are still various under-researched topics, fields, and technologies that could offer great solutions and support once fully researched. This covers nearly all fields of this interdisciplinary domain. These include data recording, data processing, and data analysis. The field also includes display technologies that enable interactive visualizations. In addition, it integrates advanced technologies such as virtual reality, augmented reality, and mixed reality. It even includes immersive analytics that require large high-resolution displays.

Also, the way in which human users consume sports data and which impact analyses have on the enhancement in sports is under-researched (Zhong et al., 2025). There are already various solutions that address some of the challenges; however, we see much room for further developments in data science, particularly when it comes to sports applications. The question of whether such technologies make for a better sports world remains open. There are many positive examples and also many negative examples with respect to this question. This means that under-researched fields do not necessarily have to be a limitation for the field of sports. In some scenarios, they could provide the naturalistic freedom in which sports were originally performed, for example, by thinking back to the old days when the Olympic Games got started for the first time.

6.2.5 Critical Decisions and Human Intervention

Technological progress brings into play more sports equipment and tools to analyze sports data and improve one or several aspects in the field of sports. However, it does not solve all the problems we used to have, and it also creates new ones. We can say that data are not the holy grail for sports data science or sports management. Each time a new technology is invented and introduced into the sports field, we receive new challenges and limitations, nearly at the same rate (Qi et al., 2024). There is a long list of such examples that are worth discussing.

For example, the video assistant referee is not a fully automatic solution to the problem of making wrong decisions during sports competitions. Such technologies typically only work for black/white decisions (see Fig. 6.5). There are no half right and half wrong, but a 100 percent solution is required. Numerous instances exist in which human intervention is required. In addition, automatic decisions combined with human intervention take much longer, making fans and spectators feel bored. Consequently, technology takes away the thrill of a sporting event; at least critical decisions do not create space for discussions anymore. The discussion now is more about technology and whether it makes sense or not.

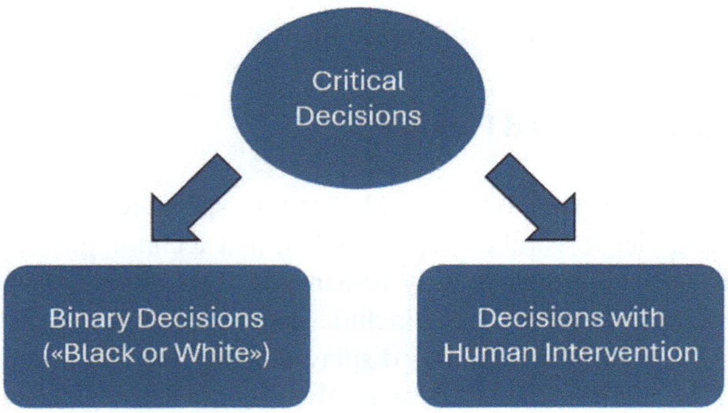

Fig. 6.5 Critical decisions in sports can be either binary or more complex so that they need human intervention. Figure created by the authors

6.3 Future Directions

Data-related aspects in the field of sports can be discussed from several perspectives, as we have already seen in this book. However, there is still much room for future directions, also some of that we cannot foresee now. This fact makes the field of sports in the context of data management and data science very interesting and intriguing. In this final section, we look at such future directions, especially in light of the impact of AI technologies (Sect. 6.3.1). In addition, display technologies could bring sports events much closer and in a much more realistic way to our living rooms (Sect. 6.3.2). Not all data in sports must have benefits and advantages that bring into play the questions of what kind of data is useful at all and whether sports could also survive without the use of data-related technologies (Sect. 6.3.3). This leads to discussions about the technological options that sports organizations have and which ones to consider (Sect. 6.3.4). Finally, in the future, the roles in data management must be clearly studied to take the best out of the interdisciplinary character of sports-related data science (Sect. 6.3.5).

6.3.1 Impact of Artificial Intelligence

Artificial intelligence cannot be found today only in typical sports applications, equipment, and technologies. Before 2000, machine learning and data science techniques have been applied to sports-related problems, such as the computation of match statistics and outcomes, player performance-value correlations on the market, or just supporting the identification of new talents (see Fig. 6.6). There are various challenges in everyday sports in which AI could create many advantages, if it is accepted as a new technology and does not violate ethical regulations and data protection issues. The most popular benefits when applying AI in sports can be found for health and fitness, sports event broadcasting, betting agencies, fan flow and advertising, or the calculation of the best team formation. Today's applications

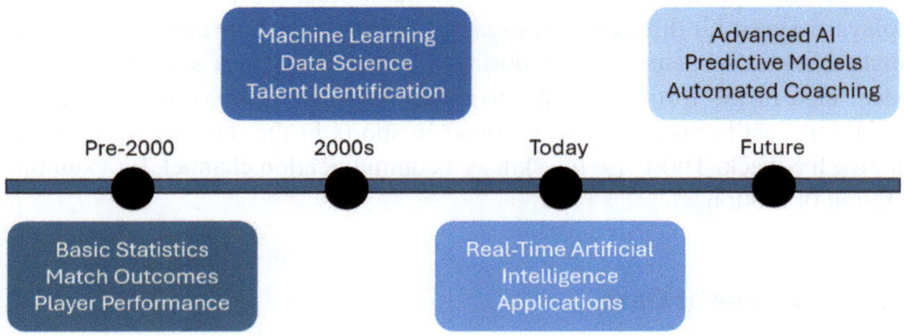

Fig. 6.6 Advanced AI, predictive models and automated coaching might be important elements of future sports data management. Figure created by the authors

do not only typically include static data but must also keep pace with real-time data for which data analyses require fast algorithmic solutions.

Famous AI examples in sports that persist to today can be found in Hawk-Eye systems that are typically used during tennis competitions such as Wimbledon or the US and Australian Open (Wang & Han, 2024). Such motion tracking systems contain various advanced algorithmic concepts that must process data rapidly and compute reliable outputs. One might say that sports are also possible without AI support, but AI can bring new opportunities to the world of sports. However, it will also bring new challenges into play. Not only sports can benefit from AI applications, but data science research also has benefits due to the learning effects when applying the developed techniques to a new kind of data.

6.3.2 Display Technologies

The displays are important for the sports field as they show the events during a sports competition to different types of people interested in sports. They can be installed inside a stadium to entertain fans, show advertisements, or provide information about current results and match statistics (Yi & Zhou, 2018). On the other hand, they might just be used in a laboratory to visually represent the results of a sports data analysis. There are various opportunities to use display technologies in the field of sports. Although there are already various display types installed in the sports domain in different scenarios and settings, there will be further developments of the technologies included to make sports an even more entertaining field. Displays played an even greater role during COVID-19 pandemic times, when many fans were unable to travel to sporting events and had to watch them remotely, in front of their TV or computer monitors in the simplest case. However, there are more advanced options to watch sports matches, for example, by making use of VR, AR, or MR technologies, which gives a more immersive experience to the sports fan.

A display is typically regarded as a medium for visual presentations. Display technology in sports started many years ago, bringing more fan experience, improved atmosphere, or excitement to the field. Small-, medium-, and large-scale displays are used for different purposes, for example, to show current game results, statistics, and also game replays during a sports event in a stadium on a video screen, also in the form of a cube to make it visible from various perspectives. In addition, tactile displays can be found in sports in the modern world to report and give feedback. Those use the skin as a communication channel, for example, by vibration or motion.

6.3.3 Overuse of Data

Although there should be enough data to make valuable analyses in the field of sports, it remains questionable if the data can solve all the problems and the challenges (Watanabe & Rewliak, 2022). In addition, data overuse can also have a negative impact on sports competitions, as sports live from the attractiveness of unclear referee decisions that give room for discussion and argument. This discussion will no longer be needed if a fully automatic decision replaces the human decisions of a referee. However, what we also learned from semiautomatic VAR systems is that fans and spectators and the mass media have enough topics to discuss, not just referee decisions alone but also more about the whole concept of including technological data analyses into the decision-making process. Although we expected automatic solutions to be much faster than pure human decisions, we see that the semiautomatic solution still takes some time to reach a final decision, and this again is negatively perceived by both fans and athletes.

The massive amount of data in sports is a positive side effect of this discipline, but to take advantage of the full potential of data analyses, there is still the challenge of filtering out which types of data metrics and measurements are the most important to solve the tasks at hand (Bai & Bai, 2021). The problem is not measuring, storing, and analyzing data, but rather identifying the relevant data portions of this kind of big data. This is challenging for static data, but even more challenging for dynamic and real-time data that require rapid and efficient algorithmic solutions. In addition, the more data are available, the more ethical considerations must be taken, which can be a time-consuming process. This means that before starting a data analysis, it can take some time, and the recorded data might already be useless before it can be used. There are two types of opinion about data in sports. A group of people will see it as a chance to improve the performance of athletes, find better training conditions, and earn more money. Others still see the issue of a degradation of the real value of sports, having benefits from unforeseen events and decisions that give room to discuss and finally entertain people (see Fig. 6.7).

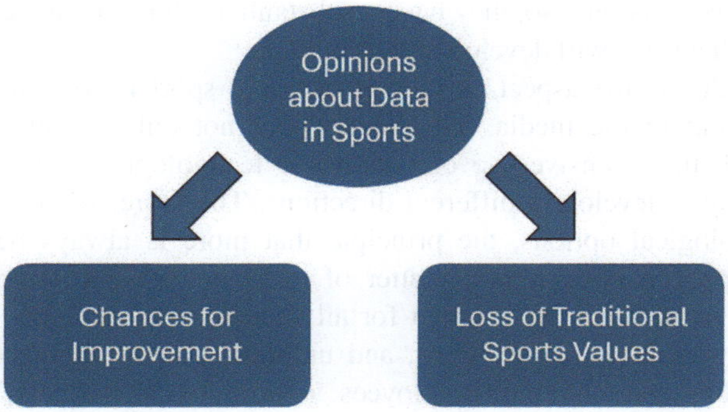

Fig. 6.7 Opinions about advantages and disadvantages of the existence of data in sports vary. Figure created by the authors

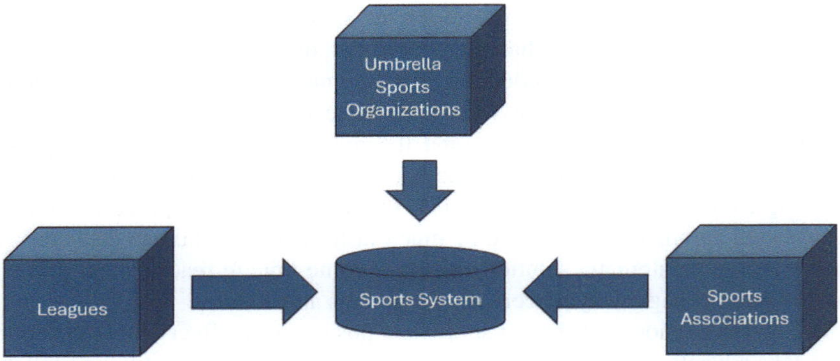

Fig. 6.8 Different organizations in the sports systems influence the rules and therefore the future use of technology in sports. Figure created by the authors

6.3.4 Technological Options

Technological options create new possibilities for sports organizations in terms of data management. User-friendly tools give sports organizations with little experience in data management access to new opportunities in this area. The choice of these technologically available options that are used has the potential to have a significant impact on the future development of the sports system. Leagues (e.g., Premier League, Bundesliga, etc.), sports associations (e.g., FIFA, UEFA, etc.), and umbrella sports organizations (e.g., IOC) play an important role in the development of sports (see Fig. 6.8). These associations and umbrella organizations determine which technologies may be used in connection with data in the respective sports and at what level. In doing so, they have a substantial influence on the direction and speed at which a sport will develop and change.

Added to this is the aspect of how attractive a sport is for fans to follow in the stadium and in the media. This means that not only is the core of sports changing with the intensive use of data-based technologies, but its commercial potential can also develop in different directions. Therefore, when it comes to the use of technological options, the principle that more is always better does not necessarily apply. Rather, it is a matter of making the right strategic decisions to create the greatest possible benefit for all stakeholders involved. This includes not only leagues, sports associations, and umbrella sports organizations but also athletes, coaches, and other club employees, as well as fans, partners, and sponsors. Numerous technological options present potential for further development at the level of leagues, sports associations, and sports umbrella organizations. This should be taken with caution. In addition, such developments are often a learning process that needs to be repeatedly adapted.

Individual sports organizations (in the sense of individual clubs), on the other hand, have more freedom and less direct responsibility for the medium- and long-term development of a sport, even though their actions also indirectly influence it. Individual sports organizations operate more independently within the sports ecosystem than associations and use the data management technologies that they believe will deliver the greatest benefits and can afford (Qi et al., 2024). Large and financially strong sports organizations have an advantage here not only because they can finance sophisticated and customized tools and technologies or even develop them themselves but also because they have the resources to hire more staff in this area or bring in external consultants. However, ultimately, individual sports organizations also have an interest in maintaining or improving the competitive balance, attractiveness, and the sustainability of sport to remain attractive to fans, spectators, and sponsors, thus creating an economic basis for their long-term existence. The technological options used to achieve this will have a significant influence on the direction in which sport will develop in the future.

6.3.5 Clear Roles in Data Management

Data-based decision-making in sports organizations is changing both the way employees work and their roles. To ensure that these change processes run as smoothly as possible, managers must have strong leadership skills. It takes time, determination, and a good strategy to firmly anchor more data-based working practices in the culture of a sports organization (Qi et al., 2024). This means clarifying the roles and, if necessary, making structural adjustments. This can sometimes be associated with uncertainty. Many sports organizations are highly resistant to change. This makes it even more important to actively shape the change, clarify roles, and support affected employees in finding their feet in changed roles or with new specialists.

There is no universally applicable recipe to clarify the roles and the appropriate structures in sports organizations. Employees who are severely affected by change often react with resistance because they feel threatened in their current role. Managers can also be overwhelmed by the change or lack sufficient knowledge of the topic. This increases uncertainty and carries the risk of disorientation. Change is particularly noticeable externally when there are changes in institutional structure, for example, when an organizational chart is altered and responsibilities are reassigned. At the same time, it can also be dangerous for a sports organization if it fails to make the right systemic adaptations. This is suboptimal because it prevents individual employees from effectively performing their duties. However, clarifying roles should not be viewed as a one-time event; rather, due to the dynamic environment of data management, it represents a continuous process. Interfaces and responsibilities must be reviewed at regular intervals and redefined if necessary.

The future success of sports organizations in the context of effective data management is highly dependent on capable leaders. They should be able to motivate or even inspire employees and provide guidance (see Fig. 6.9). Ideally, leaders will have more than a basic understanding of the technical requirements of data management, even if it is not necessary that they are familiar with all the details. The role of a chief data officer (CDO) or at least a cross-functional

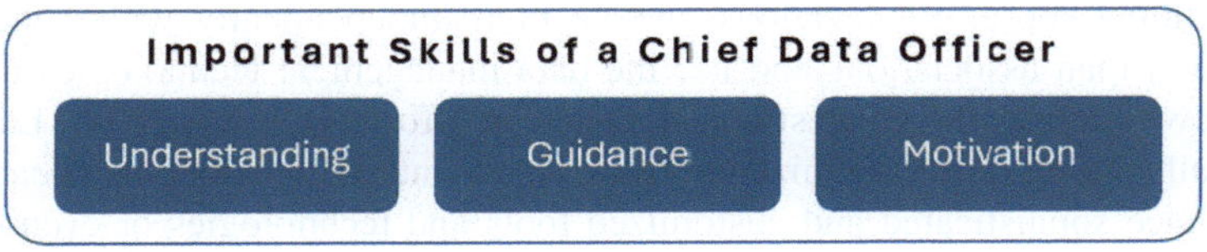

Fig. 6.9 A chief data officer faces a challenging role in sports data management. Figure created by the authors

data management officer is likely to become even more important in the future (Hermes & Riedl, 2022). This is because data management and data competence represent a cross-sectional function that is highly sought after in various areas: sports, medicine, marketing, ticketing, etc. To be able to face these challenges, sports organizations should ideally be agile learning organizations with a distinct strategic direction. It should be clear in each individual area how data-based decisions are combined with other decision-making approaches and previous practices. This is an ongoing learning and optimization process, as the world of data is also constantly and dynamically evolving. If the roles of individual employees remain unclear, the risk of inefficiency, diffuse responsibility, and loss of trust in data processes increases. However, if an appropriate strategy and a convincingly facilitated change process succeed in putting employees on the path to a more data-oriented sports organization, this can unlock many future development potentials and achieve success in both the business and sports sectors.

References

Andreoni, G., Bissolotti, L., Castagna, E., Valagussa, G., Mondini, F., Paleari, A., & Pittaccio, S. (2022). Assessment of the usability of an innovative assistive swimsuit. In L. Miesenberger, G. Kouroupetroglou, K. Mavrou, R. Manduchi, M. C. Rodriguez & P. Penáz (Eds.), *Proceedings of the 18th International Conference on Computers Helping People with Special Needs, ICCHP-AAATE*, volume 13342 of Lecture notes in computer science (pp. 469–476). Springer.

Bai, Z., & Bai, X. (2021). Sports big data: Management, analysis, applications, and challenges. *Complexity, 2021*, 6676297.

Barkham, P. (2007). The Ionic Man—will a vest decide who wins rugby's biggest prize? *The Guardian*.

Büchel, J., Engler, J., & Mertens, A. (2023). The demand for data skills in German companies: Evidence from online job advertisements. *EconPol Forum, 24*(2), 56–61.

Bongiovanni, I., Herold, D. M., & Wilde, S. J. (2024). Protecting the play: An integrative review of cybersecurity in and for sports events. *Computers & Security, 146*, 104064.

Bowles, H., & McGee, D. (2023). Data ownership, athlete rights and the global sports gambling industry. In D. McGee & C. Bunn (eds.), *Gambling and sports in a global age*, volume 18 of Research in the sociology of sport (pp. 41–56). Emerald Publishing Limited.

Burns, A., & Collins, D. (2023). Interdisciplinary practice in performance sport: A scoping review of evidence of collaboration. *European Journal of Sport Science, 23*(9), 1877–1891.

Costa, S., Silva, A. J., Dias, T., Marinho, D. A., Batalha, N. M., Roque, R., Afonso, C., Aminova, M., & Ferraz, R. (2025). Integrity and transparency in sports: A survey review. *The Open Sports Sciences Journal, 18*, e1875399X353976.

Davis, J., Bransen, L., Devos, L., Meert, W., Robberechts, P., Haaren, J. V., and Roy, M. V. (2022). Evaluating sports analytics models: Challenges, approaches, and lessons learned. In *EBeM 2022: AI Evaluation Beyond Metrics, Workshop Proceedings* (Vol. 3169).

Fattah, I. A., & Mts, A. (2023). Decision making performance of big data analytics capabilities: The mediating effect of co-collaboration. *Journal of System and Management Sciences, 13*(6), 410–431.

Glebova, E., Madsen, D. O., Mihaľová, P., Géczi, G., Mittelman, A., & Jorgič, B. (2024). Artificial intelligence development and dissemination impact on the sports industry labor market. *Frontiers in Sports and Active Living, 6*, 1363892.

Guo, X., Li, X., & Guo, M. (2024). Diversifying configurational paths for athlete data protection. *Scientific Reports, 14*, 32053.

Hadland, T., & Lessing, H.-E. (2021). *A complete illustrated history of the recumbent bicycle*. The MIT Press Reader.

Hermes, A., & Riedl, R. (2022). Chief digital officer (CDO): Literaturanalyse und handlungsempfehlungen für die praxis. *HMD Praxis der Wirtschaftsinformatik, 59*(3), 795–817.

Hussain, Y., et al. (2024). Revolutionizing sports information systems for real-time analytics: The SportFlow analytics engine. *Journal of Community, Environment & Sustainable Health, 7*(2), 105–120.

Jianjun, Q., Isleem, H. F., Almoghayer, W. J. K., & Khishe, M. (2025). Predictive athlete performance modeling with machine learning and biometric data integration. *Scientific Reports, 15*, 16365.

Khan, A., & Shafeek, M. (2024). Technological doping in sports: The new frontier of competitive advantage. *International Journal of Physical Education, Sports and Health, 11*(4), 552–554.

Khurana, R., Wang, A., & Carrington, P. (2021). Beyond adaptive sports: Challenges & opportunities to improve accessibility and analytics. In *Proceedings of the 23rd International ACM SIGACCESS Conference on Computers and Accessibility (ASSETS '21)*, New York, NY, USA. Association for Computing Machinery.

Kim, J.-H., Kim, J., Kang, H., & Youn, B.-Y. (2025). Ethical implications of artificial intelligence in sport: A systematic scoping review. *Journal of Sport and Health Science, 14*, 101047.

Li, X., & Guo, X. (2024). Factors affecting the protection of data rights in sports events: A configurational analysis. *Scientific Reports, 14*(1), 5353.

Neifer, T., Lawo, D., Bossauer, P., Esau, M., & Jerofejev, A.-M. (2020). Data storytelling als kritischer Erfolgsfaktor von data science. *HMD Praxis der Wirtschaftsinformatik, 57*(5), 1033–1046.

NFL. (2025). 100 greatest game-changers: Lester Hayes rule. Accessed August 28, 2025.

Obi, O. C., Dawodu, S. O., Onwusinkwue, S., Osasona, F., Atadoga, A., & Daraojimba, A. I. (2024). Data science in sports analytics: A review of performance optimization and fan engagement. *World Journal of Advanced Research and Reviews, 21*(1), 2663–2670.

Postma, M. (2023). *Best practices for big data management in the sports industry* (pp. 1–8). TScIT 39, University of Twente. Accessed July 10, 2025.

Qi, Y., Sajadi, S. M., Baghaei, S., Rezaei, R., & Li, W. (2024). Digital technologies in sports: Opportunities, challenges, and strategies for safeguarding athlete wellbeing and competitive integrity in the digital era. *Technology in Society, 69*, 101012.

Reddy, S. (2023). The role of data analytics in enhancing decision-making in sports management. *International Journal of Advanced Informatics and Data Science Machine Learning, 4*(2), 9–16.

Rouleur. (2025). Spoilsports illustrated: Equipment condemned by the rulebook. Accessed August 28, 2025.

Saxe, K., & Hardin, R. (2022). Psychological safety in athletic team environments. *Journal of Sport Behavior, 45*(2), 203–216.

Stoudt, S., Jernite, Y., Marshall, B., Marwick, B., Sharan, M., Whitaker, K., & Danchev, V. (2024). Ten simple rules for building and maintaining a responsible data science workflow. *PLoS Computational Biology, 20*(7), e1012232.

Tennis Museum. (2025). The history of spaghetti stringing 1971. Accessed August 28, 2025.

Wang, H., & Han, H. (2024). Analysis of the advantages and disadvantages of hawk-eye technology in tennis competitions. *International Journal of Environmental and Health Research, 14*(3), 318–325. Accessed September 13, 2025.

Watanabe, N. M., & Rewliak, J. (2022). Where analytics gets it wrong. *Journal of Applied Sport Management, 14*(4), 2.

Wikipedia. (2025). Sign stealing. Accessed August 28, 2025.

Yi, X., & Zhou, M. (2018). Detection and analysis of led display system in large stadiums. *Light & Engineering, 26*(3), 51–57.

Young, F., Coulby, G., Watson, I., Downs, C., Stuart, S., & Godfrey, A. (2020). Just find it: The Mymo approach to recommend running shoes. *IEEE Access, 8*, 109791–109800.

Zhang, J., Le, T., & Chen, J. (2023). Investigation of essential skills for data analysts: An analysis based on LinkedIn. *Journal of Global Information Management, 31*(1), 1–21.

Zhong, Y.-J., Yang, J.-W., Guo, W.-H., & Wang, Y.-S. (2025). The impact of digital technology on sports consumption: Evidence from Chinese college students. *Frontiers in Psychology, 16*, 1501327.

Index

D. Schwizer, M. Burch, *Data Excellence in Sports*, Management for Professionals,
https://doi.org/10.1007/978-3-032-10993-4

B

N

MIX
Papier aus verantwortungsvollen Quellen
Paper from responsible sources
FSC® C105338

If you have any concerns about our products,
you can contact us on
ProductSafety@springernature.com

In case Publisher is established outside the EU,
the EU authorized representative is:
Springer Nature Customer Service Center GmbH
Europaplatz 3, 69115 Heidelberg, Germany

Printed by Libri Plureos GmbH
in Hamburg, Germany